MOSCOW DMZ

The Story of the International Effort to Convert Russian Weapons Science to Peaceful Purposes

Glenn E. Schweitzer

M.E. Sharpe
Armonk, New York
London, England

Library of Congress Cataloging-in-Publication Data

Schweitzer, Glenn E., 1930–
Moscow DMZ : the story of the international effort to convert Russian weapons science
to peaceful purposes / by Glenn E. Schweitzer.
p.   cm.
Includes bibliographical references and index.
ISBN 1-56324-625-2 (alk. paper).—ISBN 1-56324-626-0 (pbk. alk. paper)
1. Economic conversion—Russia (Federation).
2. International Science and Technology Center.
3. Brain drain—Russia (Federation)
4. Nuclear nonproliferation.
5. United States—Relations—Russia (Federation).
6. Russia (Federation)—Relations—United States.
I. Title.
HC340.12.Z9D446   1996
338.4′76233′0947—dc20
95-42353
CIP

Printed in the United States of America

The paper used in this publication meets the minimum requirements of
American National Standard for Information Sciences—
Permanence of Paper for Printed Library Materials,
ANSI Z 39.48-1984.

∞

| BM (c) | 10 | 9 | 8 | 7 | 6 | 5 | 4 | 3 | 2 | 1 |
| BM (p) | 10 | 9 | 8 | 7 | 6 | 5 | 4 | 3 | 2 | 1 |

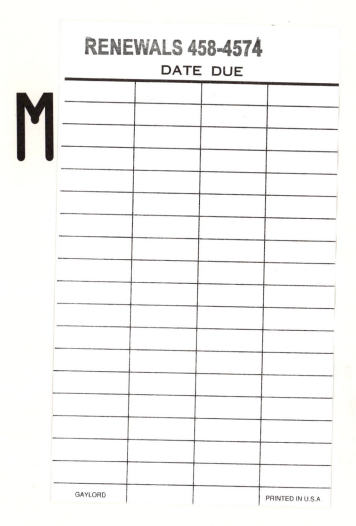

Contents

Acknowledgments

A Salute to the Contributions of Many Others

Samuel Johnson said, "Your manuscript is both good and original; but the parts that are good are not original, and the parts that are original are not good." I suspect that the reader of this book will find considerable truth in his admonition, for many of the most interesting insights in this book are the insights of others.

Many Russian colleagues throughout their country deserve my special thanks for their never-ending efforts to help me understand what was happening within a society in transition—within the government, within financial circles, within all types of technical institutions, and within Russian families. From them I learned that generalities about Russian attitudes and motivations require many caveats. I learned that there is no one more resourceful than a Russian in coping with the unexpected. And I learned that a Russian friend will be there when you need him.

The leaders of the Ministry of Atomic Energy, the Russian Academy of Sciences, the Ministry of Foreign Affairs, and other governmental and scientific organizations repeatedly went out of their way to help ensure a professionally rewarding and personally satisfying stay for my wife and me in Moscow. If they viewed my activities at highly classified Russian facilities as suspicious, they never conveyed such an impression to me; and I can assure them that I never violated their trust. They were always ready to entertain any question I had. Invariably I received a frank and prompt answer, even though the answer was not always the one I wanted to hear. What a difference a few years can make!

The International Science and Technology Center (ISTC) staff from the United States, Europe, Japan, and Russia displayed a level of loyalty and support for our collective efforts that rivaled my best experiences during a career of several decades as a manager of technical and policy programs in the United States. In many ways, I regretted the day when our tour came to an end, the day that I walked out of my office with its five chandeliers and through the vestibule with its seven flags proudly on display. I hope that this book does justice to the outstanding efforts of those who remained in Moscow.

And to the Russian people, even those who crammed me against the walls of the jammed metro and tram cars day in and day out, I say thank you. You never hesitated to let me know how it really was out there on the streets and in the crowded apartments.

Of special importance for this book was the help of hundreds of directors, scientists, and engineers of many research and development institutions throughout Russia who provided me with unexpected access to some of their most pressing problems, personal and professional, and to many innovative solutions to these problems. Unfortunately, a number of the very promising solutions languish for lack of support by Russian bureaucrats and by Western government and business leaders who are not prepared to take any type of risk by backing ideas that have not yet been *proven*. Perhaps this book will help them better appreciate the payoff from risk taking and the consequences of doing nothing.

Within the United States, the leaders of the National Research Council made possible my assignment to Moscow. To them and to the Department of State, which recruited me and provided my umbilical cord to Washington, to the Department of Defense, which helped me watch the money provided to the ISTC, to the Department of Energy, which supported several ISTC staff members, and to the staff of the American Embassy in Moscow, which shared my daily frustrations, I express my deepest appreciation.

The publishers of *Technology in Society* and *Global Governance* kindly allowed me to use material that I had previously published in their journals. I hope that this much fuller account of my experiences in Russia will respond at least in part to the many inquiries I have received from readers of these two excellent journals.

Anne Harrington, who became responsible for the ISTC activities within the Department of State in 1993, deserves special mention. She represented the U.S. government in the earliest negotiations of 1992 to establish the Center and then she joined me during the first year of our planning activity in Moscow. Her contributions to the Center have been manyfold, and she provided many excellent suggestions for improving the accuracy and utility of this manuscript.

Most important, the only person who could have made this book possible is my wife, Carole. She willingly put her very successful business career on hold to enable us to go to Russia. She mastered the basics of the Russian language, starting from scratch, so she could make her full contribution to our joint efforts. She soon knew more about Russian literature than many American academics. And she became a journalist writing insightful columns for newspapers both in the United States and in Moscow.

Carole also rescued me from drowning in a sea of paperwork. I was a *contractor* of the Department of State; but Carole handled our financial books since the department assumed that I had the administrative capabilities of the Lockheed Corporation. She directed the refurbishment of our apartment for three long winter months while we huddled in whatever corner was available. And when the U.S. agencies failed to provide adequate staff to support the ISTC, she pitched in by carrying out both financial and administrative tasks at the Center until the needed specialists arrived from Washington. If President Clinton and the U.S. Congress are serious about cost savings in the government, they should ask Carole, an experienced business executive who was exposed to the realities of government operations in Moscow, to write a book on why government is unnecessarily expensive.

Finally, Carole served as the editor of this book. But she was more than an editor, for she understood many of the developments in Russia better than I.

MOSCOW
DMZ

Prologue

*Facing the truth and publicly debating the nation's most acute
and vexing difficulties is supposed to be the strength of democracy.
Isn't it extraordinary that this has been happening ...
in the land of Stalin and Ivan the Terrible?*

Hedrick Smith, *The New Russians*, 1991

A Struggling Russia

"We no longer fear Russian military might," a Finnish taxi driver told
us. "Rather, we worry about armies of immigrants from a poor neigh-
boring country descending upon our struggling economy. Even now,
along our border with Russia, our shopkeepers set a limit of two on the
number of visitors from the nearby Russian towns who may enter a
shop at any time. The Russians simply have no money, and for many
the temptation for theft is too great."

The driver, who was an underemployed intellectual trying to
weather the recession in his own country, offered these cynical comments to me and my wife, Carole, as we headed toward the Helsinki
airport in early 1993. We were on our way back to our apartment in
Moscow after savoring a long weekend of shopping and entertainment in
the Finnish capital. Even during an economic slump, the relative prosperity of Helsinki contrasted sharply with the drabness and despair in Russia.

We had already become accustomed to the fearful commentaries of
American colleagues and friends, who frequently visited us in Moscow,
as to the new realities of Russia—commentaries that underscored
what we experienced and witnessed every day. Typical comments
were as follows:

"We must save Russian science. It's on the brink of disaster, and the
whole world will soon lose this irreplaceable intellectual resource,"
clamored the physicists and mathematicians who came laden with
computers and scientific journals for their colleagues.

3

"If the Russian economy doesn't turn around very soon, there will be another coup attempt that will succeed; and we'll be back to the Cold War," was the regular refrain of the policy experts who were in Moscow to advise the Ministry of Finance.

"It is no wonder that plutonium is being stolen from Russia. No one even knows what was stored in some of those run-down old warehouses so many years ago," reported visitors to the formerly secret cities of the country.

"The natural resources, the underutilized manpower, and the many immature markets of the country offer vast opportunities for American business in Russia. But the laws are so uncertain, the banking system so primitive, and the mafia so omnipresent that we cannot risk investment capital," was the conclusion of every Western trade mission.

"Don't drink the water or shop at the markets; and go west every two months to get aired out," advised the environmental experts who were convinced that Russia had become a giant sponge contaminated with high levels of radioactive and toxic chemicals.

Such comments certainly do not describe a superpower. But as long as Russia has nuclear weapons and missiles that work—and Russia surely does have thousands of them—it will retain superpower, or at least super powderkeg, status in the eyes of military leaders throughout the world. Nevertheless, to most foreigners, within and outside Russia, the country is perceived as a basket case in need of urgent resuscitation.

The inevitable question is, Why can't Russia use the vast technology behind its nuclear prowess to help rescue its crumbling economy?

A Foreign Response for Redirecting Weapons Talent

This question concerning a new type of benevolent nuclear genie had been foremost in our minds when we left for Moscow in 1992 to participate in the conversion of Russian military capabilities to civilian endeavors. The Department of State had chosen me to become the first executive director of the International Science and Technology Center (ISTC), which was being established in Moscow by the United States, twelve European nations, Russia, and Japan.

The commitment to the ISTC by the United States was part of the overall national effort to help Russia downsize its military establishment in a responsible way, a commitment embodied in what is commonly referred to as the Nunn-Lugar Initiative. The principal task of the ISTC was to help prevent a nuclear brain drain from Russia into countries on our not-so-favored list and at the same time to encourage Russia to use its military technologies in rebuilding a civilian science and technology base that could lead to a healthier economy.

The Europeans were represented at the ISTC by the European Economic Community and the European Atomic Energy Community. The Council and the Commission of the European Community carried out oversight and implementation responsibilities. The European Union was established in 1993 and now provides an extensive umbrella over these and other organizations. In view of the evolving nature of the many European bodies in Brussels, this manuscript usually refers simply to the European Union (EU) when discussing activities of its many subordinate institutions.

Of course, sorting out the involvement of the many Russian organizations interested in the activities of the ISTC was even more complicated. But the varying perspectives of these organizations is important to discussing the future of Russia; therefore, the book contains references to many ministries, committees, institutes, and enterprises in an effort to present differing points of view.

As to the Japanese, they usually speak with one voice in international settings; analyses of the internal dynamics in Tokyo in reaching international positions will be left for others to explore.

In the background of our international intervention into the heartland of the Russian national security establishment stood the optimistic slogans of *perestroika* and *conversion*—concepts that were tumbling into a bottomless pit of skepticism throughout Russia. The Russians had tired of the false promises associated with these concepts as they saw their earnings rapidly slipping away, their factories systematically closing, and their research institutes turning into machine shops for repairing household items. In short, both concepts had promised much but, for the Russian in general and the scientist in particular, delivered little.

Thus, however noble the Western efforts, they too would be viewed with suspicion and caution by a populace calloused to fallacies about the ease of recovery that were punctuating the entire economic revolution within the country.

Adapting to a Changing Russia

Moving to Moscow for sojourns of several years, with the requisite adjustments to the grim local scene, is almost always a traumatic experience for Americans and other foreigners. We simply do not thrive in drab and dark environments where adequate lighting is a luxury. Few of us can gracefully accept cold showers for weeks on end due to cleaning of the hot-water pipes or adjust to the lack of heat during cold snaps in October before the central heating system is activated. Hiking up twelve flights of stairs with the week's groceries because of frequent elevator malfunctions and having to remember to remove windshield wipers to thwart street thieves add to the stress. We are unaccustomed to puncturing automobile tires and twisting axles in potholes on the main streets of a nation's capital. And living without ready access to reliable medical services is risky and unsettling.

I had lived in Moscow for three years in the 1960s, but within the sheltered confines of the American Embassy compound. Then, of course, with the KGB protective services and a highly disciplined populace, life had been more predictable.

As a regular visitor to Russia since 1985, for periods of two to three weeks, I thought that I was up-to-date on recent changes. Nonetheless, I simply was not prepared for the many new ordeals and surprises, and even the simple rewards, that we would encounter during our stay. This time we would be living and working in a society that was spinning in free-fall release after the toppling of communism—like a gyroscope without an axis to center its political, economic, and emotional turmoil.

By 1992, new dangers to survival had become widespread in Moscow. For transplanted American suburbanites, the exposure to Russian urban crime was often frightening. More than 165 bombings were recorded in the city in 1993 alone. Car thefts became rampant; street muggings increased; and extortion, even within Western companies, became an inevitable cost of doing business in the unfamiliar evolutionary era of privatization.

Also, transportation hazards rose dramatically as traffic lights became inoperative, powerful foreign cars with untrained Russian drivers muscled smaller vehicles aside, and street fires from leaking gasoline trucks heralded chronic maintenance failures. As to air transportation, impoverished Aeroflot agents sold tickets for standing room in the aisles of already overloaded aircraft. Then, skyrocketing fares resulted in a dearth of passengers and lower revenues, which in turn led to a greater reliance on older planes and a further deterioration of maintenance services. The disastrous results are well known. Even train travel took on fearful dimensions as rail renegades used knock-out gases to immobilize passengers long enough to clean out the valuables in their sleeping compartments.

But my worst experiences occurred on the icy sidewalks of a city that no longer benefited from the primitive but effective chipping, scraping, and brushing by thousands of pensioners and elderly women of years past when Moscow city services were still in evidence. I simply could not find shoes or boots with effective suction cups, spikes, or other traction devices for safe passage across the glacial surfaces of Moscow. As I lay stunned on my back outside the Universitetskii metro station following my most serious fall, I belatedly decided to hire a full-time driver—one who would transport me door to door during the winter season lest I join the thousands of Muscovites with broken bones who crowded the city's clinics.

On the positive side, by the early 1990s the fears of foreigners about encounters with the security services and trepidations over making personal contacts with Russians had generally evaporated. Unfortunately, a modified menu of anxieties had replaced these earlier apprehensions. The shock waves of depression rippling among the populace and the general disorientation from economic deprivation and uncertainty could be observed everywhere: on street corners where Russians were selling their most cherished possessions, in housing renovation projects where highly trained scientists scraped wallpaper to supplement their incomes, and near metro stops where well-dressed panhandlers apologetically sought handouts.

Perhaps the most dramatic indicators of change were in the shops of the cities throughout the country. Who could ever forget walking into state stores that were well-stocked with drab, low-quality goods at bargain prices in 1985, visiting the same stores with barren shelves in 1990, and then in 1993 finding these very stores renamed "commercial shops" and bulging with the widest variety of goods from all over the world, albeit at very high prices?

Quoting from a book about Russia that I wrote in 1989:

> Each time I am in Moscow, I visit the single retail store where personal computers may be purchased. During each visit, I receive the same reply to my query as to the procedure for purchasing a personal computer. "We have no computers in stock right now, but we are expecting a shipment in several months. Come in at that time, and we will take your order."[1]

When Carole and I visited Radio Shack on Leninskii Prospekt and saw the shop's impressive inventory in 1994, I knew that the shipments had finally come in. Indeed, we could have been in the Radio Shack store on K Street in Washington, D.C.

The cultural differences between Russians and Americans no longer seemed to be a serious barrier for visitors. But sometimes it was difficult to be proud to be an American. It seemed that Russia had imported many of the worst features of our society while overlooking the best. Still, there was no higher aspiration among many Russians than to be as "cool" as the Americans depicted on Russian television screens. Every tram and metro car was full of Russians of all ages clad in shirts, coats, and caps bearing American logos.

Unfortunately, many Russians soon resented the activities of Americans in their country. The press regularly linked financial scams with unscrupulous American businessmen. The growth in crime and the proliferation of guns were quickly compared to developments in New York and Los Angeles. Nevertheless, Made-in-America consumer goods sold well everywhere, even if they were really made in Moscow. Besides, Americans were preferable to the Europeans and Japanese. Those countries had sent their armies to conquer Russia in decades and centuries past, and the Russians had still not completely forgiven them.

Of course, Russian nationalists, in particular, worried about the American influence. A common joke in Moscow quoted a Russian official lamenting,

> While the Americans never sent their armies to Russia, we are now facing a greater danger. Every day squads of Americans in three-piece suits set out from the Radisson Slavianskaia Hotel, briefcases in hand, for institutions in every part of the city.

The nationalists were particularly suspicious of the Western fascination with the way Russia was handling or mishandling its stocks of plutonium and uranium.

Shortly after our departure from Moscow, several Russian newspapers let fly with the accusation that 200 American organizations active in Russia were interested primarily in spying.[2] While rebuttals soon appeared in the press and punctuated political debates, American spying will continue to be a battle cry of those politicians longing for the good old days.

Cultural gaps between the two societies have not totally disappeared. Language difficulties, variances in work habits, differing views as to the role of women, and conflicting attitudes toward the legitimacy of profit making, for example, continue to persist. At the same time, it often seemed to us that the cultural chasms that are developing within Russian society itself, as within other societies, may be deeper than the cultural valleys separating Russia from the West. Thus, while some Americans learn to enjoy a weekend trip to the forest to gather mushrooms with the older generation of Russians, young Russians prefer to spend their spare time searching out pirated videotapes instead of carrying forth such unprofitable habits of their parents. Some Americans experience the pleasures of cross-country skiing with the help of patient Russian tutors, but Russian youths prefer to disrupt the neighborhoods on noisy motorbikes.

Also, for Russians long accustomed to a classless society, the emergence of a class of wealthy Russians appeared to be a particularly offensive phenomenon for all but the rich themselves. Some economists predict that the noveau riche class of Russians will eventually constitute the vanguard bringing economic order to the country. In the meantime, however, most of the population seem to cling to their upbringing and prefer that the entire society be on the same plane, even if that means all are poor together.

We had anticipated a new type of Russia; and on arrival in Moscow in mid-1992, we vowed to immerse ourselves to the fullest extent possible into a Russian society undergoing change. We hoped that we could understand what was happening. We wanted to *make a difference*, however small, but in the *right* direction.

In the Midst of Transition

The changes in the political and economic fabric of Russia that began when Mikhail Gorbachev took charge in 1985 defied my imagination. By every indicator, his policies of *glasnost, perestroika,* and *demokratizatsiia* turned Russia upside down. Then the attempted coup in 1991, the dissolution of the Soviet Union shortly thereafter, and the reformist zeal of Boris Yeltsin ensured that the course of history would be altered forever.

The upheaval of the Russian political landscape during the late 1980s quickly became clear although the contours of the new architecture are still being drawn and revised. Freedom of speech, freedom of the press, freedom of religion, and the right to assemble began to take on real meaning. Slowly the country moved toward democratic processes even though the effective implementation of a multiparty system encountered serious barriers.

Few experts, if any, predicted the political drama of the 1990s. In October 1993, we witnessed from our living room window the flames biting into the skyline from a blazing White House, the home of the dismissed Russian parliament. The previous day we had driven past fires set by communist demonstrators on a main thoroughfare of Moscow, as we skirted trucks of soldiers poised to repel a rebellion. No sooner was the White House recaptured by the government than gunfire erupted in our neighborhood throughout the ensuing nights. We quickly realized that the nationalistic underpinnings of communism might have been dormant but were far from dead.

While most of the political upheaval was concentrated in Moscow, life in the remainder of the country could not be ignored, as most vividly demonstrated by subsequent events in Chechnya. Beyond the capital city, I encountered so much political cynicism that it seemed clear the outlying populations wanted to forget about Moscow and simply go their own way. While political parties—or more accurately, political groupings—may be important within the parliament, outside the buildings of the legislative halls of Moscow few cared or even knew about the activities of the new political entities.

The 160 ethnic subgroups scattered throughout Russia remained a formidable force. Most saw greater local autonomy as the only political solution. They wanted control not only over local political institutions but also over local deposits of gold, diamonds, gas, and oil. Even the mafia gangs with roots in ethnic enclaves within and outside Russia demanded territorial rights for sections of Moscow and other cities that were attractive to the masters of graft, coercion, and intimidation.

At the same time, the promised dividends from economic reform remained an academic fantasy to most Russians. Many cities turned into sidewalk bazaars featuring consumer products from throughout the world, but often at prices that eluded the average Russian. Why was it that Russia turned to Turkey, China, Korea, Egypt, India, and other less developed countries to provide many of the basic commodities of life that covered the shelves of Moscow stores and kiosks, while Russian factories languished for lack of orders from customers? Why was it that inflation spun out of control and the only way the Central Bank could keep up was to print ruble bills of larger and larger denominations?

Many Russian enterprises slowly ground to a halt. Efforts to privatize saved a few; but the industrial backbone of the country, including the once sparkling plants that produced military armaments, continued to rely on state subsidies to keep inefficient production lines alive. Every month, plant managers threatened massive layoffs. Many of the best young workers took the hint and found work elsewhere, often on the streets peddling consumer goods. Still, the bulk of the workers hung on, usually working less and less; and production levels slumped lower and lower.

Privatization became the buzz word for foreign efforts to reform the economy. Soon privatization became an end in itself, as foreign experts boasted about the numbers of newly privatized enterprises, instead of talking about privatization as a means to a better standard of living.

But what did privatization mean beyond the restaurants, the small shops, and the service companies that were the easy candidates for privatization? Was the Russian economy to mirror the American approach? Was privatization the only road to rid Russia of the three economic evils: state subsidies for industry, lack of competition, and industry's responsibility to provide social safety nets for entire cities? And what was the sense in privatization if the new owners only clutched useless vouchers or traded them for bottles of vodka, while there was no capital to build a business?

To most Russians, privatization meant that many former political leaders would skim off Russian assets and become the barons of the noveaux riches. To the workers at thousands of factories that became joint stock companies and then closed their doors, it meant that they were led down a path to nowhere. To the military-industrial complex, it meant that many factories of supreme importance to the nation would be put off limits for privatization and would continue to receive state subsidies.

In the countryside, the opportunities for agricultural entrepreneurship seemed to be few and far between. The best land and the heavy equipment remained under central control in various forms. Some cooperatives managed to prosper, and indeed some cooperative leaders bought Mercedes and Volvos. Private farming did not take off. Farmers hesitated to give up a modest but certain income for an unpredictable return based on their personal capabilities—not only practical skills of working the fields but also skills to manage a business, Russian-style.

Despite economic difficulties on all fronts, somehow the Russian government still managed to find the resources to support a large weapons complex. Though much reduced from its apex in the mid-1980s, the military-industrial infrastructure continued to employ millions of specialists and other personnel at many research, production, and deployment sites throughout Russia. Transition within this military establishment is the focal point of this book.

Turmoil in the Military-Industrial Complex

Nowhere have recent changes within Russia been more traumatic than within the military-industrial complex. Once the privileged sector of Soviet life with high pay and an abundance of subsidized consumer items for all employees, this elite establishment has fallen on hard times that were unthinkable until the collapse of communism.[3]

Stigma replaced pride as the military epaulet for many young soldiers. The cleaning up of urban debris replaced the execution of military maneuvers as the daily fare of army units. Tents replaced apartments as the quarters for many military families returning from service abroad. And the shooting of urban demonstrators and even of rebellious elderly farmers helped define the new, unpleasant roles of a high-technology army.

It appeared that only the Red Army Choir survived the turmoil of the past few years, although they joined the other artists of Russia in seeking the bulk of their paychecks from tours abroad. Also, their voices no longer crackled with the authority of the past, and civilian understudies from the concert halls of Moscow were usually featured at the military performances at home and abroad.

Many industrial enterprises and research and design institutes that developed behind high security fences opened their doors to foreign visitors in the search for customers for Russian products. The doors unveiled facilities as modern as had been suspected in the West, staffed with scientists and engineers with finely honed talents. The Soviet military machine was no paper tiger, and the remains of that machine were still impressive. But few Western firms invested in conversion activities of these facilities; and the developing countries—countries interested more in well-proven military hardware than in the products of recent research—soon became the most promising customers for the products of much of this establishment.

Large numbers of the most brilliant Russian specialists were located within the military-industrial complex. Like their colleagues in the civilian sector, they soon became discouraged with the lack of opportunities to use their talents in a transformed Russia. These specialists were the target of our efforts to redirect the nation's intellectual know-how from military to civilian endeavors.

Reorienting the Technical Potential Toward Peace

With the rapid emergence of economic uncertainty everywhere in the country, the once stable, prized—and indeed prestigious—professions of the nuclear scientists and rocket engineers had plummeted to seemingly immeasurable depths. Dissolution of research teams, erratic payments of salaries, and closing of laboratories gave immediate credence to the U.S. contention that these high-tech weaponeers would be easy prey for seduction by agents from distant countries.

As to my long-time professional acquaintances in Moscow, during the late 1980s few scientists or engineers would admit any ties with the Soviet military complex, even though the Soviet press reported that one-half of the nation's military technology had roots in the Moscow region. In an about-face, however, by 1992 almost all the Russian scientists and engineers I had known earlier unabashedly claimed previous involvement in military research activities. They had become convinced that their personal eligibility for conversion programs being sponsored by their own and foreign governments was the best ticket for future financial support. Honesty had become the best policy.

This book concentrates on a reorientation of the technical potential of Russia embodied in the large pool of talented scientists and engineers throughout the country. Many examples of technical opportunities for redirection are presented. Nevertheless, such redirection should be considered within a broad context of the future of the Russian economy as well as within the framework of the overall science and technology base of the country.

Of special concern is the future of Russia's nuclear weapons specialists, for the urgent need to control the world's nuclear weapons capability was the primary motivation for our trek to Russia. The future of these experts is of course entwined with the future military doctrine of the country. Whatever the doctrine, the size of the nuclear weapons establishment will surely shrink. It is crucial that specialists who leave the establishment because of this downsizing focus their energies on civilian tasks within Russia rather than support the military ambitions of leaders of other countries.

This book is organized into several parts in addressing the Western attempts to accelerate the reorientation of the technical potential of Russia. The first five chapters trace the history of the ISTC from its inception, through the diplomatic negotiations that were essential to establish the legal and operational basis for the new international organization, and into the first year of its operation. This eyewitness account includes many observations on the inevitable entanglement of foreign policy decisions of the United States and other countries with the domestic political turmoil within Russia. It passes through the intersections where the aspirations of Russia and its people, hoping to be propelled into prosperity by modern technologies, cross the economic realities of falling standards of living. Finally, the book cannot escape the personal traumas of foreigners working and surviving in Russia where the human energy needed simply to stay healthy often drains on-the-job productivity.

The next four chapters provide crosscutting overviews of developments involving Russian weaponeers and the resultant issues that challenge U.S. foreign policy. The topics discussed will have major impacts on the direction of Russia's economic and military development and on U.S. policies toward Russia during the remainder of this century. These chapters reach a number of conclusions about the future of scientific research in Russia, the likely success of Russian and foreign efforts to convert Russian military enterprises and institutes to civilian activities, and the difficulties of preventing dual-use technologies developed in Russia for civilian purposes from being diverted to military uses within Russia or abroad. The ISTC experience provides many relevant examples that support these conclusions.

The concluding chapter poses a few questions of broad international scope. Can the lessons learned during the early days of the ISTC be transported to other programs in Russia and to programs in other countries? Isn't the concept of encouraging the scientific elite to work for peace and not for war applicable in other countries that have not yet become reliable members of the world community, such as China and North Korea? And isn't the concept of providing financial assistance directly into the hands of people rather than through the hands of Western intermediaries and foreign governments relevant in many desperate countries of the world? In short, if the ISTC is on the right course, can clones be developed?

The book draws extensively on personal experiences. Of course, I am but one of thousands of Americans with deep personal and professional interests in the future of Russia. But, I have been fortunate to have had unusual opportunities in the country over a period of three decades; and this book is an effort to share my experiences with others. I hope that the personalized episodes will be accepted in the spirit in which they are offered.

Chapter 1

Fear of a Weapons Brain Drain
Stirs International Action

Nuclear Scientists of All Friendly Countries, Unite. . . .
The International Science and Technology Center Will
Soon Be Established in Moscow.
Major M. Pogorelyi, *Red Star*, March 4, 1992

Struggling Scientists in the Weapons Complex

In the wake of the failed Moscow coup of August 1991, an increasing number of reports reached the West about Middle Eastern countries approaching Russian institutions in search of nuclear, chemical, biological, rocket, and related technologies. According to this information, the countries wanted technologies that could enhance their military capabilities to deliver lethal blows to nearby adversaries. Western concern centered primarily on transfers of technologies already embodied in the hardware for weapons systems; but the importance of foreign technical experts to help adapt, assemble, and maintain the equipment was very clear.

In December 1991, *Time* magazine published an article entitled "Who Else Will Have the Bomb?" that presented a graphic depiction of the routes of diffusion of nuclear weaponry throughout the world. The report warned that Russia "could sell nuclear equipment or provide technical aid by out-of-work scientists" to countries such as Iran, North Korea, Iraq, Algeria, Libya, and Syria. More ominously, *Time* underscored that China, which was soon to become one of Russia's closest collaborators and an international conduit in the nuclear field, was "recklessly peddling nuclear equipment and expertise to any nation willing to pay cash."[1]

Also by the end of 1991, many formerly secret research and development (R&D) institutions in Russia had begun to open their doors to

16

foreign "partners" who would finance their new civilian activities. At the beginning, the Russian government carefully orchestrated this broad effort to attract foreign clients, involving about one dozen Russian scientific and production organizations. But soon, scores of Russian institutes and enterprises joined the effort. These individual institutions began exercising an increasing degree of autonomy from central control, with their representatives exhibiting great flexibility to accommodate potential foreign customers.

During this period, visitors to Russia lamented the plight of Russian scientists, many of whom were being paid at levels below the poverty line or were not being paid at all. Much of their equipment was no longer operative or had passed into obsolescence, and most institutions had canceled subscriptions to foreign scientific journals due to the lack of funds. The international scientific community was very upset about the economic difficulties of well-known colleagues working in the universities and in the institutes of the Russian Academy of Sciences. Nobel laureates and other leading scientists in the West were soon clamoring, "Save Russian science," warning of a massive brain drain that would destroy Russian "schools of science" of critical importance to the world.[2]

Economic hard times engulfed the hard-core military scientists and engineers as well. Inflation rapidly eroded their paychecks. Their special supply lines for consumer goods disappeared. Their former patrons within the military-industrial complex pleaded poverty and advised them to find new sources of funds. The uncertainty of future funding was as unexpected as it was traumatic for this privileged class that had always been rewarded with generous subsidies and perquisites for their successes in molding the Soviet Union into a superpower.

In January 1992, *The New York Times* reported the conditions in ten formerly secret nuclear cities:

> Their disintegration is now seen as threatening to send scientists and materials flying into foreign hands in a new kind of international peril. . . . Ferment is real. Russian nuclear experts have received job offers from Iraq and Libya. . . . Bomb makers in the secret cities are striving to invent new ways of making money at home. Some of the initiatives would hinder atomic leakage, others encourage it.

But the paper also noted that "lifting some secrecy, they now want to go commercial, embark on joint projects with the West, and do nearly anything in their power to survive and avoid falling apart."[3]

The Western countries, particularly Germany, were alarmed by the increased contacts between countries on their not-so-favored lists and the Russian weapon designers, especially in view of the economic discontent among Russian researchers. A critical question being asked in Bonn and Washington was, "Will Russian scientists and engineers sell their secrets to help feed their families?"

The German government was under considerable international pressure to explain how Iraq had received advanced technology, with military applications, from German firms and what the government would do to contain technology diffusion on a broader basis.[4] The Germans, along with the Americans and other Europeans, were also sensitive to additional troublesome developments, possibly rooted in Russia. Had Libya acquired a chemical warfare capability under the guise of developing a pharmaceutical or pesticide facility? Where did Iraq initially obtain the wherewithal to begin to develop nuclear weapons and, more recently, a biological warfare capability? How extensive were North Korea's recent dealings with Russian rocket designers?

The Russian government publicly shared Western concerns over the necessity to contain the knowledge of their experts who had developed Russia's weapons of mass destruction. The government wanted to reclaim all the nuclear weapons and rockets that the Soviet Union had deployed to Ukraine, Belarus, and Kazakhstan; they were not eager for their scientists and engineers with knowledge about nuclear weapons either to remain employed in these countries or to emigrate from Russia to other countries near the Russian borders.

Thus, the weapons brain drain from Russia had become a major international security issue.

The Genesis of a New International Organization

Against this background, in late 1991 German Foreign Minister Hans-Dietrich Genscher proposed the establishment of an international program to provide financial support for Russian weapons scientists and engineers. The general idea of an international program of peaceful research for Russian weaponeers had been discussed in Europe for several years, but Genscher's personal interest raised the dialogue to a more serious level.[5]

Such a program would encourage weapons specialists to work on civilian programs in Russia rather than succumb to temptations to go to other countries where they could apply their expertise to military systems. At about the same time, American Secretary of State James Baker began exploring a similar idea. In early February 1992, at Camp David, Presidents Yeltsin and Bush discussed the establishment of an International Science and Technology Center (ISTC) and practical steps to translate the concept into reality.

Within two weeks, Russian Foreign Minister Kozyrev, together with Messrs. Genscher and Baker, issued a statement proposing establishment of the ISTC.[6] The German government, perhaps for financial reasons or because of pressure from the French, passed its baton to the European Union, which agreed to be a sponsor of the ISTC. Japan also agreed to participate. The United States then took the lead in beginning the diplomatic process to establish the ISTC, which because of the initials of the three signatories, was sometimes facetiously referred to as the "KGB Center."

Once word of this proposal hit the scientific communities, American and Russian specialists at nuclear weapons design laboratories quickly began preparing proposals for projects that would be financed by the Center. They had been in regular contact with each other for two years, dating to the time when representatives of the Russian nuclear weapons laboratories began visiting the United States in substantial numbers in search of new outlets for their talents. Most American specialists were enthusiastic about the possibilities of tapping into the high-technology capabilities of Russia.

Some American cynics likened the proposed program to a sophisticated method of bribery to keep Russian experts in place instead of flirting with Middle Eastern suitors. These same skeptics acknowledged that such bribes were warranted. Western intelligence officers anticipated an information bonanza. Overall, almost everyone in the West thought the ISTC was a good idea, with a price tag that promised to be low in view of the plummeting salaries of Russian researchers to the equivalent of $25 to $50 a month during 1991.[7]

The diplomatic negotiations began quickly, with each of the four parties (United States, European Union, Russia, and Japan) publicly committed to bringing the ISTC into being as soon as possible. President Yeltsin signed a decree authorizing the appropriate Russian agencies to work toward establishment of the ISTC.[8] Among the foreign parties, the United States pressed most vigorously on the need for prompt action. The European Union and Japan, while more conservative in their general approaches, attempted to accommodate the American eagerness. The key negotiators—Kislyak of Russia, Gallucci of the United States, and Benevides of the European Union, along with several different Japanese representatives, met first in Brussels and then in Moscow as they advanced the "KGB initiative."

The ISTC was to be a new special-purpose, intergovernmental body. Therefore, the diplomats needed an international agreement that set forth not only the purposes of the ISTC but also its legal status and the nature of its governing structure.

The diplomats and their legal advisers soon crafted a draft ISTC Agreement. Preliminary concurrence was reached on most of the difficult points. For example, each party providing funds for projects through the ISTC would determine which projects its funds would support instead of placing financial contributions for projects into a general pool. Russia would arrange tax and customs exemptions for Center activities within its territory. The Secretariat staff in Moscow would be granted a range of diplomatic privileges and immunities.

Within a few weeks, the remaining knotty issues were temporarily pushed off the negotiating table. Specifically, the parties agreed to postpone for several months the negotiation of the statute for the ISTC. This document would eventually include details concerning (1) intellectual property rights that resulted from projects, (2) access by foreigners to Russian weapons facilities where they could monitor and audit ISTC project activities, and (3) internal ISTC procedures for approving and financing projects.

By late May of 1992, the diplomats had developed a complete text of the ISTC Agreement, in English and Russian. Representatives of the four parties initialed the text in Lisbon where the negotiators had met in parallel with a meeting devoted to economic issues involving six Western governments and the Japanese government. The United States, the European Union, and Japan pledged to provide $67 million for the programs of the Center.[9]

As the champagne glasses clinked in Portugal, optimism rose in Moscow, Tokyo, Washington, and Brussels that the ISTC would be operational by the fall of 1992.

We Want You on the Ground—Yesterday

The four parties had informally agreed that the first executive director of the ISTC would be an American and the first chairman of the Governing Board would be a European. After officials of the Department of State had interviewed me as one of the specialists on the short list of candidates for executive director, a phone call summoned me to the department, where I was offered the position. It was April. I had just returned from a trip to Russia, and now I was to be shuttled back to Moscow as soon as the investigators approved yet another security clearance.

While Moscow had not been at the top, nor even the bottom, of the list of my wife Carole's preferred destinations for living abroad, she hesitantly said, "Go for it." The president of the National Research Council, where I was employed, strongly supported my participation in the ISTC initiative. Therefore, I signed a contract with the Department of State and packed my bags. The department wanted to launch the effort immediately. I left for Moscow at the end of June 1992.

Since the ISTC did not yet exist, I was temporarily assigned as an attaché of the U.S. Embassy in Moscow, with full diplomatic privileges. The only catch was that embassy housing was in short supply. I was left to fend for myself amid the burgeoning breed of Russian entrepreneurs offering leases on astoundingly expensive "privatized" apartments. At least that was the status the newly incarnated real estate agents conferred on the vacant flats. They contended that all that was needed to ensure a pleasant experience was a substantial up-front payment together with a lease with my signature and one Russian signature. The identities of the Russians who had the legal right to sign were never clear, however. Recalling that thieves had already stolen some of my clothes from my hotel room during my last visit, I was less than eager for a protacted stay in vulnerable quarters.

Alone in Moscow, I immediately set about the search for an apartment with some semblance of security, before I dared suggest to Carole that she board a flight to Russia. Fortunately, my friends at the Russian Academy of Sciences knew of my situation and offered me an apartment in an academy building where receptionists would keep an eye on the entranceway around the clock. The wallpaper was torn and hung in tatters. The windows didn't close. The kitchen held ancient and dangerous appliances. And the washing machine resembled a bucket with a stick.

Nevertheless, I informed Carole over a static-laden telephone line from the hotel that the apartment had "potential." Besides, where else could I find an apartment with an owner who had a clear title? As a further rationale, I noted that we would save the U.S. taxpayers tens of thousands of dollars because the apartments being rented by the embassy were costing three times as much, up to $60,000 per year. And some of those apartments were located twenty miles farther from the center of the city. Again, Carole's hesitant response was, "Go for it."

Carole arrived in Moscow in August. By early fall we had fully accepted our new apartment as our residence and settled in on the twelfth floor of 14 Gubkin Street. Within a few weeks, the hot-water and heating systems began to function. I had even succeeded in coaxing the Moscow city telephone department, which was being assisted by a British joint venture, to install a facsimile machine/telephone in the apartment. It would soon prove to be worth the $2,500 tab as the most convenient connection to the State Department and other overseas institutions during our stay in Moscow.

Initially, our neighbors were an odd mix of foreign scientists, Chechen "businessmen" (read mafia), and Russian transients who couldn't afford hotels. The Libyan chemical engineer who had been living down the hall for four years raised my curiosity over possible channels for diffusion of chemical warfare technologies out of Russia, while his children tore the tiles from the hallway floor and hurled these imitation frisbies at our door.

Within one year, however, most of the building residents changed, as joint ventures with hard currency for rental payments replaced visiting scientists living off the disappearing budget of the Academy of Sciences. Of course, the Chechens stayed. As their businesses prospered, they even converted several apartments into a restaurant, a barbershop, a medical clinic, and a snack bar. Altogether, at peak times these facilities provided customized services to a total of not more than three or four guests of a Chechen-owned professional soccer team.

What more could anyone desire, with an outdoor market four tram stops away, a Soviet-style department store just up the block, and only a fifty-minute commute by tram and metro to the embassy or the premises of the ISTC? The Ulan Bator movie house, Ho Chi Minh Square, and the Hanoi Restaurant added to the charm of the neighborhood. More important, a nearby medical center that the Seventh Day Adventists had just opened would become an important stop for the two of us.

But one necessity was missing. After being crushed and flattened by the hordes in the trams and metro, Carole longed for her ten-year-old Honda. It was soon on a freighter bound for Helsinki en route to its new parking spot outside our building. While gasoline was in short supply and the traffic police in search of payoffs mistakenly took Carole to be easy prey, she fearlessly dodged through the out-of-control traffic of Moscow for more than two years. Our admiring Russian friends and neighbors always saluted her with an "atta-girl" (in Russian, *molodets*) as she headed out the driveway.

In short, we made the transition to Moscow without the loss of many beats. I was on the job as scheduled. Rarely did survival measures at home interfere with my responsibilities at the ISTC. Carole took on the many problems facing foreigners in a city undergoing a transition that would surely last for many years. She hassled with the peddlers, made the monthly rounds to pay utility bills, organized the shopping runs, and prepared magnificent meals for many appreciative Russians and for foreign visitors who preferred the hominess of our modest watering hole to conspicuous consumption at the Metropol Hotel.

Searching for a Homestead for the ISTC

As we were settling into our newly found living quarters, a similar need for a suitable facility for the Secretariat challenged the parties to the ISTC Agreement.

When I first arrived in Moscow, a desk and several Russian helpers were waiting for me at the Institute of Pulse Technology in southeast Moscow, about forty minutes by metro or automobile from the Kremlin. The Russian minister of atomic energy had been the director of this formerly secret institute, which played a key role in the testing of nuclear weapons and in the design of measuring systems for other defense institutes of the ministry. The institute was experiencing a drastic downsizing as 500 of the 3,000 staff members departed in search of higher-paying jobs in the rapidly expanding commercial offices and kiosks of Moscow. The minister clearly thought that this facility with excess capacity should be the home of the ISTC. Since the Russian government had tasked him to find an appropriate facility, his views would surely carry great weight.

But the U.S., EU, and Japanese representatives were not convinced. They wanted a facility closer than eight metro stops to the center of the city. Also, they preferred a separate building rather than the wing of a research institute. In addition, the Japanese were very hesitant to have the ISTC located close to nuclear weapons activities, even if the weaponeers had terminated most of their secret research in this building.

The search for alternative facilities commanded an enormous amount of energy from the Russians and the foreigners involved in the creation of the ISTC. The first Russian offering was a new building on prime property within the grounds of Moscow State University. The partially constructed walls were already crumbling, however, and the underlying dirt foundation had turned to a sea of mud from the fresh rain. The structure would be very small with accommodations for only twenty-five people. Finally, and most important, the building was under the control not of the university but of a Russian entrepreneur who had acquired a contract to develop an industrial park for the university. His sole interest in the ISTC was to maximize his income. For example, when I asked if the road to the building would soon be completed, he replied that this depended on ISTC financing of the overall street network for a significant section of the industrial park.

The second Russian proposal was to locate the ISTC offices outside Moscow in the town of Troitsk. But foreign staff wanted to live near the political and cultural activities and the logistic supply lines of Moscow. Also, the foreign representatives insisted that the facility be readily accessible to visitors; and the drive to Troitsk in the winter was often difficult. The clinching argument for rejection came following the Russian claim that the intended building would be completed in four months. A Russian worker at the building site sheepishly admitted that construction had already been under way for seven years.[10]

The third and final alternative was to locate the ISTC along the Moscow River across from the Kremlin. But, the available building seemed to have barely survived an air raid on the capital in years past. The cost of resuscitation would have been astronomical. Indeed, every time I drove by the building, I saw yet another crumbling brick wall.

Thus, the ISTC Planning Group, which I headed, settled into the Institute of Pulse Technology in anticipation of initially locating the ISTC in the same building on a temporary basis, pending the availability of more suitable quarters for the Center. By fall, twenty-five Russian carpenters, painters, and electricians, together with a military construction squad, were reconfiguring and redecorating office space for about fifty people. This construction site was located in an impressively large sector of the second floor of the Pulse Institute, less than a few hundred feet from the Planning Group's quarters.

Every day I wandered into the construction area to measure progress. Every day I was disappointed that speed was not a priority of the crew. And every day I learned that three more months would be needed to finish the job. Nevertheless, by the end of the year new walls had miraculously appeared, lights flickered in new electrical installations, window frames had been sealed, and even the mountains of construction debris had disappeared. Still, occupancy was many weeks away when work suddenly stopped. The Russian government had not paid the workers for three months, and they moved to another job site with salary payments received in advance.

While we continued to refer to this wing of the Pulse Institute that was being readied for occupancy as the "temporary" home of the Center, it was clear that the likelihood of acquiring additional property at Russian expense was close to zero.

Meanwhile, the original Planning Group of six members had grown to twelve with the arrival of Japanese, Russian, and American specialists; and we huddled in five rooms down the hall from the facility under construction. From time to time we had temporary helpers, particularly from the United States, eager to provide us with advice for a few days on how to manage an organization. But we didn't need advice for a few days. We needed pairs of working hands—on a permanent basis. Our ISTC Planning Group was responsible for organizing a series of intergovernmental meetings to develop the basic management documents for the Center, and our most urgent need was typing power.

During the first six months in the Pulse Institute, all members of the Planning Group were convinced that the ISTC would be operational by the end of 1992. The Russian press also anticipated early action.[11] But as we scheduled and rescheduled celebratory parties to christen the elusive Center, I began to harbor doubts that the ISTC proposal would ever amount to anything more than a paper tiger. Had I really traveled to Moscow simply to add my ideas to the long lists of false promises of financial assistance that other Western specialists had deposited in every ministry and most institutes of the city? Despite these chronic doubts, I still considered the chances for success to be 50/50, although I regularly presented to the staff more positive odds of 90/10. I certainly didn't want them to go home just yet.

Setting the Policy Framework for
International Action

Beginning in July 1992, the highest priority of the four parties was to reach a consensus on a draft of the Statute for the ISTC. The Statute, along with the ISTC Agreement, would provide both the legal and political basis for the organization. Other operating documents would supplement the two basic documents. We hoped that any changes in Center policies and activities would be reflected in changes in those operating documents, without the necessity of revisiting the Agreement or Statute for further negotiation.

As we proceeded, we increasingly took on the character of the United Nations, with every phrase of every document reviewed in working groups and plenary sessions. At the staff level, I refrained from making a single decision of any consequence without consulting with my colleagues from the other countries. Our staff meetings were too frequent even to count; and I soon mastered Tom Peters's technique of "management by wandering around," as I spent most of my time in the offices of others.

Several key issues included in the Statute are discussed below. The four parties reached consensus on these issues only after many months of discussions, but in the end this deliberative process proved very useful in cementing widespread support among the parties for the approaches of the Center.

Intellectual Property Rights

Many Russian officials were convinced that American and other Western organizations active in Russia had been systematically cherry picking for their own use technologies that the Soviet Union developed at a cost of tens of billions of dollars. These officials inevitably pointed to the general lack of adequate systems within Russia to protect intellectual property and to the inadequate links between Russian laws and international legal systems as their major vulnerabilities. Specifically, the details of patent and copyright protection eluded a nation where prior discoveries had been the property of "the people." The Russian negotiators were determined to prevent the ISTC from becoming yet another venue for foreign businessmen to profit unfairly from the efforts of Russian specialists. Therefore, from the outset the issue of

Intellectual Property Rights (IPR) was a high priority in the negotiations to establish the ISTC.

For many months, negotiators from Washington, Brussels, and Tokyo faced off with representatives from several Russian agencies to develop an IPR framework. The negotiators finally presented a text in early 1993 that was accepted by the four parties.

While there were repeated attempts within the ensuing fourteen months by Russian representatives to reopen negotiations of this painstakingly drafted language, the original framework repelled repeated salvos from many quarters and remained intact. It certainly was a far better bargain for Russia than the various horse trades their institutes were developing with many Western organizations, arrangements that simply let their horses out of the barn and forfeited all Russian rights to experienced foreign dealmakers.

The central ISTC concept was that all aspects of IPR would be vested with the Russian institution carrying out the project. Nevertheless, the foreign party financing the project would have the right to an exclusive, royalty-free license for commercial use within its territory of the results of the research, provided the returns from these commercial activities did not greatly exceed the investment of the concerned party. In such a case, the licensing arrangements would be subject to renegotiation. Presumably, if the returns on a $1 million investment were $2 million, further negotiations would not be necessary. But if the returns were $50 million, the negotiating table would again be busy.

Related concepts were as follows:

1. Other ISTC parties that did not finance the project would have the right to negotiate licensing arrangements with the Russian institution, based on normal commercial terms, for introducing the products of research in their territories.

2. All parties to the ISTC Agreement would have the right freely to use the products of research for scientific and other noncommercial purposes; for example, when the ensuing technology was used by governments solely for space exploration.

3. The Russian institution would have an obligation to ensure that the research products were actively promoted at home and abroad. If, after two years, the institution did not extend itself, the institution would automatically forfeit commercial rights to the financing party.

4. Finally, technologies developed prior to the project and brought into the project would be legally protected, with the IPR for these

technologies remaining the property of the organization that brought the technologies into the project.[12]

My foregoing abridgement of the language in the ISTC Statute concerning IPR will undoubtedly trigger nervousness among the lawyer-diplomats who painstakingly crafted far more complicated phraseology. Therefore, before passing final judgment on the appropriateness of this IPR approach, those readers who may have money at stake are referred to the specific language in Appendix C.

Access for Monitoring and Auditing

No less complicated were the negotiations concerning *access* to project activities by representatives of the party providing funds and by the ISTC staff monitoring the project. Such access was to include discussions with project participants at the work sites, checking on the equipment that had been purchased, and review of the financial records and related documents.

The most volatile debates during the entire ISTC negotiating process centered on the advance notice required for access by foreigners to "closed" cities where projects would be located. Since some of these cities had been the secret birthplaces of Russian technologies designed to destroy the West, Russian reluctance to expose them to public scrutiny was understandably intense. The security agencies had developed admission procedures for foreigners that called for several levels of time-consuming reviews before approval of entry. Skeptical security officials were not prepared to go further.

Eventually, the negotiators developed a formula that required the financing party and the ISTC staff to provide at least twenty days' notice for access to project sites. At no time did the Russian representatives object to the concepts of project monitoring or project auditing. The debates revolved around the mechanics of actually conducting these activities.

A related issue was the length of time that the Russian insitution would be required to maintain records for audits following completion of a project. Finally, agreement was reached on a two-year limit for auditing rights following completion of the project.[13]

After these initial agreements, additional practical problems arose which the staff in Moscow resolved. Among them were the following:

1. Could equipment provided by the ISTC to institutes still engaged

in military R&D be used in closed facilities of the institute, namely in areas that were not open for monitoring and audit, if the equipment were brought out and shown to visiting auditors? An unequivocal answer was needed to underscore that the ISTC would not tolerate diversion of equipment to military purposes. Thus, the answer was an emphatic "no" in order to provide assurance that the equipment was not being used in weapons programs conducted behind closed doors.

2. Could researchers take personal computers provided by ISTC away from the project site, such as borrowing them for use at home? Again the answer was "no," in an effort to keep the ground rules unambiguous by requiring all equipment provided by the ISTC to remain at the project site.

3. If the Russian institution provided certain equipment for the project at no cost to the ISTC and the equipment was permanently affixed to structures located behind closed doors, could personnel supported by ISTC work on this equipment behind closed doors? This decision was positive, but with some hesitation. There simply was no other way to incorporate this equipment into the project; and more likely than not, without the equipment the project would have little meaning.

4. Could ISTC funds be used to construct new open facilities to allow project participants to move out of areas where access was prohibited? Again, this was a positive response since such a step contributed toward a clearer separation of military and civilian activities, which greatly facilitated the projects of the ISTC.

Unfortunately, even after this extensive groundwork, later complications concerning the issue of access threatened to erode Russian support for the ISTC at a critical time. These issues are discussed in Chapter 4.

Scientific Advisory Committee

The European Union insisted that a Scientific Advisory Committee (SAC) be established to review each project proposal before it was presented for consideration by the Governing Board. This procedure would mirror a standard review process already in place in Brussels within the framework of other EU programs.

The other parties were very concerned that a SAC would simply add a level of bureaucracy to an already complicated review process. The European Union persisted. The other parties argued that governments and not scientists would decide which projects should be supported and that the governmental representatives did not want to become involved in debates with advisers over which projects deserved support. The European Union continued to persist.

After lengthy discussions, the parties agreed to establish a SAC on the basis of appointments of the members by the parties. But the SAC would not meet to review project proposals. Instead, each SAC member would receive each proposal by mail, review it independently, and then submit comments to the Secretariat. The Secretariat would compile the comments and forward them to the Governing Board. This formula seemed to eliminate the possibility of a new committee with its own staff and budgetary requirements being inserted into the review process.[14]

Contributions to Overhead Charges of the Institutes

Under the system inherited from the Soviet era, Russian enterprises and institutes not only paid salaries to workers, they also supported a wide range of social services. In some cases they provided housing, schools, and hospitals; they managed transportation services; and they even operated water and sewage systems, not only for the R&D facilities but also for the residential areas. Indeed, in some small cities, the directors of enterprises and R&D institutes were de facto mayors of the towns. Within the Soviet state, this system was one approach that worked; and the workers were generally satisfied. Nevertheless, it was not surprising that overhead charges on projects sited at R&D institutions were often calculated to be as high as 700 percent, and charges in the range of 300 percent were commonplace in order to pay for the support system.[15]

In addition, the institutes were responsible for setting aside funds to cover retirement, medical services, injury and pregnancy leaves, and other costs that in the West are referred to as employee benefit packages. In the West, these charges are normally on the order of 25 to 30 percent of salary levels, whereas in Russia the percentage is about 40 percent. More important, the lack of accountability for the use of funds in Russia that have been set aside for pensions and health insurance has been perceived in the West, and within Russia, as scandalous.

The United States was determined that ISTC funds would not be diverted into covering overhead charges, despite the pleas of the Russians that someone needed to pay for the electricity and water that were necessary simply to open an institute for business. In addition to the disenchantment over waste of the money, the concern of the foreign partners centered on the possibility that ISTC overhead funds might end up supporting the purchase of automobiles for institute directors or might even be used to support subversive weapons development activities.

Consequently, the United States proposed and the other parties agreed to the limitation of overhead payments to about 7 percent of the total cost of each project. Further, the 7 percent would be paid only after an acceptable final report of the project reached the Secretariat to ensure that the project would indeed be completed and result in a tangible product. The Russian institutes were expected to cover all other overhead costs as their matching contributions to the projects.[16]

A more difficult issue was the question of employee benefits. By law, Russian institutes could not make salary payments until they had set aside 40 percent of the salary level for the various social funds. The institutes contended that they simply did not have the 40 percent, because all their money was tied to specific projects and could not be shifted to support ISTC activities.

After eighteen months of struggling with this problem, the parties accepted a scheme developed by the Planning Group whereby all payments to participants in ISTC projects would be channeled directly to those participants through cashiers of commercial banks and not through the institutes. Since technically the institutes never saw the money, they had no legal obligation to provide the 40 percent matching funds.

Nevertheless, Russian specialists were concerned that avoidance of the 40 percent match might also affect their rights to have access to pension and medical benefits. Therefore, most institutes decided to either (1) continue to pay the employees a minimum wage from institute funds, with the 40 percent match, in addition to the much larger direct payments the project participants received from the ISTC; or (2) have their employees work less than 100 percent of their time on ISTC projects with the 40 percent match based on the salary for the other time that they worked on institute projects. Either of these schemes would ensure that employees retained eligibility for all state benefits.

With these and other details coming under control, by the end of

1992 a nearly complete draft of the Statute was ready.[17] But what was happening with the diplomatic procedures to establish the ISTC formally?

Moving the Agreement into Volatile Political Arenas

Only after I was on my way to Moscow did I learn that the pouring of champagne in Lisbon in May did not really signal a consensus on the text of the ISTC Agreement to establish the ISTC. The officials in Paris had not fully expressed their views; and when they did, they dropped a bombshell. The French government insisted that a French-language version of the Agreement be equally authentic with the English- and Russian-language texts. Not to be upstaged, other EU members then demanded authentic texts in their eight languages as well, and the Japanese had no choice but also to insist on their own language.

For four months, the juro-linguists struggled to obtain linguistic conformity among eleven texts. First, they tried to communicate changes by sending telegrams among the capitals. But a change in one text could affect ten other texts; and the flurry of responses in Japanese, Greek, Portuguese, Danish, and Russian—let alone English, French, German, Italian, Dutch, and Spanish—to changes in other languages were seldom identical. Finally, when the volume of telegrams threatened to bury the texts, the wordsmiths decided to gather in Brussels, where the domino effect could be viewed simultaneously by all. At last, after weathering a constant din of simultaneous translations for several days, they reported success in September.

Then the Russian government needed additional time. During the summer, the Russian tax laws had changed. The Russian negotiators wanted to understand the implications of an Agreement that waived tax requirements. Also, they wanted to have another round of full consultations within their government.

Finally, all was ready. The Americans, Europeans, and Japanese gave their consent; and the papers were sent to President Yeltsin for his signature. Of course moving a paper through the Russian administrative apparatus offers a special type of challenge, but finally a signed decree emerged.[18] On November 22, 1992, the champagne glasses clinked again as fifteen ambassadors gathered at the guest house of the Foreign Ministry in Moscow to attend the ceremonial signing of the Agreement to establish the ISTC.[19]

Now all that was needed was the endorsement of the ISTC Agreement by the European Parliament and ratification by the Russian Supreme Soviet. The staff and I expected that both of these actions would be pro forma and that in early 1993 the ISTC would finally begin to function.

Meanwhile, just before the end-of-the-year holidays in Moscow, the Russian Foreign Ministry became concerned about the proactive orientation of our Planning Group in the Pulse Institute. We were visiting Russian institutes, consulting with scientists and government officials, and preparing official documents; yet we had no formal status. The Russians proposed that we be formally constituted as an intergovernmental Preparatory Committee (Prepcom) for the establishment of the ISTC. The other parties quickly agreed. The parties designated me as chairman of the Prepcom. The staff members working at the Pulse Institute were to have double titles as both members of the Prepcom and members of the staff of the Prepcom.[20]

At the time, I thought this diplomatic nicety was insignificant and that I would have a short-lived title. I was greatly mistaken.

Alone, but Not Alone, at Christmas

While most of the other foreigners who were assigned to the ISTC Planning Group and then to the Prepcom had departed for home for the holidays, Carole and I remained in Moscow. Despite the bitter cold, we were determined to enjoy a few days together exploring our neighborhood and other parts of the city. Of course, on working days I made the daily trek on the metro to the Center where a handful of us in winter coats and gloves crouched behind stacks of papers. My daily reports to my colleagues of new rumors that ratification was just around the corner became the highlights of our activities.

Christmas Eve found Carole and me by ourselves, listening to taped Christmas carols, flicking on Russian television programs, and gazing out over the snow-covered city.

We heard an unexpected knock at the door; and there were two Russian colleagues from the Pulse Institute who had come by metro and tram for more than one and one-half hours to wish us a Merry Christmas, not even knowing if we would be home. They had brought us all they had to offer—sacks of fruits and vegetables from their dacha. First, they orchestrated an unusual feast of vodka-laced fruits, which we promptly embalmed in Russian champagne. Then they introduced Carole to an array of new vegetables. By the time the 80-proof fruit disappeared and the vegetables had been reduced to rinds and seeds, we had made great strides toward closer international cooperation. We will long remember that touching evening in Moscow.

On New Year's Eve we decided to follow a Moscow tradition for foreigners of watching a ballet at the Bolshoi Theater, visiting Red Square, and then celebrating with champagne. The dancing at the Bolshoi was no longer flawless, since the three best troupes were traveling the world in search of hard currency; but even the fourth string was entertaining in this gem of a theater. Then we went on to the brilliance and mystery that only a lighted Red Square can project. For ten minutes we withstood the bitter cold, absorbing an indelible mental picture of the church of St. Basil's and even the red neon hammer-and-sickle emblems that still garnished the Kremlin wall.

Finally, we chose the Chechen restaurant in our apartment building for our midnight meal and toasting so that our driver could also celebrate at his own apartment. While the restaurant was convenient when there was no designated driver, the Chechens should have saved their culinary skills for the owner and his friends, who reportedly dined there every night. Their overpriced meals for foreigners needed a little more than chicken skins to contain the butter in the Chicken Kiev.

But we entered the New Year on a high note. Our apartment was scheduled for renovation in January. The ISTC was but two quick votes away from reality. Our Russian friends were concerned about our every need. Our fax machine provided a reliable link with the State Department and often the only link between the Center and the sponsors of the Center.

And we thought we would soon see some bright spots on the economic front. Indeed, Russian and American economists predicted that new forms of shock therapy were all the country needed to reverse the slide in production, to dampen inflation, and to stimulate a new breed of honest entrepreneurship.

Even in Moscow, hope could spring eternal.

Chapter 2

Planning Proceeds Despite a Recalcitrant Parliament

We have detailed files of hundreds of former Soviet Union experts in the fields of rocket, missile, and nuclear weapons. These weapon experts are willing to work in a country which needs their skills and can offer reasonable pay.
Advertising leaflet of the Hong Kong–based
Sun Shine Industrial Company, August 1993
(circulating in the Middle East)

Preparing for the Long Vigil

The falling snow quickly erased the tracks of our cross-country skis as Carole and I traversed the spacious grounds of Moscow State University in mid-January 1993.

Earlier in the week at the Pulse Institute, the Prepcom staff had frantically prepared the documents for the initial meeting of the fifty-member Prepcom. The diplomatic missions in Moscow had just dispatched to Brussels, Tokyo, and Washington, through their own channels, our latest bundles of hastily prepared manuscripts with the hope that the packets would arrive at their destinations in one week. That would be ten days before the scheduled session in Moscow.

All of us should have been hard at work at the institute on this Saturday also, preparing additional papers for distribution at the meeting. But the Institute simply would not unlatch its doors on weekends. We offered to huddle in hooded jackets and bring our own Finnish heaters so that lack of heat could not be the excuse. But the management of the institute could not afford the costs of the security guards to let us in and to ensure our safety.

The alternative of a brief outing in the snow would help Carole and me forget the paper chase for a few hours and offer escape from

Russia's economic troubles everywhere we turned. In addition, skiing and snowballs would add some levity to the deeply troubling talk about the smuggling of uranium and plutonium by suspicious global shoppers.

I had just purchased new Latvian skis at a Russian sporting goods store for $2 and new French ski boots and bindings for $40 from a street vendor who claimed he had obtained them at a discount through a local sports club. When I subsequently saw the exact boots on sale for $140 at a Swiss joint venture sports shop, I knew that uranium was not the only hot product in town.

We soon encountered a pack of hungry junkyard dogs, yelping their way through the university grounds. Hard economic times had led to many abandoned pets and to canceled city services that could corral uncontrolled animals. The police had simply shot several hundred "dangerous" stray dogs in a nearby town a few days earlier. Realizing that a dog bite would mean a trip to Helsinki for rabies shots, we terminated our skiing in this area until we could arm ourselves with mace or pepper gas. Leisure activities were certainly complicated.

Fortunately, the American Embassy dacha along the Moscow River offered even better snow-covered trails through the nearby woods and onto the frozen river, and without canine escorts. This dacha also became the site of our representational functions for the staff of the Center and friends from the diplomatic corps who preferred skiing, tennis, croquet, and poetry readings to the crowded cocktail parties of the embassies.

Meanwhile, at our apartment, a Finnish renovation team had invaded the living room armed with power saws, a mini-lumberyard, and miles of wallpaper reinforced with fiber glass to keep the poor quality concrete walls from further crumbling. Every day for ten weeks, the Finns and their Russian helpers scraped the walls down to the concrete, sanded the floors, ripped out the kitchen and bathroom appliances, and gradually transformed our apartment into livable quarters. A $55,000 renovation price tag was modest compared to the costs the U.S. Embassy was incurring to prepare habitats for new arrivals. Also, had the Finnish mark not suffered a recent fall, the price would have been $10,000 higher.

I pointed out our frugality to the State Department budgeteers when they asked why I was building a palace in Moscow. They were unimpressed.

With a warm apartment and ski trails at our beck and call, I was fortified to take on the bureaucratic hurdles that blocked the road to establishment of the ISTC.

Continuation of the Document Dance

While our personal lives went forward, activities of the Prepcom were also picking up steam. In February, delegates to the meeting of the full Prepcom arrived from Tokyo, Brussels, and Washington, as well as Moscow, to put the final touches on the administrative arrangements for the ISTC, which they thought would soon come into being. The European Parliament had formally endorsed the ISTC Agreement, and the Russian government had submitted the paperwork to the Supreme Soviet requesting ratification. In Tokyo and Washington, action by the legislative bodies was not required. Multiple drafts of about a dozen management documents for the ISTC decorated every surface in our offices at the Pulse Institute, while weapons scientists from throughout Russia began knocking on our doors in search of funds to support their conversion efforts.

In periodic reports to the four parties, I had been optimistically projecting ratification of the Agreement by the Supreme Soviet by March 1993, with the first meeting of the Governing Board of the Center shortly thereafter. The staff was already processing project proposals for consideration by the board. Money would begin flowing to the Russian weapons specialists by summer, when the Secretariat would be in its new facilities with a forty-person staff, six automobiles, and a long list of perks—or so we all thought.

Until that time, we needed to focus our efforts on completion of a number of key documents that would provide the legal, administrative, and management framework for the Center's activities. The development of several of the most important documents is discussed below.

Financial Regulations

With a draft Statute almost ready, the next order of business was to develop financial regulations for the Center. How would the money be transferred from the United States, the European Union, and Japan to the ISTC and then on to the weapons scientists and engineers? How would the ISTC manage these funds? What sorts of constraints would be placed on expenditures? What levels of budgets would be required for administering the Secretariat? How often would audits be carried out?

The staff needed to provide background information on the financial environment in Russia so that these questions could be addressed by the four parties. In a country where checking accounts were unknown and most banks were linked to mafia operations, this undertaking was not trivial. But the U.S. government had not yet provided the two financial experts to work in Moscow as promised; through default, I had become the resident expert on the details of money matters.

After many discussions with commercial banks in Moscow and with Russia's Central Bank, my Russian colleagues and I thought we had developed an approach that would avoid two of the key problems encountered by many foreign organizations operating in Russia. Of special concern were the Russian practices of (1) charging fees of up to seven percent for withdrawals of cash from bank accounts, and (2) requiring immediate conversion to rubles, whose value was dropping like a stone, of 50 percent of all foreign currency transferred to Russia for commercial purposes (an ill-defined term at best). We were determined to avoid these pitfalls by distributing ISTC funds through a single Russian bank that would agree to favorable arrangements; and we had found that bank—CONVERSBANK.

The negotiation of the financial regulations was to proceed in a work group of the Prepcom that would meet concurrently with a plenary group discussion of other unresolved issues. Since I would be chairing the plenary session while the resident financial experts were still missing en route to Moscow, we needed a specialist on financial matters to represent the staff in the work group. Therefore, the Department of State designated Carole as a financial expert to hold the fort until the reinforcements arrived from Washington. Her business background and her practical experience in dealing with financial transactions in Moscow gave her strong credentials for this task.

The discussions continued for four long days. The European Union had promised to distribute their proposals to the other parties well in advance of the meeting. But someone in Brussels forgot to meet his deadline, and the EU specialists simply brought to Moscow a new draft document with proposed financial regulations. The European Union had prepared the sixteen-page document only in English even though the Prepcom operated in two languages. Therefore, the translators had but one evening to prepare a hastily rendered Russian version.

The work group then struggled through the document, word by word, with the help of an interpreter. Curious linguistic hangups punctuated the discussions. Some Western concepts, such as allowable costs and competitive tenders, were not entirely clear to Russian accountants. Finally, late Friday evening the work group chairman from the U.S. Department of Defense announced that they had reached a consensus. Carole thought that all delegates in the frigid room during the marathon sessions were satisfied with the twelve-page text. She reported that just a few minor points needed authorizations in the capitals and then the final document could be prepared. She had missed the silent undercurrent of partisanship in the negotiating room, however, and the Moscow discussions were but the beginning of a paper odyssey that lasted for more than one year.

Once back in Washington, the Defense Department experts who had participated in the negotiations decided to propose a "few" revisions affecting about one-third of the document. These comments were largely organizational and editorial, but they nevertheless caused consternation among other participants in the work group who thought they had put the document to rest.

Not to be outdone, many months later EU experts decided to rewrite another 10 percent of the document according to their latest thoughts. The European Union wanted to have an on-site representative in Moscow to approve every financial transaction of the Secretariat involving funds provided by the European Union, including payment of taxi fares and telephone bills. This concept was completely contrary to the thrust of earlier negotiations designed to minimize bureaucracy and to provide the ISTC Secretariat with its own financial staff. In the end, the EU delegates recanted; because they themselves could not figure out how their proposed system could ever work, let alone how they would find and pay a trustworthy European to live in Moscow with the sole purpose of second guessing the Center's financial officer.

The procedures that were finally set forth in the financial regulations (e.g., banking arrangements, procurement requirements, financial reports, budget preparation, responsibilities of financial staff) generally reflected the realities of working in Moscow—poor communications, rapid turnover of experienced staff members, and uncertain reliability of vendors, including those allied with foreign firms.

Initially, the American and European representatives had tried to take their own regulations, which were in force in Washington and

Brussels, and transfer them to the Moscow scene. This was not possible because the regulations of the various parties differed. Also, the financial systems that would be used by the ISTC would be much less elaborate than the sophisticated computer operations in place in Brussels and Washington where specialists and hardware were in abundance.

Indeed, in Moscow the rule for any administrative or management system should be: the simpler, the better. While expertise and equipment could be found in the city for a price, the experts often were not available at any price when they were needed; and equipment always seemed to malfunction at the most critical times.

Nothing is dearer to the hearts of government bureaucrats than control over money. Thus, the negotiations over every word of the financial regulations continued into early 1994, when agreement was finally reached by all parties. The final document was quite general, as it should have been. Many of the micromanagement details that the Europeans originally proposed were pushed aside to be worked out as the Secretariat developed its internal operating rules.

Instructions for Preparing Proposals

Another important ISTC document was entitled *Instructions for Preparing Proposals.* This document set the standard for determining which project proposals received by the Secretariat were eligible for processing. If a proposal did not comply with the standard, it would be returned to the originator for revision and resubmission. More than fifty people participated in preparing the *Instructions*, which set forth the required format and contents of proposals. Of special importance were the sections that described the costs that could be covered by ISTC funds and those that could not.

In retrospect, despite the complexities of meshing the suggestions of fifty experts into a single coherent text, this document was quite straightforward, even for Russians, who had little previous experience in preparing proposals for a competitive review process. The document was more complete and more clearly written than comparable documents used by many organizations that provided funding for R&D projects in the West. The staff distributed thousands of copies within Russia, both in Russian and in English.

The *Instructions* were the primary reason that, within a few months reasonably well-developed proposals from all over the country started to flow through the ISTC system. Also, this document was quite valuable as an educational tool for Russians trying to adapt Western approaches to project funding under other programs. Indeed, Russian professional acquaintances considered the *Instructions* far more useful than many of the training sessions organized in Russia by Western institutions to teach techniques for preparing proposals targeted on foreign financial support.[1]

Other Operating Documents

Several other documents were linked to the project agreements that the ISTC would sign with the Russian institutes selected for carrying out ISTC projects. The discussions of these documents began in mid-1992. In September 1994, the four parties finally endorsed *Model Project Agreements*. The issues addressed in these documents came to the fore when the Center announced its first financial awards, and the ensuing problems are discussed in Chapter 4.

Finally, the Russian Ministry of Atomic Energy (MINATOM) was repeatedly concerned that the Ministry of Finance would not provide the funds for Russia to meet its legal obligations to support the ISTC, as set forth in the ISTC Agreement. Therefore, the Prepcom developed a *Memorandum of Understanding* between the ISTC and MINATOM that acted "on behalf of the Russian Federation." The memorandum set forth the obligations of Russia to provide space, staff, vehicles, and some supporting services at no cost to the Center. Our Russian colleagues were pleased that they could then go to their government financiers with this reaffirmation of the Russian commitments and seek funds. But in practice, MINATOM had great difficulty acting on behalf of the ministries that controlled Russian finances; and their internal arguments over funding were a constant problem.

A second memorandum was to call for MINATOM to provide additional services for the Secretariat, such as translators, computer support, and vehicle drivers, to be paid for by the ISTC. After more than two years of negotiation, however, we abandoned the proposal for this memorandum. It became clear that such services could be purchased on the commercial market by the Center as needed. I led the move to reject the idea of having MINATOM provide standby personnel who would always be available to help an overworked Secretariat, following a long-standing personal bias that an overworked staff is preferable to an underworked one.

In view of this plethora of documents, the Prepcom was floating on a sea of paper that became deeper every day. This apparently is often the case with international organizations that must shower the member countries around the world with excruciating details on all developments.

But we had several special problems. All documents were to be prepared in English, and some in Russian as well. But we had few people who could write English with any degree of grammatical correctness, because English was the second or third language of almost all staff members. Indeed, for many months, the two of us who could write acceptable English became funnels for all documents. Second, most documents were needed in at least a dozen copies and some in hundreds of copies; but there were no functioning copy machines at the Pulse Institute. Only through the sympathy of the U.S. Embassy were we able to make copies of our many manuscripts, as I repeatedly made trips on the metro lugging documents downtown for reproduction.

Finally, in late 1993, Los Alamos Laboratory in New Mexico loaned the Prepcom a small Canon copier designed for operation on Western electrical circuitry. A local maintenance specialist became a regular visitor to the Pulse Institute, first to adapt the copier to Moscow conditions and then to keep it running. Only many months later, and exactly two years after I arrived in Moscow, did we have in place the beginnings of an adequate reproduction capability.

The Worth of a Weapons Scientist

Since the purpose of the ISTC was to counteract the financial incentives for scientists and engineers to scout for opportunities to sell their skills to other countries, the appropriate salary levels for Russian specialists participating in ISTC projects became a hot button for debate. Later, we foreigners realized that the pay level, while important, was but one of several key factors determining the mindset of scientists and engineers caught in the downsizing of the Soviet military effort. Also of importance were the likelihood that ISTC paychecks would actually reach the scientists on time, the length of the ISTC contractual arrangements, the technical challenges offered by ISTC projects, the opportunities provided by ISTC for scientists to remain members of their research teams, and the domestic and international recognition associated with working on ISTC projects. But, at the beginning, the amount of money was the issue. Russian colleagues, who were silently aware of these other factors, apparently did not want to deflect attention from the issue of money.

The Russian Foreign Ministry quickly punctured a balloon floated by the Europeans that the ISTC adopt *standard* salary levels for specialists working on ISTC projects. The Russian diplomats successfully argued that pay levels in Russia would be only temporarily far below international levels, and ISTC documents should not suggest that such low levels were standard or even currently appropriate for highly qualified Russian specialists. Also, they contended that pay levels published by the ISTC might be used as an excuse by foreign firms operating in Russia to reduce their levels of pay to Russian specialists.

Thus, in the fall of 1992, the four parties instructed the Planning Group to encourage salary levels in the project proposals to the ISTC that would take into account the salaries currently paid by Russian institutions together with supplementary income earned by financially astute weapons specialists. Also to be considered were the salaries being offered by foreign companies and organizations operating in Russia and the Russian practice of providing bonuses of 25 to 30 percent for participants in international projects.

I interpreted these less-than-clear guidelines to mean we should

> pay what it takes to attract key weapons specialists to participate in ISTC projects in competition with other income opportunities, but don't pay more, since the limited ISTC funds should reach as many weapons specialists as possible.

The staff then initiated a survey of pay levels within a few "typical" Russian institutes and a review of published information about pay levels. The two key conclusions from these efforts were as follows: As a whole, scientists and engineers were paid far below the levels paid to many other professionals and well below the average paid to all categories of workers. Second, within Russian R&D institutes, it was common practice for many researchers to supplement their official salaries with additional income. This income was derived either from part-time work of their institutes on special contracts with foreign organizations or from their personal dealings in buying and selling goods, which had nothing to do with the institute.

This study led to a staff recommendation that the ISTC should pay three times the official salary levels for government scientists as published by the Russian Ministry of Labor, noting that such a policy would encourage the participants in ISTC projects to hold down one job instead of the usual two or three. Translated into dollar terms, this meant that the ISTC should pay scientists between $200 and $300 per month.

Then, in February 1993, a Western delegate to the meeting of the Prepcom surprised the assemblage by proposing that the ISTC should simply match the official salary levels of the Russian government. He argued that this policy would enable the ISTC to spread its money among a larger number of Russian specialists than would the policy previously articulated by the four parties or the policy proposed in the staff study. Apparently, his views did not reflect a well-developed position of his government; for after a negative response by other delegates to this one confusing signal, such a proposal was never again raised. In future meetings, all participants recognized that unless the ISTC supported attractive salary levels for Russian weapons specialists, the Center would have little impact in deterring leakages of knowledge to foreign countries.

The four parties also considered several other issues related to pay levels. These were as follows:

1. If the project were sited in a *hardship* area, such as the Urals or Siberia, or in a closed city, or both, the participants should receive bonuses of 20 to 30 percent in accordance with Russian practice.
2. Participants working on two different ISTC projects should be paid the same level under each project unless they had significantly different responsibilities in the two projects.
3. Institute directors who had many administrative duties could participate in projects, but they could not serve as project leaders or charge large portions of their time to the projects.
4. All pay levels would be calculated on the basis of dollars or ruble equivalents of dollars so as to help cope with the rapidly changing currency exchange rate.
5. Finally, there would be no escalation clauses in the project agreements to enable salaries to keep up with inflation. The parties wanted to commit firm levels of funding to projects once they were approved without having to set aside additional funds for coping with unpredictable swings in the economy.

Thus, inflation would be addressed in two ways. First, as noted, payments would be calculated in dollars, which were less sensitive to inflation than rubles. Second, paying quite high levels at the outset of the project should ensure that the payments remained relatively high in the wake of anticipated inflation one or two years later.

Although the salary issue was temporarily resolved, it would re-appear many times during the course of establishing the Center and launching the projects.

Mired Down in the Supreme Soviet

While this frenzy of activity was underway at the Pulse Institute, Russia's parliament, the Supreme Soviet, was determined to lose the rubber-stamp reputation of its Soviet predecessors. Apparently the po-litical training programs of the U.S. Information Agency, which spon-sored many planeloads of Russian legislators traveling to Washington to watch proceedings on Capitol Hill, were having an impact.

As soon as the proposed ISTC Agreement arrived at the Supreme Soviet for ratification at the beginning of 1993, it was referred to five committees of the lower house for consideration. "Not to worry," was the daily refrain of Russian officials involved in the preparations for the Center. Of course, they were observing this new type of parlia-mentary procedure for the first time, while still viewing the body as a rubber stamp.

The ratification procedures began amid general confusion as to how an agreement that touched on the interests of so many committees would be handled. Finally, the International Relations Committee as-sumed primary responsibility and established a coordinating commis-sion that included representatives of all interested committees. At the outset, the commission organized three formal hearings on the ISTC and many informal meetings between deputies of the parliament and representatives of the Russian government. Issues that would delay ratification soon became well-defined.

In view of the many other topics before the legislative body and the limitations on the number of deputies and staff members, the leaders of the five committees decided that the chairman of the International Relations Committee should personally shepherd the ratification document through the parliamentary process. Two other deputies quickly assumed the roles of chief advocate and chief opponent.[2] Thus, the fate of the ISTC was in the hands of three people.

From the beginning, the committee chairman was generally positive about the Center; but he was very clear that he would not endorse the ratification document until a complete consensus developed within his committee. He did not want to be embarrassed by opposition arising within the full parliament after the committee supported ratification. The deputy who was the chief advocate was a physicist from a weapons laboratory; the spokesman for the opposition was a navy submarine captain. Unfortunately, the former suffered a concussion during a fall at his dacha near St. Petersburg and was unavailable for several weeks at crucial times in the process. The latter became diverted to the task of heading off an attempted Ukrainian takeover of large portions of the former Soviet Black Sea Fleet. He also became scarce as he undertook shuttle diplomacy to Sevastopol and Kiev.

When the International Relations Committee found time to focus on ratification, two core concerns of opponents were the penetration of foreign governments into the security affairs of Russia and the distortion by foreign governments of the scientific priorities of the country. The opponents emphasized that the $67 million committed to the ISTC by the foreign parties was a trivial sum in exchange for such extraordinary powers to be given to these governments. Another important factor was the distrust of Russian Foreign Minister Kozyrev by many deputies; they believed he had sold out to the West on other fronts. Therefore, his support of the ISTC automatically triggered opposition from this faction.

The Russian press was replete with reports about the financial woes of laboratories throughout the country. When the newspapers learned about the ISTC proposal, the reactions were as mixed as the number of reporters writing their stories. The conservative paper *Den* was particularly sharp in its criticism of those who "defended Western interests."[3] The more balanced paper *Kommersant* reported concerns over a CIA plot but eventually concluded that this wasn't really the case.[4]

The more specific complaints of the opponents included the following allegations:

1. Diplomatic status for Secretariat staff members would give them license to spy without the fear of punishment if they were caught.
2. The Agreement mentioned that the ISTC could earn "profit" for

which there would be special currency exchange privileges. This not only opened the door for illegal currency operations by the ISTC in Russia but would encourage such activities.

3. The Agreement was silent on intellectual property rights, even though Western firms had been systematically "stealing" Russian technologies as a result of their "legal" activities in Russia.

4. Finally, the Agreement placed inadequate limitations on the rights of foreign participants in ISTC projects to have access to highly sensitive Russian facilities for monitoring and auditing projects.[5]

Fortunately, the negotiators addressed these specific arguments when preparing the ISTC Statute, which all four parties approved in draft form in February 1993. Supporters in the Supreme Soviet pointed to the Statute to ensure their colleagues that the interests of Russia would be adequately protected. Opponents countered that the Supreme Soviet was not being asked to ratify the Statute, noting that the Statute could be changed by the mistrusted Kozyrev anytime *after* ratification of the Agreement without approval of the legislative body.

In retrospect, the negotiators of the ISTC Agreement, particularly the Russian diplomats, should have been more sensitive to the possibility that skepticism had replaced the rubber stamp within the legislative branch of the Russian government. They should have insisted on slight modifications of several provisions of the Agreement, as well as inclusion in the Agreement of several additional provisions that appeared in the Statute. These steps could have eased the ratification process.

Examples of such modifications and amendments follow. First, there was no need to link the ISTC with "profit" in the Agreement. Apparently, the negotiators thought that revenues from licensing or other arrangements could cycle back to replenish the Center's budget. Nevertheless, words other than "profit" could have been used to set forth the concept. Second, the Agreement should have at least indicated that the approach to IPR would be based on "equitable" sharing of the payoff from research results. Such a general statement would have gone a long way in countering the disaster scenarios invented by the parliamentarians. Finally, with regard to access to closed facilities, the Agreement could have explicitly recognized the Russian right to protect portions of facilities not involved in ISTC projects.

Of course, such technical fixes would not have overcome the general mistrust of the Russian foreign minister. But they would have eliminated many of the complaints over details and thereby shortened the review process. As will soon be apparent, earlier action could have been a decisive step.

Confrontation with ISTC Opponents

For six months the Prepcom staff waited for action by the Supreme Soviet, each day scanning the Russian newspapers in search of the upcoming agenda for the legislature. Each day we would predict "two more weeks until the parliament acts." Through it all, both the U.S. and Russian governments told me to stay out of this internal affair of Russia. "We know how to work with the parliament. Just leave it to us," was a constant reminder from the Foreign Ministry that taxed my patience.

But a Russian colleague, who had deep roots throughout the Russian weapons community and was anxious for the Center to begin providing funds to his acquaintances, was less constrained. He developed personal relationships with the key deputies of the parliament, with the quiet approval of the Russian bureaucracies. Government officials were not eager to risk becoming too involved in internal negotiations with the parliament because they might end up on the wrong side of the debate. But my colleague flashed his trump card as a physicist who represented suffering Russian researchers fighting to gain a seat at the political game table. From him, I learned that the picture being painted by the ministries was much rosier than reality warranted: *The ratification was in deep trouble.*

By sheer luck, I spotted the chairman of the International Relations Committee of the Supreme Soviet, set apart by his bright pink shirt, at the Fourth of July reception hosted by the American chargé d'affaires. When I introduced myself, he immediately asked, "Where have you been?" And he added, "You should come and see us."

With this invitation, I decided to become directly involved with the political action. Without endorsement but with no objection from Russian officialdom, I invited my Japanese and European colleagues from the Prepcom and representatives of the U.S., Japanese, and EU missions in Moscow to join in a show of force as we visited the International Relations Committee in mid-July 1993. Much to our surprise and satisfaction, all the key players of the parliament were present, both deputies and staffers.

For more than an hour, the navy submarine captain fired the torpedoes aimed at the advocates of ratification—torpedoes loaded with arguments about IPR, access, profit making, and espionage opportunities. By the end of his last salvo, we knew that the ISTC was listing badly and was on the verge of sinking. Our tenure in Moscow had surely come to an end.

But then the chairman of the committee interjected, "These are problems which we can work out. All we need is a supplementary protocol, among the Western countries and the parliament to provide us with reassurances in these areas. We are not asking to change the Agreement. That would be too complicated. We simply want a document signed *at the same level as the Agreement* which provides the necessary assurances. We will work with you to develop the language for such a document."

Thus, the message was, "Don't fold your tent just yet."

Following the meeting, I met privately with the chairman, who had suddenly become my good friend. He confided that he wanted to push the Agreement through, but he needed to provide the submarine captain with *something* so the captain would not make a fuss when the formal ratification vote was taken.

The next day, I visited the chairman again to report the great difficulty the three foreign parties would have in negotiating directly with the parliament. He replied that he knew we had no choice but to work through the Foreign Ministry, but he wanted to impress his colleagues that they too could deal with diplomats. He urged me, "Tell Kozyrev to send me a letter, since he has been ignoring us." He added, "Then the committee will work out the details."

Elated, I gently nudged the Russian Ministry of Foreign Affairs to be more aggressive and talk to the committee. The Foreign Ministry did indeed send a letter to the committee although not over the signature of Kozyrev but penned by his deputy foreign minister. They did not need a new flash point. Negotiations between the executive and legislative branches of the Russian government finally took on a degree of urgency within Russia's White House.

Searching for Weapons Scientists

Despite the apparent movement within the legislature, we knew that the remainder of July and August would be a slow time in Moscow.

Many legislators would be on vacation, and the Supreme Soviet might close its doors entirely for a few weeks.

The staff and I decided to use the time to visit institutes located in small towns around Moscow where we might find clusters of weapons scientists who still didn't know about the ISTC. We had initiated these outreach visits about nine months earlier and uncovered many former weapons scientists anxiously awaiting someone interested in their civilian research plans.

During these visits, we discovered in these satellite towns not only different lifestyles but different approaches to R&D activities and divergent attitudes about the future of the country. A few examples of our trips follow.

Chernogolovka

Chernogolovka is a two-hour drive, to the northeast of Moscow. Now a "science city" of 20,000 people with ten research institutions, the town was established shortly after World War II to carry out research on rocket fuels for the Soviet military effort.[6] The location was close enough to Moscow to allow the scientists to stay in touch with government agencies and other research institutions but far enough away to permit unnoticed use of testing ranges for different chemical reactions that involved large explosions.

Research on rocket fuels remained one of the mainstays of the town for many years. But as the ten institutes gradually found homes in Chernogolovka, other types of both military and civilian research activities were added, including a surge of research in the 1980s on space-based laser systems to destroy missiles.

In their new efforts to appear less insular, local scientists downplayed these classified research activities as being the reason for years of secrecy about the town. Instead, they pointed out that the nearby air force target range had made access to the area too dangerous for foreigners. Now, even the air force is less concerned about visitors to the area, they added.

Desperate for new sources of funds, the heads of several institutes had invited us to view their facilities. Our initial visit centered on new ideas of 500 rocket scientists who thought they could uncover the causes of most industrial explosions. Also, they wanted to develop techniques to incinerate chemical wastes. But most of our hosts were

Chernogolovka, February 1993. Prepcom members from the United States, Japan, France, Germany, and Russia meet with rocket propulsion scientists at the Institute of Chemical Physics.

well into their sixties with little experience in relating research to anything other than the interests of the air force. Were these old warriors really equipped to develop products that would sell on the commercial market? Convincing the new generation of Russian business leaders that this vintage of research could be of value seemed like a tall order.

The first priority of many scientists in Chernogolovka was to obtain invitations to go west, and 80 percent of the key researchers of one small facility, the Landau Physics Institute, had actually succeeded. A second priority was to establish small enterprises that could produce consumer items, using the facilities of the institutes. But there had been little success. A more profitable activity of the enterprises was to buy apartments and dachas, refurbish them, and then sell them to the nouveaux riches in Moscow who were looking for weekend retreats.

Upon our departure from Chernogolovka, the rocketeers presented us with a wooden stump carved into the shape of a brain. This symbol of the brain drain—or of a brain that needed financial nourishment—

Brain—or bomb? This wood carving, a gift from scientists at Chernogolovka, became an ISTC mascot.

became the Center's first mascot. Ironically, for many visitors to the ISTC the wooden brain took on the more ominous look of a mushroom cloud from a nuclear explosion.

Many of the scientists in Chernogolovka were probably good candidates for ISTC projects—former weaponeers with international ambitions. Nevertheless, two keys were needed if they were to unlock the doors to mainstream civilian research. First, they needed to abandon their nostalgia for the "good old days" of unlimited subsidies. Second, they needed to find important low-cost projects that would help the country and serve the interests of the West. They could then realistically think about linking an aging workforce with aggressive young Westerners who could take their products to market.

But how could they use their many indoor and outdoor explosion test areas? Only in 1995, when Russia faced the task of cleaning up the debris in Chechnya, did I have a perfectly compatible idea, namely, research on techniques for removing land mines from war-ravaged areas—in regions of the former Soviet Union, in Afghanistan, in Africa, and in Southeast Asia. I immediately passed on this idea to the combustion engineers of Chernogolovka.

Zelenograd

Another stop was Zelenograd, not far from Sheremetevo International Airport beyond the northwest edge of the city.[7] This is the site of the Soviet attempt to clone Silicon Valley.

During the 1960s, most of the country's advanced microelectronics research activities were concentrated in Zelenograd. At the same time, the Soviet leaders decided that production facilities would be dispersed throughout the Soviet Union; and the major production plants for microelectronics were established not in Zelenograd but in the Baltic republics, in Belarus, and in several cities of Russia.

Thus, with decentralization following the collapse of the Soviet Union, the specialists in Zelenograd had only limited capability to produce electronic components in their experimental factories. Since their R&D efforts lagged well behind the West, outside interest in the city's research efforts was minimal. Even the production facilities in the city often stood idle. The growing disdain within Russia for items made in Russia placed locally manufactured computers on the top of the list of unwanted products. Thus, the research centers and enterprises of Zelenograd had no choice but to pin their futures on joint undertakings with IBM, Samsung, and any other foreign firms they could attract to the former nerve center of the Soviet electronics industry. They had some success in the hunt for foreign collaborators who were willing to make modest investments in the city. Also, they found takers in Bulgaria for their electronic games, in Poland for their watches, in Hong Kong for their silicon wafers, and in India for their gallium arsenide devices.

The scientists were happy that a few foreign firms were interested in their products and were providing new sources of income. At the same time, the foreign firms seldom entrusted the Russians with challenging research tasks, preferring to let them concentrate on routine production of relatively simple electronic components.

Meanwhile, a different type of brain drain was underway in Zelenograd. A substantial number of Russian electronic engineers went to Syria on multiyear contracts where the pay was very good, at least by Russian standards. The nature of their assignments in Syria was never clear to us.

Our sense was that the impoverished Zelenograd researchers saw an influx of Western firms as their only hope of retaining their position as a prosperous community. They had already become accustomed to foreigners dictating the terms under which they would use their technical know-how.

It seemed unlikely that the ISTC would play a significant role in their activities in the near future. We doubted that their Western partners were interested in having a somewhat cumbersome international organization in the midst of their direct dealings, which apparently were already turning a profit for the partners.

Obninsk

To the south of Moscow is the "atomic city" of Obninsk, the home of the first Russian nuclear power reactor.[8]

In this town of 100,000 people are four institutes that have been involved for many years in nuclear activities in support of both military and civilian programs. The Institute of Physics and Power Engineering, the oldest and largest institute in Obninsk, was diversifying into many areas of nuclear research. There also were institutes directed to agriculture, medicine, and geophysical processes. From cancer treatment chambers to chambers for growing a variety of crops to artificial cloud chambers, the city was truly a metropolis of large scientific equipment. This of course meant heavy reliance on electricity at a time when the price of energy was climbing rapidly.

A significant portion of the research in Obninsk has been directed to assessing the aftermath of the Chernobyl accident. Indeed, contamination from Chernobyl reached Obninsk, conveniently providing field laboratories for the agricultural researchers. But the plans for investigating the long-term effects of the disaster have always outrun the financial support for such investigations.

At Obninsk, the Prepcom staff gave its first formal presentation on procedures to be followed in seeking financial support from the Center and in carrying out Center projects. Fifty specialists from the various institutes crammed into a small conference room to watch our multinational team present approaches to project design, financial control, and report preparation. Our intepreter translated from English and Japanese into Russian over the background of a humming overhead projector that had long passed the limits of its warranty. The audience was attentive, until time for the hourly cigarette breaks; and after three hours of briefings, three breaks, and not too many yawns, the audience was still prepared to remain and hear more details on the Center's plans for financial support.

The future of ISTC projects in Obninsk was far from clear. On the one hand, the scientists who attended the briefing session seemed so desperate for new sources of support that they would have agreed on the spot to carry out any type of project of interest to the Center. At the same time, other leaders of the scientific institutes had been on the forward edge of nuclear developments in the country for decades, and they seemed confident in their ability to pull the city through its difficult days. Very frankly, I did not expect a flood of proposals from Obninsk. If nothing else, I sensed there would be in-fighting at the institutes over areas of responsibility when money was at stake. I clearly underestimated the power of the purse, however; by 1995, the proposals from Obninsk had begun to pile up on the desks of the ISTC.

Kaliningrad

Another interesting cluster of weapons specialists was located in the town of Kaliningrad, just beyond the northern edge of the capital city. There the rocket designers had been working on novel ways to extinguish the fires burning in the oil wells of Kuwait. They had developed a steel flying saucer, about two feet in diameter, to be launched from a helicopter. The whirling projectile would hit and crimp the vertical pipe in the oil shaft just below the surface of the ground, cut off the oxygen supply, and extinguish the fire. They had conducted a number of helicopter flights to perfect the aiming of this spinning metal disc; but by the time the new technology was ready, Red Adair and his colleagues had already put out the 500 or so fires in the Gulf region.

We were interested in reports of research on synthetic diamonds, and our hosts did not disappoint us. They had a shock tube from the 1950s that was over 200 meters in length. Their idea was to force shock waves through the tube with such impact that they would compact carbon powder into gems of industrial quality.

Another proposal was to prepare for the predicted impact on earth of one or more large meteorites during the next century. They were ready to build 200 low-cost rocket launchers that could be deployed around the world to shoot down any incoming meteorites headed for populated areas.

We were hesitant to mention any more topics, because they would surely have a solution given the slightest encouragement. Indeed, this was the most imaginative group I encountered during my stay in Moscow. Despite their enthusiasm, we decided to concentrate on industrial diamonds and let others evaluate their flying saucers and anti-meteorite weaponry.

Unfortunately, our excursions were always too brief. But even short visits made us realize that the ISTC could provide critical support for struggling scientists and keep them off paths fraught with troubles for the entire world. In many ways the visits were the highlights of my stay in Russia, but I knew that our immediate tasks were waiting for us at the tables of the Pulse Institute.

Unexpected Help for Ratification

"The first weapon scientists to protest were at the two top-secret Russian nuclear weapons centers who called for thousands of their colleagues to go into the streets to draw the government's attention to their demands for a living wage." Thus, the *New York Times* reported the growing turmoil throughout the weapons community where paychecks had suddenly stopped for three months.[9] Meanwhile, the officials of MINATOM acknowledged to us that many members of the scientific elite were receiving lower pay—when they received it—than workers on the Moscow metro.

When queried by the U.S. Embassy about the *Times* article, I noted that for more than one year protests had become commonplace within the Russian science community. At the same time, lumberjacks, miners, and gas field operators also had been threatening to organize strikes. But this was the first time that scientists from the core of the weapons complex, the most loyal of all scientists, had stepped forward. They finally received their back pay, but at an average level that was equivalent to $40 per month.[10]

We became aware of three letters sent by scientists to the leaders of the Supreme Soviet about the situation in Arzamas–16 and Chelyabinsk–70. The chairman of the Supreme Soviet reacted by instructing the International Relations Committee to expedite its deliberations on the ISTC Agreement.

These developments also provoked serious discussions within the Prepcom staff as to the utility of the Center, with its limited resources, in resolving such crises. During the discussions, our Russian colleagues repeatedly pointed out that the Center had a value beyond simply providing funds—a value as a rallying point for an unappreciated and unfocused scientific community.

They argued as follows: The ISTC process offered the hope that conversion of some parts of the laboratories to civilian activities could proceed in an orderly fashion since ISTC funds were real and not mythical like so many government funds. Also, the ISTC proposal process, which emphasized the development of linkages between military and civilian researchers, was forcing secret laboratories to work in partnership with open laboratories and foreign collaborators. This new networking would become a very important contribution of the ISTC. Finally, they underscored that the ISTC emphasis on putting money directly into the pockets of scientists, and avoiding corruption along the way, offered the potential of changing the way research is funded in Russia.

Such thoughts were quite inspiring for the foreign members of the staff, and we all vowed to dig in our heels and push even harder.

Meanwhile, as a testimony to the perceived importance of the ISTC, Arzamas–16 had 107 proposals in the pipeline; and we received a list of 26 proposals during a visit to the Institute of Inorganic Material in Moscow.

Within a few days, a contingent of weapons specialists from Arzamas–16 was in Moscow meeting with deputies of the Supreme Soviet and appearing on television. They were pleading for greater allocations of government funds for their research center, the original nuclear weapon design laboratory. They also urged ratification of the ISTC Agreement as a new source of funds. This position was a sharp departure from earlier days when Arzamas scientists could always obtain whatever funds they needed from MINATOM, or its Soviet predecessor organization, with little justification.

Up until that time, the leaders and scientists at Arzamas–16 had shied away from the ISTC believing that involvement in the programs of a multinational bureaucracy was the last thing they needed to complicate their lives further. Indeed, they had strongly criticized the concept of the Center, criticism that had reached parliamentarians in Moscow. This turnabout to public lobbying for the ISTC, whether the result of financial desperation or proddings from MINATOM, provided critical pressure within the parliament to move ratification to center stage.

The West's arch enemies of years past and the Center's chief antagonists of recent months had suddenly become our allies. And the scientists at Arzamas–16 sustained this support throughout my tenure at the ISTC.

On the Verge of Compromise

The vacation schedule for the Supreme Soviet during late summer of 1993 was uncertain as the deputies remained at their desks to exchange daily political salvos with the Russian government. For Russians to sacrifice their vacations was extraordinary indeed, but the political barbs between the parliament and President Yeltsin were so pointed and so frequent that the deputies felt they were struggling for survival. They finally decided to take a recess in late August, but they were promptly recalled to Moscow to continue to cover their flanks from the attacks of an increasingly belligerent president. And Carole and I cut short our rest and recreation trip to the United States to be in position when the parliament reconvened to talk ratification.

Even though the political sniping picked up where it had left off, optimism was rising at the Pulse Institute. We hoped the deputies would take time out from the political bombardments to complete the ratification procedures.

The Foreign Ministry had intensified its efforts to reach a compromise with the Committee on International Relations. The key to the compromise was to be the requested document signed by representatives of the four parties, who would be at the same level as the signers of the Agreement. This meant that the Russian deputy foreign minister and the ambassadors of the three other parties in Moscow would sign.

The document would simply say that the parties intended to adopt the Statute for the ISTC, which had already been negotiated in the Prepcom, following Russian ratification of the Agreement. The Statute included extensive provisions on IPR and access that responded to criticisms of the opponents in parliament. Also, the Statute included reassurance for the parliament that the Russian government must approve every project that involved Russian institutions and that appropriate limitations would be placed on the use of ISTC funds.

In addition, the Foreign Ministry would sign a separate agreement with the leaders of the parliament stating that the government would not approve any changes in the Statute without first consulting with the parliament. The submarine captain could then say that he had jerked Kozyrev's chain.

The captain had just returned from his latest naval negotiations in the Crimea. He apparently would grudgingly go along with this formula, and the other opponents would follow his lead. This time I felt confident with my report to Washington, Brussels, and Tokyo that in "two more weeks" ratification would be completed.

And then our world collapsed. Yeltsin could no longer accept the opposition he encountered on seemingly every issue before the parliament. With the stroke of a pen in mid-September, he simply dissolved the Supreme Soviet and assumed all legislative powers for himself. He announced that elections would be held in December for a new parliament. After fourteen months of consulting, advising, negotiating, and lobbying, the founders of the ISTC proposal confronted the reality that the Center was perched squarely over the abyss of obscurity.

But couldn't Yeltsin assume ratification powers himself and sign another decree establishing the Center? Or must the ISTC Agreement await the arrival of a new parliament with a different cast of characters who would start the ratification process from ground zero—while harboring yet another host of hidden agendas and secret liaisons. This time, it would take more than two weeks to sort things out. More likely, two years would be needed.

The staff and I agreed to proceed with business as usual, even though there was little real business. We would continue our efforts to develop additional proposals that would increase the pool of Russian specialists with vested interests in the outcome of the ISTC debate. And we would project an image of optimism that the Center concept was still alive and that a new international organization was on the verge of reality.

Privately, we wondered how soon we would be packing our bags.

Chapter 3

Diplomatic Dodges
Around the Parliament

Nothing is more permanent than that which is temporary.
A modern Russian proverb

A Funeral Pyre for the Center

The initial reaction at the Pulse Institute to the dismissal of the Russian Supreme Soviet by President Yeltsin was cautious relief that the major roadblock to the ISTC was history. The Russian staff members pointed out that Yeltsin had already signed two decrees supporting the establishment of the Center. According to their logic, the simple solution was for him now to pen a third document that would establish the Center immediately. They added that all the decree needed to say to comply with the entry-into-force provision of the ISTC Agreement was that Russia had completed "the necessary internal procedures" to bring the Center into existence.[1]

Of course, the upper levels of the Russian government were in a state of disarray trying to find their way through the political fallout from the abolition of the parliament. Many of the former deputies of the parliament refused to leave their offices in the White House, and several of the leaders threatened to depose the president by whatever means necessary. Thus, the ISTC was not near the top of the government's agenda.

Soon the White House became the center of a military insurrection, as automatic rifles and machine guns somehow made their way through clandestine routes to the ensconced legislators and their legions of supporters. During my frequent visits to the American Embassy just across the street from the White House, I repeatedly encountered angry demonstrators armed with communist flags, posters, and bullhorns, pressuring their way to the entrance of the White House. Growing encampments of security forces and army troops barred the mob from the building, which had been transformed into a formidable fortress under government siege. Contingents of military vehicles lined the nearby streets. Increased action appeared imminent.

Then following a Saturday visit to the commissary located within the embassy compound, Carole and I drove by several fires set by demonstrators in the middle of the Garden Ring Road just two blocks from the embassy. After weaving in and out of trucks loaded with armed troops at the edge of the demonstration, we pointed our car across the Moscow River and quickly retreated to our apartment a few miles away.

The next day, the rebellion began in earnest. We learned from a timely phone call received by a Russian friend whom we were visiting that Yeltsin's former vice president and a retired general had left their White House stronghold. Commanding a sizable force of enraged Russians, they stormed the mayor's office. Then the heavily armed procession headed for the major television station, Ostankino, with plans to take control of the airwaves.

Having heard this news flash, we again pointed our car toward our apartment, where we became transfixed by the Russian television broadcasts. It was hard to believe that intensive shooting had erupted in several parts of the city. Reluctant military and security forces finally came to the aid of Yeltsin; but, as we later learned, this solution came only after the troops had witnessed the killing on the street of some of their colleagues by snipers in the White House.

On the following day, special forces stormed the White House and took control; but not before army tanks had blasted the building at point-blank range and fires had badly charred the top five floors. Throughout all the unnerving events, CNN fed its footage live to a secondary Russian television station that continued the street coverage after a ravaged Ostankino station lost its broadcasting capability. The CNN coverage, which graphically showed a rampaging mob incited by former national leaders bent on destroying people and property, was a major factor in swaying the public and the army to support Yeltsin. Without such backing, the outcome of the political battle might have been much different.

On Monday evening, as Carole and I stared through our living room window in disbelief at the White House burning in the distance, both the frustrations and accomplishments of our fifteen months in Moscow flashed through our minds. We thought our tour of duty had certainly come to an end. Only a fragile flicker of hope suggested that somehow the Center would not also go up in flames in a devastating conclusion to such a concentrated preparatory investment by so many people. But how could Yeltsin possibly focus on the Center with his country on the brink of collapse?

The next day I went to the Pulse Institute to face the gloom of the staff. We agreed to gather our thoughts and then to plot a strategy once the smoke had cleared. In the meantime, we would watch out for our personal safety. As it turned out, we were not being alarmists; that evening, a staff member called me from a metro station where he had taken cover from a hail of bullets. He quickly accepted my invitation to take refuge at our apartment for the night. Although the stillness of the night was broken by the sound of gunfire in our normally quiet neighborhood, knowing that we were twelve stories above the street provided some degree of security.

Resourceful Russian Diplomats

The idea of a quick Yeltsin signature on a decree to launch the Center was overly simplistic. Following the failed rebellion, Yeltsin had promptly called for parliamentary elections in December; and he obviously hoped that many of his followers would win seats, particularly in the new lower house—the Duma. Though technically Yeltsin may have been empowered to rule by decree, his advisers cautioned against gaining the reputation of a dictator who flagrantly disregarded the legitimate interests of parliament—even though no parliament existed. He needed to avoid creating public opinion, with its associated voting power, that depicted him as a despot interested only in self-aggrandisement.

At the same time, the four parties had invested too much effort into establishment of the ISTC to abandon the proposal or to mark time for six to nine months, or longer, while a new parliament took the reins. Some members of our international staff of a dozen people had been in Moscow for more than one year carrying out preparatory work; and as we have seen, many senior government officials from Washington, Brussels, and Tokyo had visited Moscow on several occasions to shape the structure of the Center.

More important, the situation with Russian weapons scientists and engineers was becoming increasingly critical as thousands of under-employed and underpaid specialists left their institutes to seek their fortunes in commercial activities on the streets and in secluded offices of Russia. Also, rumors were flying that matchmaking services for unemployed weapons specialists had increased in Hong Kong and Trieste, with entrepreneurs from the Third World trying to recruit Russian weapons specialists to work in distant countries in the Middle East and Asia.

Meanwhile, Yeltsin had issued a general decree that set forth the legal basis under which he would assume the powers of the legislature, very carefully noting that assuming the powers of taxation and related financial issues required special attention. And the establishment of the ISTC with its special tax privileges clearly fell within this latter mandate. The essence of the special procedure was that the State Legal Office needed to agree that the approach was appropriate in the absence of a legislature.[2]

After several weeks of discussion involving the Prepcom staff, representatives of the foreign missions in Moscow, and senior diplomats at the Ministry of Foreign Affairs, the Russians reached into their diplomatic bag of tricks and proposed an approach whereby the four parties would establish the ISTC on a *temporary* basis, or in diplomatic parlance a *provisional* basis. The Foreign Ministry had several other international agreements ready for ratification by the parliament, and they intended to apply this approach to these agreements as well. All the while, messages flew back and forth among Moscow, Washington, Tokyo, and Brussels.

Foreign Ministry officials contended that this formula balanced the necessity for prompt action with the political recognition of the legitimate role of the parliament. The implication was that as soon as the newly elected parliament became organized, the government would ask it to consider ratification of the ISTC Agreement along with the other international agreements. Thus, so they argued, Yeltsin could not be accused of seizing dictatorial powers. The Russian legal experts pointed out that a similar approach had been used in 1992 in Helsinki when a number of countries adopted, on a provisional basis, an international agreement on the reduction of conventional armed forces in Europe.

Quickly, the representatives of the four parties began drafting a Protocol on the Provisional Application of the Agreement Establishing an International Science and Technology Center. This was to be a very brief document—contrary to what the document's title seemed to indicate. The key concerns of the United States, subsequently echoed by Japan and the European Union, were that (1) all provisions of the ISTC Agreement would be in force; (2) procedures would explicitly enable other countries also to adopt the ISTC Agreement on a provisional basis; (3) a review of the protocol, particularly the implementation of the associated ISTC Agreement, would be carried out in two years; and (4) Russia, as well as the other parties, would be required to give six months' notice if they intended to withdraw from the protocol.

With regard to the final point, the Western partners and Japan were concerned that they would commit money for long-term projects and then the Duma would force Russia to withdraw from the protocol. The Russian institutions might terminate their projects but keep the unspent money.

The Prepcom had developed procedures that called for the ISTC to commit funds not more than six months in advance. Thus, the proposed withdrawal requirement would ease concerns. Also, such a provision in the protocol would mirror the original six-month withdrawal provision of the Agreement.

After several weeks of daily visits by our foreign contingent to the Foreign Ministry where we met with Russian lawyers and diplomats, we finally crafted a protocol, both in Russian and English.[3] It was already late November. A new parliament was to be elected in early December and would begin its work in January. Would this procedure, which assumed that there was no parliament, be appropriate if it were not completed by the time of the election? The Russian experts assured us that if the protocol were signed by the four parties prior to the time the new parliament became operational in early January 1994, there would be no legal or political problems.

Reassured, we intensified our consultations with Brussels, Tokyo, and Washington. And we continued our daily discussions with Russian officials.

An Eleventh-Hour Protocol

I had thought that turning a very brief protocol into a signed document would not be a difficult chore, since the four parties had already signed the ISTC Agreement underlying the protocol. But I was wrong. Diplomatic and political complications quickly became apparent.

There were absolutely no problems in Washington. Department of State officials exhibited great flexibility in accommodating every minor requirement of the other parties. The United States was ready to sign at any time, with no further approvals required by the executive or legislative branches.

In Brussels, however, the various bodies of the European Union were under great pressure not to make any mistakes in dealing with Russia. The EU Court of Auditors had just found many irregularities in other EU programs being carried out in Russia. Therefore, EU officials were cautious in agreeing to anything without first obtaining many signatures in Brussels, which would diffuse responsibility. With this mindset, they decided that the new protocol was in fact a new international agreement that required endorsement by the European Parliament, even though the European Parliament had endorsed the ISTC Agreement one year earlier. This meant that while the European Union would sign the protocol, the protocol could not enter into force until it had subsequently passed muster with the European legislators who sat in Strasbourg, France.

In Tokyo, there was no requirement for action by the legislature. Nevertheless, the Japanese Foreign Office considered the protocol to be sufficiently important that the cabinet would have to approve the protocol before it could be signed; and the cabinet had strict operating procedures. First, the cabinet would consider the protocol only after Yeltsin had personally approved it. Second, the cabinet required one week to study the protocol before acting. Finally, the approval of the cabinet would be valid for a period of not more than one week to help ensure that the political conditions at the signing were the same as the conditions on the day the cabinet met. If the signing date slipped, the cabinet would have to reconsider the issue. On top of this, the Japanese cabinet would begin its holiday recess on December 24.

In Moscow, all that was required was a new decree or instruction issued by Yeltsin. But the administrative problems of moving a document from the Foreign Ministry to the president's desk were not trivial. En route it would need another round of signatures of endorsement from several ministries, from the prime minister, and from the State Legal Office—all at a time when the country was in the midst of political revolution following a near civil war.

In view of the Japanese requirements on timing, Yeltsin needed to sign the document no later than December 17, so that the Japanese cabinet could approve the document at its last meeting of the year on December 24. Everyone expected the document to be signed well before that deadline, but this was the outside date. The new Russian parliament would be in session after the first of the year, and, according to the Russian experts, adoption of the provisional procedure would not be feasible after that date.

Would the Prepcom again become a mere spectator to the internal workings of the Russian bureaucracy as was the case through most of the deliberations of the Supreme Soviet earlier in the year?

No!

A Russian colleague at the Prepcom, after consultations with MINATOM and the Foreign Ministry, took the lead in forcing the paper through the system. He agreed to throw caution to the wind and play a role that few Russians would be willing to accept—prying into the business of a cluster of Russian agencies on a daily basis. First, he became acquainted with the secretaries in the approval loop, including those in the Foreign Ministry, in the prime minister's office, and in the president's office. Then he worked the telephones constantly, inquiring, cajoling, and—when necessary—pressuring the paper handlers to move the document forward.

He kept us informed on a daily basis, writing on the blackboard the number assigned to the document as it left the Foreign Ministry, the new number assigned as it arrived in the prime minister's office, and then the number assigned as it left the prime minister's office. After several weeks, we even had the number assigned to the protocol as it arrived in President Yeltsin's office on December 13, accompanied by an internal visa scrawled with signatures too numerous to count.

Now it was critical to capture the attention of the president within two or three days. My colleague talked to the president's secretary and to the chief of office administration who handled every piece of paper. How could the protocol and the proposed decree be moved to the top of the pile? We needed someone to intervene, reported my colleague.

At home late Tuesday evening, December 14, I made a desperate phone call. I explained the urgency of our problem to a colleague at the Russian Academy of Sciences. The next morning one of the most senior academicians agreed to urge a long-time friend and close adviser to Yeltsin to move the protocol to the top of the president's in-box. On Friday morning, December 17, the academician called to inform me that the adviser had found the document, that he had put it

Ministry of Foreign Affairs, December 27, 1993. Diplomats sign the protocol provisionally establishing the International Science and Technology Center.

in front of Yeltsin, and that Yeltsin had signed a decree.[4] Two hours later the Foreign Ministry called to say that the signing of the protocol by the four parties was being scheduled for December 27. The Japanese immediately accommodated the latest proposal.

I sent a fax to Washington, saying, "Yeltsin signed. Foreign Ministry proposes December 27 signing by four parties. Thanks for hanging in there with us."

The Department of State replied, "You don't know how many people you made happy with your fax."

On December 27, in a quiet ceremony at the Foreign Ministry, a deputy foreign minister and senior diplomats from the United States, the European Union, and Japan signed the protocol. The next day, I took a bottle of champagne to the Academy of Sciences and toasted my friends who helped us when the chips were down.

A Wave of Eager Weaponeers

Now the goal was to ensure that all elements of the Russian weapons community learned about their new opportunities. The Center was no longer a paper tiger. It would soon be a real tiger with the scent of green printer's ink.

During the intensive negotiations to complete the protocol, we had taken several time-outs to welcome little-known visitors to the Pulse Institute. They were chemical and biological weapons experts and rocket designers who had come out from behind closed doors during the past year but who were having difficulty preparing proposals that could command support from the ISTC. They simply were not experienced in specifying in advance the details of activities they intended to undertake. They were accustomed to receiving large blocks of money to explore general areas of R&D and then develop the details as they proceeded. But that was not how the ISTC system was to work. The financing parties wanted to know in advance the details of the projects they were going to support.

Going back to 1992, the impetus for the proposal to establish the ISTC was the concern over the proliferation of nuclear weapons technology. Not unexpectedly, almost all of the early proposals submitted to the Prepcom were from Russian nuclear scientists and engineers who had become quite skilled in preparing proposals according to the ISTC *Instructions*, which MINATOM had distributed widely throughout its institutes.

At the same time, the spread of chemical and biological technologies was also very worrisome; but the Russian specialists in these fields apparently had never heard of the ISTC or at least were inhibited from visiting the Pulse Institute. Therefore, early in my stay I decided to try to stir up some interest among the biologists and chemists. And I requested a meeting with Yeltsin's special adviser on biological and chemical warfare.

When my colleagues from the original planning group and I had met with the special adviser in late 1992, he was concentrating on replying to Western charges that Russia was not living up to its international legal obligations concerning limitations on chemical and biological warfare agents. But he was also vitally interested in finding new employment opportunities for specialists from the R&D institutes who had supported the Soviet military efforts and who now had little to keep them busy. He had heard only vague generalities about the ISTC, but he was intrigued by the possibility of available funds to support his colleagues. He agreed to contact the leading chemical and biological warfare specialists in the field and put them in touch with us.

After several months, the director and senior managers of the central R&D institute that had developed most of the chemical agents showed up at the Pulse Institute. They were eager to expand their new, nonmilitary efforts. But at the outset, they had great difficulty defining concrete project proposals that met the ISTC standard. By the fall of 1993, they had improved their approaches considerably; they finally submitted a number of acceptable proposals. Among the topics of interest to them were new ways to detect chemical pollutants in the environment, new approaches to the treatment of AIDS, and methods for decontaminating chemically impregnated clothing and other material.[5]

Similarly, many months after I met with the president's special adviser, representatives of BIOPREPARAT, an organization that had been responsible for developing Soviet biological warfare agents, visited the Pulse Institute to obtain instructions they could pass on to their specialists concerning ISTC programs. They were interested primarily in the development of new vaccines and in the use of biological techniques for cleaning up the environment. After a number of meetings between our staff and the specialists from the institutes, we received a steady flow of proposals for converting biologists from military to civilian tasks.[6]

A third group of interesting weaponeers who visited the Prepcom staff during the fall of 1993 was from a major research institute in the town of Miass in the southern Urals, the Machine Building Research Institute, which specialized in the design of submarine-launched missiles. They told us that they were among a group of twenty-five Russians who had tried to go to North Korea one year earlier, only to be apprehended at the Moscow airport and sent back to Miass. They had hoped to work for $25,000 per year in a rapidly expanding technology center in North Korea that allegedly was developing communication satellite systems. Their institute in Miass, along with some government agencies, had obviously endorsed their Korean trip. Apparently, at the last minute one or more Russian security agencies became concerned over the transfer of rocket know-how to North Korea.[7]

Back in Miass with no more orders for missiles, environmental monitoring activities had attracted their attention. Specifically, they were working under contract with the environmental offices in the nearby city of Chelyabinsk to improve the monitoring stations for measuring air and water pollution. Also, they were trying to develop better communication networks throughout the city and the region for the collection and processing of environmental information. One idea was to establish in the region a system of environmental alert stations that would immediately notify the regional government of accidents that resulted in the release of atmospheric pollutants, particularly radioactive contaminants. Finally, they had established a new line of medical diagnostic equipment that was becoming quite profitable, or so they claimed.

While the rocket scientists showed considerable interest in the activities of the Center, they apparently were doing quite well in pursuing their contracts with the Chelyabinsk officials and with local hospitals. They did not submit any proposals to the ISTC until late 1994.

Of course, many scientists from around the country made the Pulse Institute a new stop on their Moscow itineraries. In addition, we were increasingly proactive in reaching out to attract scientists who were not yet in the loop but who were of particular concern from the point of view of proliferation.

Our goal was to amass as many high-quality proposals as possible as quickly as possible. Because of the time lost during the ratification process, the Governing Board needed to move quickly in approving projects.

Sand in the Starting Blocks

The protocol was behind us, and proposals were piling up. But still more delays pushed back the first meeting of the Governing Board and the opening of the Center.

The European Union had prepared the necessary documents for the European Parliament in early January and had sent them to Strasbourg for the February meeting of the parliament. But due to an administrative slip-up, the packet of papers arrived in Strasbourg four hours after the agenda for the meeting had been settled, an agenda that did not include consideration of the ISTC. After a month's delay, the European Parliament endorsed the protocol in March, and at long last the Governing Board could meet.

But then a further complication arose. Ten days before the scheduled meeting of the board to launch the Center, the Russians requested an additional postponement since their key specialists would be out of the country on the designated date. Keeping in mind that this first meeting of the Governing Board had already been scheduled and rescheduled nine times dating back to 1992, none of the parties were sympathetic. Airline tickets had been purchased, schedules had been juggled, and some of the delegates were virtually en route. Finally, the Russians fielded an alternate team for the meeting.

Meanwhile, the sponsoring governments realized that the Center finally existed, and they needed to come through with their long-standing personnel commitments. Slowly, additional staff began to arrive. We ran out of room as soon as the first one showed up. We took turns at the computers, and we took turns at the desks. But how long could this go on?

Need for a Facility Committee

It was clear that our new facility would not be ready for the first meeting of the Governing Board. Indeed, it would not be available for the second meeting. While construction was nearly completed by the second meeting, the fire inspector would not approve occupancy until a formally established facility committee from various Russian organizations went through a checklist to ensure that the facility was completely finished and met all its standards.

The major problem related to the fire code. The newly installed rugs needed a coating of fire-retardant chemicals, which were in short supply in Moscow. Finally, sitting in our temporary offices down the hall from the new space, we unexpectedly smelled the pungent odor of a strange chemical and knew that the rugs would never burst into flame.

While we continued to wait for the facility committee to pronounce the premises suitable, safe, and sanitary, I had inserted a special requirement into the preparations—a requirement that was extraordinarily popular with the staff. I suggested that a Western company install modern Western fixtures in the restrooms, which had already been refurbished Soviet-style with an array of green fixtures predating the 1917 revolution.

The configuration of the ladies' restroom, in particular, was unusual. The Russian toilets were located at the very edges rather than in the centers of the stalls. They were comfortable for one-legged people; but for the rest of the female staff, there would be problems.

Although we were prepared to pay up to $25,000 for minor restoration work, we soon learned that restroom repair was difficult to arrange in Moscow. There was no longer prestige or financial reward for a firm to become a contractor of an international organization.

First, we contacted a Finnish company. Unfortunately, their engineer arrived for his initial appointment without his passport, and the security guards of the Pulse Institute detained him for twenty minutes before he could inspect our restrooms. Understandably upset, he decided that much more money could be made refurbishing apartments for the more accommodating wealthy Russians who would welcome him with open arms. He declined the chance to prepare an estimate.

After several other refusals by Western companies, a Danish company agreed to carry out the work. When they were 90 percent finished, but had been paid only 50 percent of their fee, they stopped work. They too were responding to the more attractive lure of the rich Russians. Five months later, they finished the job. Soon the restrooms became tourist stops for visitors from Russia and from abroad.

With the meeting of the Governing Board finally scheduled and the restroom restoration on a fast track, we thought that at last we could come to grips with the substantive issues facing the board. But two more diversions took center stage.

If Only the President Had Asked

The first diversion had a serious impact on the preparations for the initial board meeting. My ten-year old computer and printer, which had produced most of the important documents for the Prepcom, were about to expire. Also, our demands for reproduction were out of control. The bundles of papers in need of cloning had become too voluminous to carry back and forth to the American Embassy's reproduction office.

I thought that we had cleverly anticipated the need for computers, printers, faxes, and copy machines at the beginning of my stay in Moscow. We had convinced the Department of State to set aside $100,000 for advance purchases of equipment so we could start quickly once the ISTC was to come on-line.

In late 1992, the department instructed the U.S. Embassy in Bonn to purchase five computers, five printers, three fax machines, and one large and four small copy machines for the ISTC. Despite our pleas to let us buy the equipment through dealers in Moscow who could provide warranties and service contracts, the department would not budge from its procurement regulations which had centralized all purchases in Bonn.

In early 1993, we received a telegram from the embassy in Bonn reporting they had purchased the equipment. They said they would store the boxes in Bonn until we had moved into our new facility and could receive the equipment.

Nine months later, a surprise call from the local embassy officer responsible for government property in Moscow instructed me to claim my twenty-seven boxes of equipment immediately. While my name was emblazoned on the boxes, there was no paperwork. After I negotiated for three hours with the embassy administrative staff, they agreed to store the boxes in a vacant but highly classified section of the embassy, since there was no other storage option. Any reluctance they harbored over keeping the property at the embassy quickly disappeared when the American security officer learned that the Pulse Institute would not provide us with keys to their storage areas, although they would gladly keep the boxes under their control.

Six months later, in February 1994, the ISTC Secretariat desperately needed two computers at the Pulse Institute. After I obtained a signed statement from MINATOM agreeing to provide security for the equipment at our temporary quarters, the embassy sent all twenty-seven boxes to the Pulse Institute, but still without the benefit of paperwork. We opened up two computers and printers and temporarily stored the other boxes in the institute's storage room, since our offices were jammed with people.

Much to our surprise, we had received Hewlett Packard (HP) Model 386 computers, which were out-of-date for the software the staff had brought to the Center. More significantly, the computers could not even be assembled because the frames for mounting the hard drives and the memory extensions were the wrong size, and the wrong drivers for the printers had been included. Fortunately, the American HP representative in Moscow had a patriotic streak that dominated his profit instincts; he arranged for the replacement frames to be shipped to us, but only after a wait of six weeks. We found drivers that would work, and we slowly developed an expanded computer capability.

Within a few weeks after the signing of the protocol, we managed to obtain two more temporary rooms at the Pulse Institute where we could assemble the remaining equipment. Then the second surprise: the copy machines were missing. With no paperwork, we could provide little assistance to the Department of State as it launched investigations in Bonn and Moscow. Within a few weeks, we received the verdict. The copy machines were nowhere to be found.

Finally, two weeks before the meeting of the Governing Board, I received another unexpected call from the Moscow embassy asking me where they should deliver twelve more boxes addressed to me. They had been stored in the classified Xerox room of the embassy, and the embassy's reproduction specialists were cleaning house. The next day, two apologetic embassy employees showed up at the Center with five broken copy machines. They explained that they had been forced to let President Clinton's party use them several months earlier, and his entourage smashed them up pretty badly after only three days of use.

On inspection, we noted from the dials that none of the machines had made many copies of documents. A novice had broken several parts when trying to force the large machine to perform in impossible ways. Someone must have turned the four smaller ones upside down. This seemed the only explanation because carbon had spilled everywhere requiring cleanup operations of several days. We hired a local contractor of the Rank Xerox Corporation who, for a price, put the machines into working order. Finally, the Center settled the bill for obsolete and inoperative computers, damaged copy machines, and faxes with receptacles in need of replacements.

If only the President's staff had asked to use our new equipment, we would have found good operators for the machines. We understood that the president's entourage, reported to number in excess of seven hundred people accompanying him to Moscow, could hardly include one or two reproduction specialists.

But, despite this diversion, the Secretariat was almost ready.

Blocking the Front Door

The final barrier to the first meeting of the Governing Board was literally the front door to the Center itself—a door that couldn't be opened.

For two years, the American, European, and Japanese delegates and the Prepcom staff had repeatedly emphasized to the Russian government the importance of having a visitor-friendly entrance to the Center. While the Pulse Institute needed to have several security guards to prevent any unauthorized penetration of its facilities, the Center located in the same building would have many visitors of its own. They certainly would not appreciate the security procedures that had evolved

At the first meeting of the ISTC Governing Board, March 1994, the author (left) confers with representatives of the European Union—from Brussels, Rolf Timans (Germany) and Paolo Fasella (Italy), and the EU's representative in Moscow, Ambassador Michael Emerson of the United Kingdom.

from the days when the Pulse Institute was so secure it was known simply as a post office box, procedures that were not to be relaxed anytime soon.

Therefore, we had devised a scheme whereby the front entryway to the Pulse Institute would be divided in half. One sign would direct Center visitors to the left, where a receptionist would greet them and arrange for their visits. A matching sign would direct institute visitors to the right, where they would display their badges and present their briefcases for searches.

But the Pulse Institute refused to open the door for the Center's side.

After months of discussions, the reasons for the institute's intransigence finally emerged. The ISTC Agreement obligated the Russian Federation to provide security services for the Center, including someone during the day who would help the receptionist keep vagrants and other undesirable visitors off the premises. This meant that the Pulse Institute, which had assumed this responsibility for Russia, had two choices. It could either use its regular security guards, who would work overtime; or it would have to hire new personnel. In either case, there would be an expense which was to be reimbursed by the government at a time when no Russian organization paid its debts. In addition, it turned out all security guards really worked for the Ministry of Internal Affairs and that Ministry was determined to reap a substantial profit from any additional reponsibilities.

This combination of requirements simply was too complex for resolution by the time of the first board meeting—and the foreign delegates were simply furious. By some miracle, the institute managed to open the doors for the two-day meeting, but immediately closed them thereafter, providing the glaring exception to the rule that *Nothing is more permanent than that which is temporary.* Only after a period of nine months, extending over three board meetings, was an open-door policy finally implemented.

Chapter 4

The International Center
Goes into Fast Forward

1992 "KGB" Brain Child Finally Stops Nuclear Brain Drain

Business World Weekly, Moscow, October 5, 1994

New Members Knocking at the Door

When the United States, the European Union, Japan, and Russia began developing the concept of the ISTC in early 1992, three additional Western countries immediately expressed interest in becoming members of the Center. Canada, Sweden, and Switzerland were ready to join and to commit funds to projects.

However, the four original parties, particularly the United States, were concerned that such additional participation at the outset would complicate the formal negotiations to establish the ISTC. The United States eventually convinced the three aspiring countries to wait until the ISTC Agreement was firmly in place and only then to accede to the Agreement as new members. While this approach was accepted in Ottawa, Stockholm, and Bern, none of the countries anticipated the long delay before the Center would become a reality; nor did they realize that other complications concerning their memberships would arise later.

Throughout the tortuous diplomatic process to establish the Center, both the Canadian and Swedish Foreign Offices were able to protect the funds that had been earmarked by their governments for the ISTC. Once the ISTC came into being, they were poised to contribute $2.5 million and $4 million, respectively. Unfortunately, the Swiss supporters of the Center were less successful; and the Swiss government was not in a position to make a contribution, at least not in 1994.

Despite the prospects of a welcome funding boost, political difficulties arose as both Sweden and Canada linked their accession to the

Agreement with their holding of seats on the ISTC Governing Board. The European Union had difficulty granting these two potential members, who would make relatively small contributions to ISTC projects, the same status in the governance of the Center as the United States, the European Union, and Japan, with their much larger financial commitments.

The United States argued in favor of board membership for the two countries. In Washington, officials noted that Canada and Sweden had originally agreed to delay their involvement in the ISTC on the assumption that they would have equal status with the original four parties in the governance of the Center. Also, their financial contributions would be comparable to the larger contributions of the United States and the European Union if considered as percentages of their GNPs.

Governing Board membership was vigorously debated for more than a year, both through diplomatic channels and at meetings of the Prepcom. The board finally resolved this point, as described below, at its second meeting.

The ISTC Agreement, of course, identifies Russia, the United States, the European Union, and Japan as the original parties. The Statute states that one additional country from the Commonwealth of Independent States (CIS) can serve on the Governing Board at any given time, with the seat to rotate among new CIS members on an annual basis if more than one of the CIS members seeks a seat on the board. The Agreement and Statute are silent on new financing parties holding seats on the board, leaving the policy to the discretion of the board.[1]

The board, at long last, decided that its membership could expand up to a maximum of eight. If all eight seats were filled, the board would maintain the original balance in the Agreement: that is, a ratio of three seats for financing parties to every seat taken by a CIS member.

Thus, up to three *new* financing parties could be accepted for board membership. To be eligible for a seat on the board, a new member would be required to contribute at least $2 million to ISTC projects for each year it served on the board. Finally, if more than three new members made this minimum contribution and sought board seats, the three seats would rotate annually among the interested new members.

Although the policy on Governing Board membership had not yet been adopted, the board at its first meeting in March 1994 formally welcomed the interest in ISTC membership expressed by Sweden, Finland, Canada, Georgia, Armenia, Belarus, and Kazakhstan. The board expressed its willingness to accept these seven new members after they completed the necessary formalities, with the issue of board membership deferred to a later date.[2]

At the same time, both Sweden and Finland were to become members of the European Union in 1995, thus raising questions as to double representation. The board concurred with the views of the European Union to accept them as ISTC members, however, at least during 1994. The board would then await the outcome of discussions within the European Union as to whether Finland and Sweden could maintain their ISTC memberships after joining the European Union, a body that presumably represented the interests of all its European members in its role at the ISTC. Thus, Finland and Sweden acceded to the Agreement, at least temporarily.

The policy concerning membership on the Governing Board was not resolved until June 1994. Under the guidelines, Canada could have become a board member for one year if it agreed to commit at least $2 million during that year. Not satisfied with this arrangement, Canada decided to pursue its programs in Russia on a bilateral basis.

The policy concerning additional CIS members in the ISTC was clear, but the administrative aspects of joining the Center posed some difficulties. Prospective CIS members were required to take two significant steps. First, they needed to complete procedures within their own governments to ensure that all the provisions of the ISTC Agreement would apply within their territories, including exemption of ISTC activities from taxes and customs. In the cases of Belarus and Kazakhstan, these exemptions and other aspects of the ISTC Agreement required parliamentary action.

Second, each new member needed to provide the ISTC Secretariat with certain documentation about its interests in ISTC activities and to inform Brussels, Washington, Tokyo, and Moscow through diplomatic channels about their steps to accede. This requirement caused difficulties in Armenia and Kazakhstan. Each government had very limited administrative capabilities. They both were trying to correspond through diplomatic channels with many countries on a host of issues, and it was difficult to juggle formal correspondence about the ISTC at the same time. For example, in Armenia all documents forwarded to senior officials of the government needed to be in the Armenian language. The correspondence from the ISTC languished on a table in Yerevan for many months simply waiting for an overworked translator to address the documents.

Finally, in June 1994, Georgia formally became a member of ISTC; in December 1994, Belarus and Armenia joined; and in June 1995, Kazakhstan completed its membership formalities.[3]

As each new member acceded to the ISTC Agreement, a new flag was installed in the vestibule of the ISTC facility. Finding flags of uniform size in Moscow was not always possible; and ironically, for many months an oversized flag of Finland provided by the Finnish Embassy dominated the six smaller flags in the entryway. Some visitors from Finland thought that this recognition of the importance of their country was linked to the very positive full-page report about the ISTC published in the leading Helsinki newspaper. Others attributed it to the success of the Finnish national hockey team in recent international competitions where supporters vigorously waved large Finnish flags.

Coping with Chaos in Georgia

Intertwined with the discussions by the Governing Board regarding new CIS members was the issue of ISTC representation offices in these new member states. Georgia was the first new CIS member of the ISTC, and my trip to Tbilisi in the summer of 1994 was to resolve the question of how the ISTC Secretariat in Moscow would carry out its responsibilities in Georgia.

Georgia was not only in a state of political turmoil but on the brink of a civil war. The region of Abkhazia on the Black Sea had essentially seceded from the country. Opposition forces were intent on overthrowing President Shevardnadze, using force if necessary. Pistols and machine guns were in evidence everywhere. Our hotel displayed a sign instructing guests to check guns with the concierge before going through the metal detectors at the front door. Local scientists had not been paid for two years, and Georgian currency (coupon) was essentially worthless.

The board of the ISTC had approved one project in Georgia. In addition, the Secretariat decided to organize a seminar in Georgia to acquaint foreign specialists with the technological potential of the country. These two activities were the focus of our mission.

Upon arrival in the capital with several staff members, I learned that the president wanted to see us. Before the meeting, I asked our local escorts whether we should speak with him in Russian or English since we wanted to use our limited time most effectively. They suggested flexibility on our part. When Shevardnadze began the meeting in the Georgian language, I realized that my question had been out of place.

The president knew all about the ISTC, stating that he had discussed the concept in detail with the Italian premier one year before it was formally proposed in 1992.

Shevardnadze was surrounded by a mixture of elderly scientists and young policy advisers in their twenties and thirties who were concerned with economics, press relations, and international cooperation. His office was in a building pockmarked from recent armed street battles, and the president appeared very tired. Nevertheless, the distinguished diplomat displayed an unforgettable degree of optimism that his country would eventually spin out of its current downward economic spiral.

He noted that Georgia was temporarily in desperate financial straits in view of the severance of most of its foreign contacts following the disintegration of the Soviet Union. He thought that the ISTC could play a very important role in bringing Georgian scientists back onto the international scene and urged the ISTC to establish a branch office in the country.

Remembering that the primary mission of the ISTC was to find alternate occupations for weapons scientists and engineers, I inquired as to the size of the weapons manpower pool in Georgia. He replied that it was surprisingly large, since the USSR had entrusted the Georgian Republic with leadership R&D roles in several areas of high technology that could serve the Soviet military establishment. He added that several organizations in Iran, Turkey, and other Middle Eastern countries had recently made overtures for Georgian high-tech specialists to practice their trades in those countries.

Subsequent discussions with the president's key aides revealed that at least 2,000 scientists and engineers with military-relevant high-tech skills were still in Georgia, in fields such as nuclear power systems for space activities, miniaturized synchronous motors, and electro-optical devices. Another 10,000 to 15,000 specialists with more conventional, but still significant, weapons R&D capabilities also were in the country. Apparently the Soviet leaders, particularly Stalin, felt that *christian* Georgians and Armenians were more trustworthy than the less enlightened populations of other republics outside Russia; therefore, the Soviet government was willing to allow them to develop potentially dangerous skills.

Very few of the Georgian weapons specialists were engaged any longer in R&D, since money even to open the doors of the laboratories could not be found. We suspected that a significant number were involved in paramilitary activities, which seemed to be brewing everywhere around us.

The one ISTC project in Georgia was in good hands. We were amazed to find tucked away in an otherwise dirty building of Tbilisi State University adequate clean rooms where scientists were carrying out research on the use of gallium arsenide in electronic devices. Also, we learned that the preoccupation with gallium arsenide, which had been extensively studied in the West, was attributable to the fact that deposits of arsenic abound in the country. At the same time, the participation of well-known German collaborators in the ISTC project would ensure that the R&D was useful and not purposeless activity.

One problem confronting us was the procedure for transferring money to the scientists working on the ISTC project. According to a local German financial expert, only one banking operation in the entire country was honest and reliable. We decided to funnel our money through that bank. The president of the bank was Shevardnadze's economic adviser, and his good reputation provided us with some confidence that the money would reach the intended recipients. While the Georgian scientists would have to pay a 5 percent fee for withdrawing from their bank accounts payments transferred to those accounts from the ISTC, the bank paid interest of 22 percent for foreign currency deposits. This meant that if the scientists left the money on account for three months before withdrawal, they would receive the total amount.

Despite the political importance the president attached to having an ISTC branch office in Georgia, it was difficult to justify such an investment with only one ISTC project in progress in the country. As an alternative, we designated Tbilisi State University as an information center for the ISTC; and we purchased from a local vendor, recommended by the American Embassy in Tbilisi, a computer/printer system and a copy machine for the information center. We reasoned that this equipment could do double duty in providing support for the ISTC project located in the same building. The university was, of course, delighted. The Georgian Academy of Sciences, which the president had suggested as the site for the branch office, was not.

Being sensitive to the financial crisis throughout the country, we assumed responsibility for the expense of hosting a banquet which our

Georgian colleagues gladly attended. But they refused to be outdone. Somehow, they extracted a special allocation of funds from the president's account and organized a luncheon for us on our last day there. It was impossible for us to pay for this affair, which undoubtedly used up much of the country's protocol budget for the year.

Racing Up the Spending Curve

Once the ISTC had been formally established, pressure mounted in Moscow and Washington to begin supporting as soon as possible the recycling of weapons specialists. Of course, the Russian scientists and engineers who had proposals waiting in line were ready to begin work at a moment's notice.

In Washington, the Congress had become impatient with the Clinton administration's lack of skill in promptly dispensing through a variety of programs money appropriated for assisting Russia. These funds were designated for accelerating the downsizing of Russia's military establishment (Nunn-Lugar funds) and for moving Russia toward a market-driven economy and a pluralistic democratic society (foreign assistance funds). The U.S. agencies, and particularly the Department of Defense, were interested in showing Congress better balance sheets immediately.

An additional reason for jump-starting the ISTC was rooted in the widespread criticism of many American programs that simply funneled money to American consultants, rather than to the Russians who were supposed to be the beneficiaries of assistance. The ISTC approach of transferring cash directly to Russians would provide a small counter-weight to such criticism.

At the first Governing Board meeting, the American delegate agreed that the United States would sponsor projects that would consume more than $10 million of the U.S. contribution to the ISTC. The Japanese and European delegates were not as well organized; the initial projects they supported would total only a few million dollars. Fortunately, the Secretariat staff had used the many months while waiting for this meeting to work with numerous groups of Russian specialists in developing several dozen good project proposals to consume the available funds.

For the first year of the Center's existence, the backlog of interesting proposals prepared during the waiting period ensured that all the financing parties could commit monies as quickly as their bureaucracies would release the funds. By the end of 1994, the United States had committed essentially all of its original pledge of $25 million for the ISTC. The rate of commitment by the Japanese and the Europeans had also gained momentum, and even the Finns had begun earmarking funds for specific projects from their contribution of $1 million. At the end of the year, all the parties had designated a total of about $50 million for projects. These projects would employ more than 5,000 scientists and engineers, primarily from the weapons complex, for up to three years, depending on the lengths of individual projects. By fall 1995, the participants numbered over 10,500.[4]

Then the question of additional commitments became an important issue in Washington. I and others urged that additional funds be devoted to the ISTC. If the ISTC was to be effective in encouraging large numbers of Russian weapons specialists to convert to civilian activities, they must be assured that the program would continue for some time. They should not have to take time off from their work on ISTC projects to worry about how they would return to their old professions of making bombs and rockets.

As we see in Chapter 5, I estimated that the target for ISTC activities in Russia was about 60,000 *dangerous* scientists, engineers, and technicians whose skills would be of significant benefit to certain countries interested in weapons of mass destruction. Of course, some of these specialists would continue to work on weapons programs regardless of the ISTC; but probably two-thirds of them were susceptible to enticement to important conversion programs such as those being supported by the ISTC—if the programs were to continue for a number of years.

The initial ISTC projects indicated that for each $1 million, about 100 weapons specialists could be employed on ISTC projects for one year. This would cover not only the payments to the weapons specialists, but also the costs of participation by a limited number of nonspecialists with expertise of special importance to the projects, the costs of small pieces of equipment and supplies, and the costs of travel. Thus, the original commitment of about $70 million would translate to about 7,000 years of effort by weapons specialists. Since many participants spent less than full-time on projects, I estimated that 20 percent of the dangerous specialists who might be enticed by ISTC projects would benefit financially from the initial commitment of $70 million.

The advocates of additional resources for the ISTC were successful in Washington; and in early 1995, the U.S. government pledged additional funds for ISTC projects. Meanwhile, this new influx of funds placed considerable pressure on Japan and the European Union to be forthcoming, as the flood of good proposals continued to engulf the ISTC Secretariat.

Related to the amount of money to be provided for projects was the sensitive issue of how much of that money would go to Russian specialists and institutions and how much to foreign collaborators. From the outset, the Europeans and Japanese had assumed that all money pledged by the financing parties would go to Russia. The United States argued that it would be necessary to devote some portion of the funds from each project, say 10 percent, to cover the expenses of foreign collaborators.

We in the Secretariat preferred the position of the European Union and Japan. The Russian press constantly quoted Russian government agencies that were complaining that the so-called foreign aid of the West never arrived in Russia but was diverted to Western consultants whose advice was either not needed or called for capital investment that was nonexistent. We often heard similar complaints from Russian acquaintances. We wanted to be able to say that the ISTC pledges of $70 million meant $70 million for Russia.

A second concern related to the practicalities of trying to administer from Moscow contracts and grants with foreign institutions. Communications simply were too difficult. Therefore, the Secretariat suggested to the board that should one of the parties wish to use some of its money to pay foreign partners, that money should not be sent to the ISTC in Moscow but should be administered from Washington or other capitals.

In the end, much to our relief, the position of Japan and the European Union prevailed during the deliberations of the Governing Board, with the proviso that in exceptional cases the board could accommodate special needs of collaborators. For example, if the participation of a foreign specialist was absolutely essential to the carrying out of a project and he simply could not convince his government to fund his participation from other sources of funds, the board could authorize paying his travel expenses through the ISTC. This exception procedure was not invoked during 1994. All funds transferred to the ISTC for projects went to Russian specialists and Russian institutions.

At the same time, the financing parties insisted that foreign collaborators who were interested and could successfully find their own funding support should have opportunities to participate in the projects.

First, Western and Japanese experts were concerned that the Russian institutions might repeat investigations already conducted elsewhere. International involvement in projects would reduce this possibility. Second, a foreign presence in the projects would help the governments providing the funds to keep abreast of technical achievements and facilitate the international diffusion of successful R&D efforts in Russia.

Often the financing party would find the collaborator for a specific project; but on some occasions the Russian institutions needed, on their own, to locate foreign collaborators sufficiently interested to pay their own way. This was not always easy for Russian institutions that had been under cover until recently and had very few Western contacts. Of course, whenever possible, the Secretariat assisted these institutions in their search for interested foreign partners.

Bowing to the Tax Inspector

When the Governing Board approved the first wave of projects, the Secretariat had the task of putting money in the hands of project participants as soon as possible. The outflow of specialists from Russian weapons laboratories was increasing every day. At the same time, the number of foreigners, with undisclosed missions, moving from Third World countries to Russia was also rapidly growing.

Though speed was of the essence, negotiation of the contractual arrangements with the Russian recipients of ISTC funds would surely be a lengthy process, since the Center's requirements had no precedents in Russia. There would be an attendant delay in putting weapons scientists to work. Therefore, the board decided to authorize the twenty-three Russian institutions selected for the first projects to begin work immediately on the basis of letters of commitment from the Center. Using their own funds, prior to the signing of the project agreements between the recipient institutions and the ISTC, they could spend up to 5 percent of the funding levels approved by the board. When a project agreement was eventually signed, the Center would immediately reimburse money that was due to the individual participants in that project and to the recipient institution. If a project agreement was not signed, however, neither the institution nor the participants would be reimbursed.

In general, this approach worked. Many desperate scientists began to work, assuming they would eventually be paid. They were not being paid by their institutes, so they had nothing to lose.

With this advance funding policy being carried out, the negotiation of the project agreements began in earnest. The first major stumbling block was a widespread concern among Russian institutions that they would become targets of investigations by local tax inspectors, despite the tax-exempt status of funds provided by the Center. Tax inspectors were not impressed by international agreements, decrees signed by Yeltsin, or orders transmitted by ministries. They needed specific directives from the chief of the tax service instructing them that institutions receiving funds from the Center were exempt from value-added tax (VAT) and that participants in Center projects need not pay income tax. Unexpectedly, about three months after the Center began its operations, the former exemption was included in a general regulation of the tax service concerning grants from noncommercial foreign organizations.[5] Exemption from income tax was more difficult.

If funds for salaries were channeled through the institutes, the likelihood that a significant portion of the funds would be diverted to the tax service, as well as to the pension fund, would be very high, regardless of any instructions to the contrary. Only the bravest of institute directors would challenge the long-established tax practices, codified in many operating documents. Institute accountants, accordingly, required that the tax service and pension fund receive their shares before salaries were paid. These accountants often had close ties, and sometimes family ties, to the tax service.

Therefore, the board decided to abandon the concept of salaries. The Center would simply make grants to the participating specialists. We would channel the money directly to them every three months. Of course, this meant that eventually the ISTC financial officer would be arranging for more than 5,000 individual grant payments every three months; but at least we would know that the weaponeers we were pursuing would walk away with Western dollars and not Middle East *bakshish* in their pockets.

How did we do this?

First, the project agreement with the institute identified the scientists, engineers, and support personnel who were to receive grants and specified the daily rates for their participation in the project. The agreement stated that the ISTC would, in effect, serve as the chief cashier for paying the participants, with assistant cashiers located in a commercial bank. At the conclusion of each quarter, the project manager from the participating institute informed the Secretariat of the number of days each grantee participated in the project. This notification determined the size of the grant payment for each person for that quarter.

Second, the ISTC signed a letter of agreement with each participant, confirming the arrangements for direct payment. This letter gave the participant a paper trail as to the source of his or her newfound income. In order to appease the curious tax inspector, the letter also emphasized that the funds were from a grant that was exempt from income tax.

Finally, after receiving instructions from the Secretariat as to the size of payments, together with the names and passport numbers of the persons to receive the money, the cashiers in a Russian bank handed dollars to each participant each quarter for a fee of 0.5 percent.

Initially, this system did not work perfectly. After the bank found ways to expedite the processing of hundreds of payees in a single day, however, the cash flowed without too many interruptions. Were the institute directors happy? Of course not. They lost their sense of power when they were not personally directing the dispensing of money. Were the institute accountants happy? Of course not. Their status in the institutes was dependent on having control of money. Were the scientists happy? Of course. For the first time in a number of years, they were receiving, on time, the amounts of money they were promised. Were the tax inspectors happy? Probably not, but they may still find ways to be heard.

A Revolutionary Philosophy: No Work, No Pay

One additional problem of vital interest to all participants in ISTC projects needed to be codified in the project agreements, namely, the *details* of the program of grant payments.

As noted earlier, the board had provided guidance for determining the levels of payments to be made to participants. By the time the first project agreements were to be signed, the level for senior scientists and engineers was on the order of $300 per month plus bonuses for those who lived in hardship regions of the country.

But we were concerned about the poor work habits that had developed in Russia, the loose procedures for controlling payments to workers in R&D institutions, and the responsibility of the Center in the event of an illness or other problem that prevented a participant from reporting to work. Specifically, we were shocked to learn that some professors who would be participating in ISTC projects were entitled to fifty-four working days of annual vacation, that Russian employees routinely received double pay while on vacation, that women were entitled to up to two years of maternity leave, and that there were few limitations on paid sick leave. Would the ISTC be making payments for contributions to projects by Russians who were home on extended sick leaves or off on six-week vacations?

An EU specialist suggested that the Center pay "by the day." If a participant in a project was at work on a given day, he or she would be paid. If not at work, for whatever reason, no payment would be made.

This approach would remove the ISTC from entanglements in any of the previously mentioned problems.

The board adopted this system. The daily rate was based on an assumption that an employee should work 220 days per year, thus allowing about forty days for holidays, annual leave, and sick leave. If the annual pay level was $3,300, the daily rate would be $15.

The participants in a project could work whatever days the project manager deemed appropriate, including weekends or holidays, within the budget limitations of the project agreement. The Center would pay for four-hour increments only, with the maximum time charged on any day being eight hours. Thus, a participant who worked only two hours would not be eligible for payment for that day. If a participant worked more than eight hours, payment would be limited to eight hours. There was no concept of overtime or extra pay for weekends or holidays. Unpaid vacation periods were optional. Sick leave was the employee's responsibility.

In short, this concept was very simple and contained safeguards to deter abuse. The Russian authorities assured us that the Center was not violating any labor practices as long as the employees agreed to these terms when countersigning our grant letters. Of course, the institute directors were in a quandary because we were challenging long-standing concepts; and they were afraid that their employees would expect new types of welfare support from the institutes.

With these financial problems and other difficulties resolved during the course of the early negotiations of project agreements, in October 1994 the Secretariat was able to present to the board for approval a *Model Project Agreement*, which was to be the framework for ISTC projects. The importance of this document cannot be overstated, for it defined the relationship between the Center and the institutions throughout the CIS countries that joined the Center. It included not only important concepts but also details about doing business, Western-style, in the CIS.[6]

Many provisions of the ISTC Model Project Agreement can be used by other Western organizations interested in serious cooperation with Russian institutions but without the luxury of time and expertise to develop comparable documents on their own.

Shunning Scrutiny in the Secret Cities

A second complication arose as the Secretariat began negotiating project agreements with institutes in the very tightly controlled cities of Arzamas–16 and Chelyabinsk–70. In these cities were located many of the key Russian nuclear weapons designers. They had been the highest-priority targets of the ISTC program, for it was potential leakages of secrets from these guardians of the most sensitive parts of nuclear weaponry that gave rise to the ISTC concept in the first place. Indeed, without the active involvement of these key groups, the ISTC program would fall short of meeting its goal in a very visible way and would soon be in deep political difficulty, both in Russia and abroad.

Under the ISTC Statute, representatives of the financing parties and the ISTC Secretariat had the right to visit project sites to monitor and audit project activities. Though the Statute called for at least twenty days' advance notice of impending visits, there was an exception provision, stating that the Russian institute conducting the project and the financing party could specify other access arrangements on a case-by-case basis.[7]

Within a few months, the Secretariat had concluded more than fifty project agreements with Russian institutions, other than those in Arzamas–16 and Chelyabinsk–70, which included the standard language on the twenty-day notice. Directors of very sensitive facilities were among these initial signators, including the director of the Institute of Automatics in Moscow, which remained deeply involved in nuclear weaponry.

But the directors of the institutes in Arzamas–16 and Chelyabinsk–70 were not prepared to sign project agreements that guaranteed access for foreigners based on notice of only twenty days. They argued that they could not make decisions on visits to their cities without the concurrence of security agencies. Since they had no authority to speak for these agencies, they could not make firm commitments. They pointed out that standard operating procedures called for advance notice of forty-five days, but even with such notice they could not guarantee that a foreign nominee would necessarily be approved by the security services.

As a compromise, the Secretariat and MINATOM developed a format whereby the financing parties and the Secretariat would prepare lists of their *potential* visitors to Arzamas–16 and Chelyabinsk–70 for monitoring and auditing of ISTC projects. These lists would be prescreened and approved by the various Russian security agencies. The lists could be updated annually, or more frequently if necessary. Then the institute directors would have the authority to guarantee that anyone on the approved lists could visit the cities after a twenty-day notification period; the directors could sign the project agreements because they would not have to defer to the security agencies that had already approved specific individuals.

The Governing Board discussed this proposal at length. It was noted that the plan was similar to the *list procedure* used by foreign inspectors checking for compliance with arms control agreements in Russia, an activity that also involved access to sensitive sites. Nevertheless, two problems arose. The European Union expressed concern that the Russian security services might disapprove for arbitrary reasons a candidate for the list. The Russians agreed that should such a problem arise, consultations would be held between Russia and the financing party to reach a satisfactory resolution. Second, the Secretariat was concerned that the Russian security services might delay approval of the lists; the Russians agreed that a forty-five-day review period for authorization of the nominees for the list could be specified.

The board did not accept the list concept. The Western parties considered it too complex and inconsistent with the intent of the Statute. Negotiations were undertaken to reach agreement on other formulas, such as forty days instead of twenty days. In the end, the parties agreed to try thirty-five days for the closed cities.

Nevertheless, the Russian security forces are undoubtedly intent on preserving their final bastions of full authority. Difficulties will probably arise as foreigners continue to attempt to visit the birthplaces of Russian nuclear weaponry.

Arzamas—16, June 1994. ISTC staff members and officials from Washington, Brussels, Tokyo, and Moscow assisted in the development of the initial wave of civilian projects to be carried out at this birthplace of Soviet nuclear weapons.

Enter a Skeptical Duma

Meanwhile, the Foreign Ministry had delayed submitting to the new Duma the necessary papers for ratification of the ISTC Agreement. The Ministry of Finance remained unenthusiastic about the Agreement, and the Foreign Ministry spent a great deal of effort to ensure that their financial colleagues would not oppose ratification once the papers were sent to the Duma.

While the Duma had yet to consider the ratification issue formally, many key members of the Duma were well aware of the importance of involving specialists from Arzamas–16 and Chelyabinsk–70 in ISTC programs; without the strong support of scientists from these two centers for the ISTC, ratification of the Agreement could be stymied.

But was ratification necessary? Technically, the ISTC could continue functioning indefinitely as long as the Duma did not take action that would force the Russian government to withdraw from the Protocol on Provisional Application of the ISTC Agreement. Such negative action seemed unlikely in the near future for several reasons. First, the Duma was preoccupied with many heavier issues. Second, the Russian government would presumably argue vigorously for preservation of the ISTC. And finally, members of the Duma would probably be split on the merits of the ISTC.

Nevertheless, ratification was highly desirable. A more *legitimate* basis for the ISTC would ease some of the internal Russian problems with tax inspectors, with budget officials holding up administrative support for the Center, and with security officers reluctant to grant exceptions for foreigners traveling to sensitive facilities. More permanent status for the Center would make ISTC projects more attractive to weapons specialists who had the option of working either on weapons or on ISTC projects.

From the perspective of the foreign members, ratification would provide considerable reassurance that Russia's commitment to the Center would not be jeopardized should Yeltsin disappear from the scene. Such reassurance would have significant impact on the willingness of the parties to provide additional funding for ISTC projects. This issue of Russian commitment would undoubtedly come to a head at the time of the two-year review in early 1996 specified in the protocol and the Agreement. Thus, in the summer of 1995, after another round of debates among Russian government agencies as to the merits of the Center, the Foreign Ministry formally requested the Duma to ratify the ISTC Agreement.

The Center Launches Out on Its Own

When established in March 1994, the Center became the only stand-alone international organization cosponsored by Western governments and Russia with headquarters in Moscow.

While the ISTC followed UNESCO on the diplomatic list, it did not have a comparable umbilical cord to administrative and financial support services in Paris or any other capital. The parties to the ISTC Agreement were of course prepared to help whenever possible; but the Secretariat was largely on its own to turn the organization into a full-fledged diplomatic mission.

Many diplomats in Moscow who had become accustomed to buying favors as the only route around administrative roadblocks would probably flinch at the alternative *legal* methods the Secretariat was forced to employ to achieve the goal of establishing a new diplomatic enclave in the city. These methods might best be described as persistent, presumptuous, and pushy.

The first requirement, of course, was to have staff assigned to the Center. One by one, the staff arrived, primarily sent by MINATOM, with a few key people from Tokyo, Europe, and Washington. A dozen of the staff members had been working in the Prepcom, and they continued to be the core of the operation. By the end of 1994, the staff had grown to about thirty-five, with a few more still to arrive.

All staff members were assigned on secondment from governments: they were paid by their own governments, and the Center had no payroll. This led to a particularly difficult situation for the Russian staff members, who were to be paid government-level salaries. They did not have the opportunity to augment these salaries with special pay supplements and second jobs, as had become commonplace for talented and not-so-talented governmental employees throughout Moscow. The board helped solve this problem by approving a system of financial incentives for the Russian staff. These incentives were cast as *representation allowances* and *allowances for advanced professional training*, two techniques invented by the Soviet bureaucracy decades earlier to avoid the tax inspector.

As to the well-being of the foreign staff, the principal issues were housing, visas, and identity cards asserting certain diplomatic privileges and immunities. Housing was and will continue to be a major problem for foreigners living in Russia. As an international organization, however, the Center became eligible for the protocol services extended by the Russian government to the embassies. The organization providing these services controlled many apartments in Moscow. Though this widened the choice, the problems of skyrocketing rents, poor maintenance, isolated locations, and inadequate security in crime-infested neighborhoods remained formidable obstacles to settling into the Moscow scene.

The identity-card issue was resolved after a false start. The ISTC executive director and deputy directors were entitled to full diplomatic privileges, while the remainder of the staff had a more limited set of privileges. The Russian Foreign Ministry issued the Japanese deputy an identity card for junior staff; however, after we insisted that the Foreign Ministry experts read the ISTC Agreement carefully, they promptly corrected the mistake and issued a diplomatic card.

Visas have frequently caused consternation for visitors to Russia. For many years, I traveled to Russia using an ordinary American passport; never did I receive a Russian visa more than one or two days before my departure from Washington. When assigned to the U.S. Embassy in Moscow with a diplomatic passport, however, I received a multiple-entry visa valid for two years, with no worries about the next trip. The challenge for the Center was to move into this diplomatic mode rather than to be forced to rely on cliff-hanger scenarios.

In the end, our experience in dealing with the Russian Foreign Ministry belied many of the previous complaints I had voiced and heard from others for years about the inability of the ministry to approve visas on time. The head of the Consular Department of the Foreign Ministry laid out very clear ground rules for us. If the Secretariat decided to support a visa application for a visitor to Russia, the Secretariat should provide the Consular Department with certain information concerning name, date and place of birth, passport number, and date of issuance and expiration of the passport. For a single-entry visa, the department needed one week's advance notice. For a multiple-entry visa, it needed one month's advance notice. In addition, the Center should allow two working days for a request to be transmitted from the registration office of the Foreign Ministry where the Secretariat deposited the requests to the Consular Department, which was in a different building.

We followed these instructions to the letter, never asking for shortened time periods for visa approvals. In every case, the visa was approved on schedule.

A final protocol problem related to my car, and presumably to the cars of my successors. As the chief of a diplomatic mission, I was entitled to a special license plate reserved for ambassadors and heads of international organizations—the ultimate in vanity plates. Also, if the Center had a flag, I could fly the flag from the crushed front fender of our ten-year-old Honda. But only six more months remained of my Moscow assignment, and I had been quite content using the same license plate assigned to operators of the copy machines at the embassy who, as previously noted, deserved as much credit as I did for the start-up of the ISTC.

The U.S. Embassy had helped me obtain these license plates during a very painful experience. The Russian traffic police were interested in only one aspect of a car being registered. They wanted to see personally the number on the engine block. Brakes, headlights, and horns were irrelevant. Broken windshields were fine. But the number on the engine block had to be clearly visible. Finding a rust-encrusted number near the bottom of the engine block of a ten-year-old Honda had been a challenge that only a skilled embassy engineer could resolve. And with a powerful flashlight spotlighting the number, he had ushered us through the Russian inspection line during a snowstorm.

To comply with my newly elevated diplomatic status, I would have to subject myself to deregistration of the car to turn in the old plates, reregistration for the new plates, and then deregistration to turn in the new plates when I was ready to ship the car home. Each time, the nearly invisible number on the engine block would be the center of attention.

The deputy chief of protocol officially summoned me to the Foreign Ministry to explain to him why I had not assumed my status as the head of a diplomatic mission. "You are missing a number of diplomatic receptions and other special events," he noted. I then explained the problem with my car, emphasizing that I wanted to devote my remaining energy to pressing forward with the programs of the Center and not to hassling the traffic police over new license plates. When I pressed him to come to my aid with the traffic police, he replied in perfect English, "No one can deal with the traffic police. You should simply keep your license plates until you leave Russia."

Unfurling the ISTC's (unofficial) banner in the summer of 1994. From left to right, ISTC deputy executive directors Vladimir Kruchenkov (Russia), Atsushi Shaku (Japan), Alain Gerard (France), and the author.

Thus, while my deputies and I were all scientists and engineers, we had passed the diplomatic litmus tests of conquering the problems of housing, identity cards, visas, and even license plates, with the skill of seasoned ambassadors.

The ISTC Moves into Its New Quarters

Finally, on August 1, 1994, more than two years after my "urgent" arrival in Moscow, I moved into a private office adorned with five chandeliers and a suite of jet black furniture.

The Secretariat's new office complex stretched over one-half of a floor of the Pulse Institute. The hallway was very long and was blandly painted in a color born of a marriage of pale yellow and dull olive. The walls reflected the light from the few overhead lamps, and the corridor was so long that some visitors thought they were peering into a hall of mirrors.

Even though the other offices were not completely finished, my move into the new complex was important politically. Much to the relief of Russian government officials, I could finally report to all members of the ISTC board that the Secretariat occupied its own facility. Within several weeks, the remainder of the staff had also moved.

Fortunately, our Russian administrative officer, who had spent a number of years at an international organization in Vienna, was skilled in overcoming problem after problem. His principal task was to calm me down every time I saw something else that needed attention—windows that leaked when it rained, air conditioners that didn't work, and empty spaces for wastebaskets that failed to appear.

At the same time, I often challenged his initiatives, only to back down when he eloquently explained the reasons for some of his unorthodox approaches. For example, he told me he had purchased some new chairs, even though we already had an abundance of serviceable, though elderly, models. I agreed that maybe a few high-class chairs for important guests were in order, but I certainly flinched when I learned he had bought sixty of them. He then patiently took me around to show me where each one was needed.

A staff member assigned by Finland became our chief purchasing agent. Every day he would come back to the Center with something new as he earned the title of our "Flying Finn." The projectors, the surge protectors, and the office supplies kept piling up. The paper shredder was one of his few mistakes; it would take only three sheets at a time. We needed an industrial-size shredder.

Meanwhile, we encountered a recalcitrant crew of customs inspectors at Sheremetevo Airport who had difficulty accepting the notion that the ISTC had certain diplomatic prerogatives. Even when confronted with international agreements, instructions from the ministries, and a directive from their immediate bosses, they preferred to rely on financial incentives that we simply were not prepared to provide.[8]

The financial officer somehow managed to produce cash whenever we needed it. I am not sure how many money belts he wore during his frequent visits to the bank, but I held my breath that he would not become a target for the mafia.

Among the highlights for the staff, aside from their new private offices, were the banquets scheduled on the occasions of Governing Board meetings. The first was held in the Guest House of the Foreign Ministry, quite elegant but also a little too proper. The second was at the House of Scientists, which was more modest but still maintained some of the trappings of the prosperous days when scientists were among the leaders of society. The third was at the charming House of Writers, where our youthful support staff showed those of us from past generations how Western music is transforming life in Moscow. Had I stayed in Moscow for another meeting of the board, I planned to rent the foyer in the spectacular Institute of Paleontology, where a background of dinosaurs would remind us that nuclear weapons could easily send us back to our roots.

Thus, after not only months but years of massaging papers, maneuvering through diplomatic minefields, convincing key scientific leaders that life could be better, and finding places for the dedicated staff members to work without constant interruptions—the ISTC was on its way. Even a skeptical press began to change the tone of its reporting.[9]

No longer would the telephones be answered with the typical Russian response "Allo." The first executive director's first directive proclaimed that every voice would ring out, "International Science and Technology Center"—either in Russian or in English.

Chapter 5

Putting the Weaponeers to Work

U.S. Paying Millions to Russian Scientists Not to Sell A-Secrets
The Washington Post, September 24, 1994

Identifying "Dangerous" Weapons Specialists

When the ISTC concept was first put forth, some Western experts estimated that about 200 Russian specialists had the capability to design a nuclear weapon. They should constitute the primary target of the activities of the ISTC, these experts contended. The Western fear was that one or two seasoned veterans could take charge of a program in a developing country and successfully lead an effort to develop a nuclear capability. And if these experienced hands took an entire Russian team with them, the consequences could be serious indeed.[1] This was a very limited perspective of the potential proliferation problems that would confront the ISTC.

While only a handful of Russian scientists had a sufficiently broad base of experience to *lead* a weapons program, many developing countries already had their nuclear leaders. Highly specialized expertise that could contribute to efforts underway was of comparable, if not more, interest. Such interest greatly expanded the number of players at the international nuclear roulette tables. Also, the Western experts apparently assumed that Russian specialists would spend extended periods of time in the countries of proliferation concern since a new weapons program could not be initiated overnight. But the practical aspects of emigration to developing countries by Russians with heads full of secrets and hearts laden with extended-family ties presented formidable barriers. Also, long-term career opportunities in such far-off assignments were uncertain even by Russian standards. A few specialists might try to dodge the KGB-trained security authorities and opt for a permanent life of obscurity abroad, but such cases would be rare.

At the same time, we witnessed the emergence of a variety of new channels for transferring abroad technical information originating in Russia. Many weaponeers were making short-term visits to other countries. Foreign representatives in Russia with undisclosed home affiliations increased. Also of great significance, electronic communications from remote locations in Russia to other countries developed quickly.[2]

Thus, tens of thousands of *narrow specialists* residing in Russia with no intention to emigrate should be of no less concern to the ISTC than the handful of better-known weapons-design gurus, who were also unlikely to spend their lives in uncertainty in distant countries.

What was the market for the wayward weaponeers? In 1993 the Russian Foreign Intelligence Service identified a number of countries of proliferation concern. Its report discussed the capabilities of sixteen countries: Algeria, Argentina, Brazil, Egypt, Israel, India, Iraq, Iran, North Korea, Libya, Pakistan, Syria, Taiwan, Chile, South Africa, and South Korea. Some of these countries received a clean bill of health with regard to nuclear weapons, but others were reported to be moving into the nuclear arena in a significant way. The report did not address China, Ukraine, or any of the other states of the former Soviet Union, although many Russian organizations were more concerned about these neighbors than the ones on the list of the Foreign Intelligence Service.[3]

As to ISTC interests in the nuclear brain drain, China, India, and Pakistan have had substantial nuclear weapons programs for a number of years; but they could undoubtedly use special in-depth experience to refine their approaches and help assess their capabilities and their shortcomings. Some countries, such as Iraq and Iran, seemed interested in developing capabilities for the production of enriched uranium as a significant step toward a weapons capability. The aspirations of North Korea encompassed an entire set of nuclear capabilities from producing the material for the bomb to disposing of wastes in a surreptitious manner. These and other aspiring nuclear powers could also capitalize on the experiences of Russians in carrying out computer simulations of nuclear tests based on the weapons designs they were pursuing.

Of course, many countries had foresworn nuclear weapons through their signatures on the international agreement on non-proliferation.[4] At the same time, the uncertainty of the political courses of some of these countries and their neighbors could in the not-too-distant future provoke changes in their perceptions of the need for equipping themselves with nuclear weapons. Other countries were reluctant to tie their hands permanently by participating in this international agreement, believing that they must retain the nuclear option. And still other countries, regardless of their international obligations, could become shadowy havens for terrorists with nuclear ambitions and the desire for know-how from abroad to fulfill those ambitions.

Thus, the number of nations that should be of proliferation concern to the parties that established the ISTC was quite large. In almost every scenario depicting the future behavior of states intent on acquiring modern military firepower, the experience available in Russia could be helpful if the country were to choose the nuclear weapons path—experience embodied in specialists ranging from chief designers for entire weapons systems to technicians skilled in the proper settings of triggering devices and in handling other individual weapons components.

Of course, nuclear weaponry was not to be the only concern of the ISTC. Rockets and aircraft that could deliver the weapons were also of intense interest. As vividly demonstrated by Scud missiles during the Persian Gulf War, these same rockets and aircraft could deliver conventional explosives (or conceivably chemical or biological agents) if nuclear programs did not materialize. Again, some countries could benefit from the expertise of chief designers of rocket systems. Others, which already had their designs or even the rockets, would simply need more focused expertise in guidance systems, special lightweight materials, and electronic devices, for example, to ensure that the delivery systems worked effectively.

As to biological and chemical warfare ingredients, the temptations for many dozens of countries to investigate potentially dangerous viruses, microbes, and molecules were manyfold. Laboratories devoted to pharmaceutical and pesticide research, for example, can easily conceal additional capabilities for exploring the harmful effects of dangerous chemicals on unsuspecting people. Experienced Russian scientists could save such laboratories considerable time and effort by sharing their problems and solutions in converting chemical and biological formulas into deliverable weapons.[5]

The Foreign Intelligence Service report estimated that more than 100 countries had the industrial base to develop and/or produce chemical warfare agents in very modest facilities. Building a wall around only Russia obviously would not prevent these countries from acquiring chemical warfare capabilities; but as part of a broad international effort, such an embargo on brains to pariah states would complicate the aspirations of terrorists.

Similarly, biological agents are relatively easy and inexpensive to produce in countries with pharmaceutical or fermentation industries. But weaponization of these agents is not so easy—and indeed may be very dangerous for inexperienced technical personnel. This is the area where experienced weaponeers can be particularly helpful.[6]

Against this background of technical realities, I reached the following conclusion: Rather than the original estimate of a mere 200 dangerous Russian scientists of proliferation concern, the number of Russian specialists who developed and designed weapons of mass destruction and their delivery systems and who should be of interest to the ISTC was about 60,000.

These 60,000 specialists had many years of experience in honing their skills throughout an extensive complex of R&D facilities that at one time housed over one million scientists, engineers, and technicians dedicating their careers to nuclear, biological, and chemical weapons and to rockets and other delivery systems.[7]

What about the other 940,000?

Almost all countries of proliferation concern have a number of well-trained scientists and engineers with skills that are relevant to weapons programs. Many studied in elite institutions in the United States or Europe. Therefore, most of the one million Russians with skills important, but not unique, to weaponry would not be of high-priority interest to countries with hidden agendas involving weapons. The additional insights they could provide would not warrant the difficulties in recruiting them. But the 60,000 core specialists had many years of direct hands-on experience in the laboratories and on the test ranges where components and materials for thousands of real weapons were developed and fired. Such experience was lacking in most other countries.

According to my estimates, this manpower pool of dangerous people in Russia includes about 30,000 who learned their trade in the aerospace industry, about 20,000 in the nuclear field, and 10,000 from the biological and chemical warfare sector. The aerospace experts are largely products of several hundred institutes and enterprises that in 1994 fell under the organizational umbrellas of the State Committee for the Defense Industry and the Russian Space Agency. The nuclear specialists are primarily from the thirty R&D institutes of MINATOM; the chemical specialists honed their skills in a handful of institutes under the Committee for the Defense Industry; and the biological experts toiled in a half-dozen laboratories of BIOPREPARAT, which is a subsidiary of the Ministry of Health, and in several laboratories of the Ministry of Agriculture and the Ministry of Defense. A small percentage of specialists in various fields had been housed in forty to fifty institutes of the Academy of Sciences, thirty to forty universities and colleges, and a few institutions that became independent, such as the Kurchatov Institute of Atomic Energy. Additional specialists came through the system of the Ministry of Defense, which still tightly guards the identity of its institutions.

An estimated 50 percent of these dangerous minds were spawned in institutions in and around Moscow. Perhaps 15 percent had been concentrated in the St. Petersburg area. Most of the remainder were dispersed in the industrial cities and the secret atomic cities that stretched across the Urals and Siberia.[8] A few were linked to shipbuilding enterprises, marine-oriented research facilities, and naval bases in the north, on the Black Sea, and in the vicinity of Vladivostok.

In addition to the 60,000 in Russia, a few thousand dangerous descendants of the Soviet legacy remained in the former rocket facilities of Ukraine, at the nearly dormant mining and testing complexes of Central Asia, in Armenia and Georgia (as previously noted), and at a few institutes and enterprises in Belarus and the Baltic countries.

What are they doing now?

Clearly, many of the 60,000 specialists, perhaps one-third, continue to work full-time in the greatly reduced weapons programs of Russia. At the same time, an estimated 15,000 of the other specialists have already left the state institutions; they are spending most of their time on the streets or in the closely guarded commercial offices of Russia searching for new ways to make money, with little interest in moving to the Third World. The remainder are still in their familiar institutes, where they are underemployed, with time on their hands and uncertain paychecks in their futures. These underemployed specialists are obviously a primary target of ISTC programs. Conceivably, a few departed specialists could be enticed back to their former workplaces, but those who remained in place when the job outlook was bleak are not eager to share the proceeds from ISTC projects with deserters from the inner sanctum.

The ISTC Secretariat identified the following skill categories of weapons experts who were likely participants in Center projects:

Nuclear weapons design, fabrication, and testing
Nuclear materials research, development, and processing
Biological weapons
Chemical weapons
Rocketry, including fuels
Submarine research, development, and design
Other launching platforms
Non-nuclear materials
Lasers
Electronics
Other aerospace

As expected, the initial waves of project proposals for ISTC support came largely from specialists in the nuclear categories. About one half of them were weapons designers and testers, and 15 percent were specialists in nuclear materials. Over time, all the categories were represented; but the nuclear weapons community remained the most aggressive promoters of their projects.[9]

In summary, the Secretariat knew where the majority of the potential clients were located. And gradually these and other clients heard about and searched out their potential benefactors at the ISTC Secretariat, who had access to new sources of funds.

Indeed, many dozens of scientists and engineers from the outlying regions of Russia somehow found funds within their institutes for trips to Moscow, justifying their travel on the basis of necessary consultations at the ISTC Secretariat. This we knew for certain, since every day the ISTC official stamp was applied to our visitors' travel documents so that they could collect per diem when they returned home.

Thousands of Scientists on Center Projects

At the beginning of the negotiations to establish the ISTC, the U.S. delegates emphasized that the Center should be open to all former weapons specialists who wanted to compete for funds—the individual professor, the private entrepreneur, the retired weaponeer, and of course the research teams of the large institutes. In practice, almost every proposal came from the research teams. The bulk of the weaponeers who still had access to the means for carrying out R&D projects remained loosely clustered in these teams.

Very few individual researchers could tap into the state facilities and support services necessary to conduct serious research. Also, each application for support by the ISTC needed the concurrence of the Russian government or another CIS government, depending on the location of the proposed research. Individual researchers were intimidated when seeking favors from the government, which was staffed by bureaucrats accustomed to dealing with large organizations; and individuals simply were reluctant to push proposals through all the necessary procedural steps, particularly the step of governmental concurrence. Of course, the Secretariat was prepared to help them. But sooner or later, the individual applicants would have to show to their governments that they would not be using state facilities or resources free of charge. They would then need to justify to the bureaucracy why their governments should support their proposals, possibly in competition with proposals from state organizations.

The average size of initial projects supported by the ISTC was between $500,000 and $600,000, although they ranged from $37,000 to $3.2 million. Most of these projects were 10 to 100 times larger than research projects at Russian institutions being supported by other foreign organizations operating in Russia. For example, almost all the grants of the well-known Soros Foundation and other private foundations in the West ranged from $500 to $50,000. Most U.S. government agencies limited their awards to about $50,000; and the European program to support individual researchers in Russia also made awards in the tens of thousands of dollars, at most.

But the ISTC was interested in employing as many weapons specialists as possible, and for periods that would sustain meaningful research, usually two to three years. Most ISTC projects costing $500,000 involve fifty to sixty weapons specialists, including a significant number participating on a part-time basis. Smaller projects employ fewer specialists while requiring almost as much administrative effort on the part of the ISTC. Therefore, large projects have been considered by some Western officials to be the most efficient way to use the resources of the Center, all other factors being equal.

Usually two, three, or four separate Russian institutions collaborated on each project. Frequently, one of the institutes had been historically of civilian orientation as the weapons specialists increasingly linked themselves to colleagues with experience in the civilian sector. One approved project was to establish communication linkages among geographically separated researchers at eighteen institutions. Another effort was designed to document the extent of radiation contamination throughout Russia and involved more than twenty-five institutions. These projects were very complicated to organize and administer. It was also difficult to sustain them at a high level of performance, since the financial resources were diffused so widely that the senior managers of the participating institutes were not particularly interested in having only a small piece of a project. Nevertheless, the projects commanded financial support because the topics were significant, and the participants had been important weaponeers.

Most of the lead institutions for the early ISTC projects were located in Moscow and the Moscow region, where, as noted earlier, many military complexes punctuated the landscape. As to affiliations of the lead institutes, the largest percentage was subordinate to MINATOM, followed by institutes of the Russian Academy of Sciences.

Of course, we were concerned that the academy institutes housed relatively few of the key weaponeers and that they might be diverting funds from the primary targets of the ISTC. Nevertheless, the academy institutes played a very useful matchmaking role in bringing together many Russian military and civilian organizations and then linking them with organizations abroad. In a number of projects involving academy institutes, the bulk of the money ended up in the hands of specialists employed in defense-related institutes that served as subcontractors for the projects.

As to the fields of application for the first 100 approved projects, there was a surprisingly even distribution across more than ten fields, including new sources of energy, controlled fusion, safety of nuclear reactors, nuclear contamination of the environment, non-nuclear contamination of the environment, medicine and pharmacy, new types of plastics, electronics and computer sciences, space and aviation technologies, and basic research, particularly in physics. In general, the next several waves of approved projects followed this pattern with the noticeable exception that research in basic physics assumed a somewhat dominating position. The pioneers of fission and fusion were determined to find still new ways to manipulate the atom.[10]

While the Secretariat had considerable influence on the size of the proposals, the number of participants, and the collaborative arrangements among institutions, we had very little impact on the topics chosen by the Russian applicants. They seemed to be tied almost entirely to long-standing latent interests of Russian specialists. With rare exceptions, Russian weaponeers were very hesitant to become risk takers and to launch into completely virgin territory, even if they knew there would be an increased likelihood of receiving financial support.

A final aspect related to the extent of interest in the results of the research being sponsored by the ISTC. In the early stages of the formation of the Center, government officials in Washington, Brussels, and Tokyo encouraged their private companies to become involved in the activities of the Center on the assumption that many products for the commercial market would emerge from the Center's programs.

The overwhelming majority of the projects, however, were not targeted on commercial applications that could be marketed in the private sector. Instead, the weapons laboratories were better equipped to carry out broadly based research in physics, chemistry, biology, geophysics, and other disciplines that would be of interest primarily to the general scientific community and to government agencies that fund research. Also of interest were applied products that would support the missions of governmental agencies such as software for assessing environmental problems, power supplies for space probes, and methodologies for determining the operating condition of nuclear reactors. Of the initial projects, fewer than 5 percent appeared to be headed toward commercial markets. It was questionable at best whether any of these activities would net patentable results. Why, then, did we spend so much time on the IPR issue?

Was the ISTC encouraging too much esoteric research at a time when Russia needed practical applications? Was the ISTC really contributing to its charter to assist in the transition to a market economy? Yes, much of the initial research was too abstract, in my view. No, the research topics had little to do with the workings of the economy.

Nevertheless, as noted earlier and further elaborated in the next section, a number of projects were directed to important goals, such as environmental protection and nuclear safety, in addition to advancing basic science and introducing new products into the commercial marketplace. But many Russian skeptics over the role of the ISTC insisted that the profit line should be the ultimate test of the success of the Center and of the participating weapons scientists.

Of course, as we see in Chapter 7, the task of conversion of the research orientation from providing products of interest to the government to providing results for the commercial marketplace was always easier said than done. Would it have been any more appropriate for the Center to devote millions of dollars to inventions directed to commercial customers who had little real interest in paying for the resulting products?

The hope was that gradually this bias away from the marketplace would change as the Russian institutions thought more about the follow-on funding to sustain related research activities and interacted more with other organizations that were at the commercial table. But in the immediate future, who besides the ISTC or the Russian government will pay the bill for follow-on activities if a strong Russian economic recovery is not forthcoming? In any event, even under the best of circumstances it will be a long process until Russian R&D is sharply skewed to the interests of the private-sector marketplace. Unfortunately, many Russian researchers feel they have already spent too much time worrying about the *relevance* and *marketability* of their research.

Revealing Radioactive Contamination

The ISTC Agreement identified environmental protection, along with nuclear safety and energy sources, as a priority area for projects. With this in mind, I visited one of the country's most infamous radioactive zones—the contaminated territory adjacent to the town of Ozersk, previously known as Chelyabinsk–65.[11] The Mayak enterprise, with its uranium reactor fuel-reprocessing plant and an adjacent plant for processing plutonium for military uses, dominates this town. Mayak means *lighthouse*; but after I reported to Carole on the environmental conditions at Mayak, she recalled the recent fire there and then remarked that the firm should have been named *firehouse*, convinced that I would soon be glowing in the dark.

In 1989, chauffeured in a Soviet armored personnel carrier, I toured a radioactive waste site about a mile from the demolished Chernobyl reactor. Now, in 1994, I was ready for a trip through the Mayak complex in a truck with steel plates for protective shielding around its passengers.

This vehicle took me to a nearby lake that had been a receptor for large quantities of radioactive waste from the Mayak plants in the 1940s and 1950s. The nuclides then leaked into an entire system of pristine streams. Also, radioactive waste material had accumulated on the shore and was blown into adjacent areas. Work had been under way for almost twenty years to fill in the lake with rocks and dirt, and we watched a steady stream of armor-plated dump trucks carrying the fill material to the lake. While this cover would prevent a sloshing lake, it also would seal the existing pollution into the bed of the lake close to the water table.

Next, we headed out to the center of a 100-kilometer radioactive trace that scarred a nearby forest. This unwelcome ragged seam sown by radionuclides was the result of an explosion in 1957 in a waste container stored not far from the lake. I noted that our truck was closely followed by a mobile crane, lest we became mired in the mud. Such consideration for my safety added an unusual touch to Russian hospitality. We examined the many plots of grain and vegetables being grown in the middle of the trace, which had become a field laboratory to measure the rate of uptake of radioactive particles from the soil into the crops.

Mayak was not the only Russian enterprise that contributed heavily to radioactive contamination of the country. Nuclear reactors produced plutonium for weapons and generated large amounts of glowing waste near the Siberian cities of Tomsk and Krasnoyarsk. Some of the most lethal liquid waste was injected into holes deep into the ground, while other waste simply drained from the reactor sites into rivers flowing northward toward the Arctic region.

Then, for many years, the Soviets had discharged leftover liquids from their nuclear icebreakers and nuclear submarines into the Barents Sea in the north and the Sea of Japan in the east. As foreign countries began to detect the spread of these wastes, the international pressure mounted for the Russians to construct and operate modern disposal facilities. But the Russians simply claimed poverty, and every year the issue of uncontrolled marine dumping of waste ignites new anxieties and tempers around the world.[12]

Many Russian nuclear weapons specialists have become interested in trying to assess the messes, but few have devoted their talents to devising realistic solutions for cleaning up the disaster areas. The contamination is so pervasive in some areas and the population has lived around it for so long that no politician or specialist is driven to find an acceptable and affordable path that could make a significant difference.[13]

With this background, the ISTC began supporting a number of projects to try to set the stage for greater national efforts that could begin to reverse nuclear contamination within the country. Like most of the other environmental efforts throughout Russia, the ISTC projects steered away from difficult cleanup activities and stressed still more assessments of problem areas, through monitoring of the air, water, and soil in the field and through modeling of the environment on computers. Also, the Center supported a number of activities to help guide the handling of solid nuclear wastes in the future. These included investigations of potential sites for permanent storage of reactor refuse as well as research on the properties of different radioactive materials found in many waste mixtures of the country.

The costs associated with containment of wastes within specified geographic areas that have already been evacuated will be staggering, let alone the costs of any efforts to clean up the contaminated areas. The ISTC never had the resources required for nuclear cleanup activities. But the parties hoped that the Center's projects would provide the Russian government with better information and technical options for their future decisions on the disposition of the many zones of contamination.

Calloused to Environmental Calamities

In many ways, the chemical contamination that is omnipresent throughout the metropolitan and industrial areas of Russia is a more serious threat to human health than radiation pollutants, which are relatively easy to detect and measure. Russians can usually stay away from the radioactive zones, but they have no choice but to live within the chemical zones.

Estimates abound as to the percentage of drinking water that is unsafe, the number of square miles of lakes and rivers that should be avoided, and the frequency with which air pollution alerts are warranted.

A "pollution map" of Moscow showed that at the corner of our block, where children regularly played, high levels of heavy metals permeated the soil. Also, according to the map, apartment complexes within several miles of our neighborhood had been built on the sites of waste dumps that were simply bulldozed over, and a healthy dose of a broad mix of chemical air pollutants regularly blanketed the city. Rocket scientist or not, you could smell the odors in the air and sense the stench in the rivers. No wonder Russia gives low priority to the long-term effects of chemical pollutants on global warming when the near-term effects of chemical contaminants have contributed directly to the decline in average male longevity to fifty-nine years.

Pollution studies immediately became a popular topic for proposals prepared for the Center. The chemical weapons experts, of course, wanted to transform their skills in detecting battlefield molecules to skills in measuring common pollutants in the cities. The biological warfare specialists devised new ways to measure the impact of pollutants on human beings. Do they cause allergies? Do they cause skin cancer? And, of course, what happens when they penetrate the skin, are breathed, or are ingested? These issues have been explored in the West for many years, and unresolved questions persist.

But maybe the Russian chemists who knew how to make molecules that destroy the body would have some new ideas as to how to *protect* the body, if they were only given the chance. The parties to the ISTC Agreement were willing to offer that opportunity, but wanted to keep this group on a short leash. They released the funds for projects in bioecology in small increments. The rigor of Russian investigative methods was questioned. In warfare, there are only two points on the curve—alive or dead. But investigations of pollutants require many points on many curves. While the Russian specialists were not happy with wearing choke chains, they were prepared to comply with the strict rules as long as the new source of income would ensure that food would slide easily by the chokers on a regular basis.

Then the Russian aerospace crowd arrived. There must have been a dozen institutes in Russia that had their own experimental airplanes, and each one wanted the ISTC to outfit a plane with remote-sensing equipment to spot pollutants from afar. Spy planes suddenly became environmental observation platforms. Combat helicopters would be converted to mobile monitoring facilities. Even dirigibles were to be revived so that they could hover over the cities and take air samples for twenty-four hours at a time.

Despite all the talk generated by the managers of these institutions, they had great difficulty submitting proposals to the ISTC. Indeed, as of the end of 1994, not a single remote-sensing proposal had commanded financial support.

As a long-time environmentalist, I was delighted to see this flurry of interest in a greener Russia. But the weaponeers wanted only to *assess* the problems of chemical contamination as monitoring and modeling schemes dominated the list of approved environmental projects. Who was going to clean them up? Many of the chemical problems could have been attacked one by one on a very limited geographic basis, unlike the situation with the widely contaminated radiation zones. The Center had funds for million-dollar projects that could have been a good start.

Russia may soon be littered with pollution graveyards, huge areas of its territory hastily fenced and marked "off limits." Fortunately the country is large, with lots of space to spare. But the costs of relocation are so great that few people will pay attention to "off-limits" signs. And even if there are fences around the graveyards, what steps can be taken to prevent the theft of the metal fences to be sold as scrap?

New Sources of Energy—And Old Ones Too

Another priority area for the ISTC was the development of new sources of energy. Presumably this included innovative ways to use the country's vast oil and gas reserves to generate electricity and provide heating for the cities. For example, the Russian aviation experts had extensive experience in developing jet engines. Surely they could find ways to adapt their techniques to more cost-effective gas-fed power plants. Also, the nuclear experts had very sophisticated electronic systems to control the workings of complicated weapons. Couldn't these control techniques be used for more efficient regulation of the fossil power plants? But we received only one or two innovative ideas related to conventional power generation. The weapons specialists who knew about the ISTC had been so firmly wedded to nuclear power that they simply did not talk to specialists responsible for the bulk of Russia's electrical supply.

Also, the Secretariat expected a flurry of proposals directed to non-conventional sources of power—small hydroelectric stations, solar stations, windmills, and even tidal power schemes. This area turned out to be a dry well. I had been a skeptic about Russian capabilities in these areas when I saw their original facilities in the 1960s, which never amounted to anything more than tourist attractions. But I was hopeful that recent advances in solar receptors and wind devices might attract the attention of Russian scientists concerned about the requirements for small, remote power sources throughout the vast country.

The Secretariat also anticipated outbursts of interest in research on energy conservation. Again, the relevant specialists, if there were any in the weapons complex, were avoiding us. We did have one memorable discussion with a remote-sensing expert from the Moscow Energy Institute, a technical college. He was seeking new sources of income to pay the ruble starved faculty.

He had flown in an airplane over Moscow with an infrared device measuring temperature differences on the ground below. It was the middle of winter, and his idea was to see which apartment buildings were leaking heat by detecting temperature glows just outside the walls of the porous buildings. He discovered that all the buildings leaked. While this finding was interesting, it was not very helpful in advising the city administrators where to concentrate their efforts to seal the numerous leaks.

We were flooded with proposals in two other areas: fusion energy and new types of nuclear power reactors. The fusion scientists had been at work in the USSR for more than thirty years, and the early Soviet achievements picked up an admiring following in the United States and Europe. While the Russian effort had slipped somewhat in comparison to recent foreign achievements, it nevertheless remained impressive.

Fusion proposals arrived at the Pulse Institute from the first day I was in Moscow. The connections with foreign colleagues of Russian fusion researchers were very strong, and often both Westerners and Russians brought in the proposals. The advocates saved the Secretariat a great deal of time in that they prepared the best-structured proposals we received. We did our duty and promptly dispatched the proposals to Brussels, Washington, and Tokyo, as well as to the Russian government. But several members of the staff had serious reservations about the payoff from putting ISTC funds into this futuristic area of research which promised results in not less than twenty to thirty years. Nevertheless, when the proposals arrived in the capitals for review, the fusion enthusiasts were waiting; they convinced the governments to fund many of them. Thus, fusion activities became a significant component of the ISTC portfolio.

As to nuclear reactors, officials in Tokyo, Brussels, and Washington wanted the Russian nuclear reactor specialists to concentrate on making their existing facilities safer. But many Russian thinkers preferred to develop new *types* of reactors and leave the old ones in the care of those with lesser high-tech capabilities. The Secretariat received proposals to put reactors in missile silos, on barges, and on remote islands.

Every possible reactor concept was of interest—using plutonium, uranium, thorium, and even materials that had not yet been discovered and named.

The Russian specialists argued that they had more advanced technology than anyone else. This was true in two areas. Their nuclear submarine reactors were a different design from those in the West. They were based on lead-cooled systems that the Russians wanted to adapt to land-based power reactors. Also, the southern Urals houses the world's largest breeder reactor, which had been generating new fuel while burning the old for more than ten years.

But as long as the operating Russian reactors posed a hazard—and the Western experts were convinced that they did—the proposals for new reactor designs and related investigations did not garner much support. The Western argument was that these new fantasies would simply divert attention from old, and very real, problems.

Overall, the response of Russian institutions in the energy sector to ISTC funding opportunities was much narrower than had been anticipated. It appeared that some of the most interesting Russian ideas were already being supported by large programs of the bilateral aid agencies and by foreign commercial interests, particularly with regard to the oil and gas resources of the country. We welcomed such support as long as these programs were not abruptly terminated.

Avoiding Another Chernobyl

While visiting the large nuclear reactor complex outside St. Petersburg, I was impressed by the facts and figures presented to demonstrate that these four reactor units had operating histories comparable to those of the best reactors in the West—and better than any other operating reactors in Russia. Prominently displayed *authentic* data from the International Atomic Energy Agency confirmed the Russian safety claims. The reactor units were of the same type as the ill-fated unit at Chernobyl.

Nevertheless, many other foreign visitors to the complex contended that the units were a hazard and should be shut down. They pointed to design flaws that greatly increased the likelihood of accidents; and knowledgeable visitors were not persuaded that all the necessary upgrades in operator training, emergency procedures, and redundant systems were in place. Of course, the constant threats of strikes by dissatisfied operators added to the litany of problems associated with this station and other Russian stations as well.

In mid-1993, the director of the station informed the ISTC staff of his plans for upgrading the facilities, clearly implying that he had everything well under control. His strategy was quite simple. First, the reactors would continue operating indefinitely since they supplied one half of the electricity for the region, including electricity for export to Finland. At the same time, he would replace the units, one by one, with completely modified units that incorporated corrections of all the design flaws that had been pointed out with the old models. Indeed, one unit had already been completely overhauled. He was a persuasive salesman who had the strong backing of MINATOM, as indicated by the financial support the ministry provided to him.

Turning to proposals to the ISTC, the foreign partners were hopeful that the Russians would not ignore safety features for the operating reactors despite their apparent fascination with new models. Reactor safety was one area where funding was not a problem. If the ISTC funds ran out, both the Americans and Europeans had special allocations for reactor safety projects outside the framework of the ISTC.

But Russian nuclear power station managers thought that ISTC involvement in their daily operations was unnecessary and undesirable. Dozens of teams of foreign advisers had already walked through all twenty-nine units in the Russian power station complexes, and the Russian managers did not need any more advice or research. For each station, the manager had prepared a punch list of needed hardware to enhance safety (e.g., better dials and other display panel features, redundant electrical and mechanical switches, and computer training systems). All they needed was money, or so they thought; they surely did not want more visiting experts. Yet the top priority of most foreign collaborators was to offer advice.

Several MINATOM officials acknowledged that their operating reactors needed more attention. While blaming the situation on the lack of funds, they identified the following measures that could be taken to improve the performance and safety of their Chernobyl-type plants that raised the greatest concerns; and they noted that ISTC should play a role in some of these areas:

1. Ensuring that the *void reactivity coefficient* resulting from the design of the reactor would not turn a malfunction into an uncontrollable runaway situation.

2. Improving inspections of the structural metals and the measuring devices in the reactors.
3. Improving the systems that signal operating difficulties and trigger shut-downs of the reactors.
4. Adding new systems to shut down the reactors automatically in time of difficulty.
5. Adopting new measures to facilitate safety responses to simultaneous difficulties within several fuel channels.
6. Making reactors more resistant to earthquake tremors.
7. Replacing old fuel channels.[14]

A few Russian scientists were interested in collaborative efforts with American experts, through the ISTC or through other routes that included direct assess to cash, to address some of these problems. At the same time, most of their colleagues clung to a still greater interest in collaborations leading to the *next generation* of reactors instead of continuing to focus attention on existing safety problems.

The Russian government seemed more realistic than the Russian scientists in defining the next generation of reactors. To the officials, this meant twenty-one new reactors, based on slight modifications of currently operating reactors, to be installed by the year 2010.[15]

Meanwhile, the reactor operators could not have cared less about the future. They wanted to be paid for the electricity they had already generated, and their discussions about the nuclear future of the country focused on strikes.[16]

Almost all Russian proposals to the ISTC that addressed near-term reactor safety problems were immediately approved. The initial projects emphasized three aspects of nuclear reactor safety: improved concrete for reactor shielding that would withstand very intense radiation rays without crumbling; additional systems for detecting leakages of radioactive gases that could signal the start of a disaster scenario; and mathematical modeling of reactor behavior as the basis for better isolating those components where safety measures are needed.

All these activities seemed obvious in their importance in averting another Chernobyl-type scenario. Of course, they did not address the basic design problems of the reactors that were already operating, and some Western experts estimated that $20 billion would be required to *fix* the existing reactors so that the possibility of another massive failure was remote.

The Russian nuclear power industry supplied 11 percent of the nation's electricity. Leading the skeptics over industry practices were specialists at the State Committee for Nuclear Protection (GOSATOMNADZOR). With list after list of safety violations reported by its inspectors, the committee reported that the problems were not confined to the reactors but permeated more than 14,000 enterprises that were in the chain of activities, from the procurement of materials and equipment for the reactor stations to discarding waste materials.[17]

GOSATOMNADZOR confirmed the critical impact of the failure of Russian enterprises to pay their debts. Users of electricity did not pay the local power companies, which did not pay the electrical distribution organizations, which did not pay the nuclear power stations, which did not pay their suppliers and sometimes did not even pay their employees. Is there any wonder that the incentive to pay attention to safety had reached a low ebb?

While the ISTC projects were interesting and important, they were far too limited to have a decisive effect, at least in the near term, in reducing the likelihood of a meltdown.

Nuclear Material on the Loose

In August 1994, one of the worst fears of the Western parties to the ISTC Agreement burst into headlines in Moscow and throughout the world: "Russian Official Admits Nuclear Smuggling" (*The Moscow Tribune*); "Doesn't Your Neighbor Have Uranium for Sale?" (*Moskovksyi Komsomolets*); "Atomic Bombs Can Be Acquired Privately in Russia" (*Novaia Ezhednevnaia Gazeta*); "Waiting for the Little Tyrant with the Big Bomb" (*The Guardian*); "Wanted To Buy: Do-It-Yourself Nuke Kits" (*Time*); and "Germany Reports Upsurge in Nuclear Smuggling Cases" (*The Washington Post*).

By the end of the year, five cases of theft of nuclear materials in Russia were repeatedly cited by the media in Moscow and in other capitals.[18] The Russian minister of atomic energy shrugged these thefts off as acts of *provocateurs*.[19] Some journalists supported his claim that foreign "sting" operations were designed to ruin Russia's reputation, with one paper noting, "Federal Agents Peddled Uranium, Paper Says."[20]

Meanwhile, six foreign television crews descended on my office in the new ISTC facilities during a one-week period in August. German,

British, and Japanese reporters wanted on-the-scene commentary as to the source of the plutonium and uranium supplies that were showing up in Germany. Apparently, they were having difficulty finding any Russians willing to talk or any foreigners sufficiently knowledgeable to talk. But they knocked on the wrong door, for we were not an intelligence organization monitoring the storehouses of materials needed in making weapons.

At the same time, our staff included several experts in the field of fissionable material. We had adopted a policy of being as open as possible with all persons interested in the Center. Consequently, we became momentary celebrities, particularly to viewers of German television, commenting on the latest nuclear thefts.

But what could we say? Having no concrete information as to the sources of the stolen material or the identity of the thieves, we focused on the Center's role as a possible deterrent to such activities in the future. First, the Center was attempting to find gainful employment for large numbers of weapons specialists. Presumably, many of them did have the technical know-how to contribute to criminal operations such as the theft from storage sites in Russia of dangerous fissile material that could be sold in the West. If they were employed on ISTC projects and received regular paychecks, the incentive for them to undertake such activities would be reduced.

There was great confusion as to what quantities of which specific materials were involved. We simply noted that research institutions, which were the organizations most interested in the ISTC, did not need as large quantities of dangerous materials as were in custody of other organizations in the weapons complex. These larger quantities were undoubtedly stored in facilities under the control of organizations that were unfamiliar to us.

Finally, we pointed out that the Center had launched two projects that could contribute in a small way to containing the problem of nuclear theft. One project was directed at developing more sensitive devices for detecting nuclear material being taken through airports either in luggage or in parcels being shipped. While many schemes had been explored in the West and in Russia, the techniques that were known to Russian weapons scientists might be somewhat different and might attract broad international interest.

A second project was designed to strengthen the capability of the state committee, GOSATOMNADZOR. The objective was to design and implement a system to keep track of nuclear material at a facility near the city of Tomsk. This committee had extensive responsibilities for ensuring that materials were accounted for in facilities all over Russia. But the committee was poorly financed and staffed and was short on equipment and experience. By supporting their efforts at a specific facility, the parties thought that they could help GOSATOMNADZOR develop a model that could be replicated at other facilities. It was important that this small watchdog agency with a broad mandate to keep tabs on nuclear material develop its technical capability and assume its legitimate position in working with all types of organizations within the country.

While the ISTC had neither the mandate nor the financial resources to address the vast problem of corralling nuclear material throughout the country, the Center could serve as an important venue for demonstrating new technologies and new approaches for responding to this problem.

A Long Shopping List, a Limited Budget

As can be seen from the foregoing discussions of only a few of the areas addressed through ISTC projects, the new international organization has a long shopping list of important problems before it. None of these problems will be solved in the immediate future.

Nevertheless, a key role of the Center will be to spotlight issues, demonstrate that policy concerns can be translated into programmatic actions, and emphasize that solutions must, in the first instance, come from the Russian specialists themselves and not from the imposition of impatient foreign governments.

Chapter 6

Harnessing Hostile Technologies
for Peaceful Purposes

*The diffusion of military technologies into the civil sector was of a
"semi-military" character. Dual-purpose technologies were then
developed in the civil sector that could be used for military purposes.*
Russian Ministry of Science and Technology
Policy Report, September 1993

Avoiding Support of Weapons Development

"ISTC Project Number 29 is providing technology for improving Russian weapons." An American critic of ISTC programs greeted me with
these disturbing words at a conference in Washington shortly after I
had finished my assignment in Moscow.

"Project Number 29 is not supporting the weapons program of Russia in any significant way," I replied in my standard rejoinder to such
allegations about ISTC projects. I dutifully added, "The project is an
appropriate activity to encourage Russian weapons scientists to apply
their talents to basic research of broad international interest."

The critic had read only the title of the project, *Hydrodynamical
Aspects and Turbulent Mixing for Optimization of Laser Target Compression*. He apparently had assumed that designers interested in laser
weapons or fusion bombs would surely abscond with the results of the
research intended to support their hidden activities. Had he examined
the details of this project directed to the challenge of eventual development of new sources of fusion-driven energy, he would have quickly
realized that the activities were far removed from any type of near-
term applications. Perhaps of more relevance to the dual-use argument,
the project used nonfissile materials, whereas experiments with even
distant relationships to weapons generally use fissile materials.

Conceivably, physicists in the weapons complex could be interested in any aspect of physics research. If for some reason weaponeers were particularly attracted to the general research area of Project 29, they might use their time far more profitably reviewing reports in Western journals on related research instead of devoting much attention to this important but narrow activity.

Understandably, the potential for double-edged use of the results of projects supported by the ISTC has led to continuing uneasiness in some Western military circles over the role of the Center. Indeed, in my experience, a key question discussed by the Secretariat staff when reviewing every proposal coming into the Center was whether the project could be of significance for weapons development. We were concerned over two possible channels for feeding weapons activities: Could the anticipated results of the project have relevance in responding to military requirements? Would the carrying out of the project provide researchers with new opportunities to simultaneously investigate problems of special interest to military scientists?

The staff of the Secretariat discouraged the submission by Russian institutions of many proposals for projects whose by-products could potentially aid weapons programs. But our provisos did little to stem the tide of such proposals.

Of course, this dual-use orientation of Russian specialists was to be expected. The weapons experts were naturally interested in using as many of their unique skills as possible, skills that had been skewed for several decades toward developing the *enabling* technologies for weapons. They quickly realized that many of the same technologies also *enabled* the production of civilian items.

Nuclear Testing for "Peaceful" Purposes

I was confronted with an extreme case of a civilian-oriented project replete with weapons-development potential immediately on my arrival in Moscow in mid-1992. Weapons specialists at the nuclear center at Arzamas–16 had established a separate enterprise named Chetek, designed to carry out underground nuclear explosions for peaceful purposes under contract with any interested parties at home or abroad.

In earlier years, these and other Russian experts had designed and directed almost 100 underground nuclear experiments for peaceful purposes. They had, for example, recorded the underground tremors from nuclear detonations deep in the earth as part of a program to prepare geophysical maps related to the oil and gas potential of vast areas of Siberia; and they had investigated the feasibilty of using huge underground cavities (forged by nuclear explosions) as storage facilities for bulky items, ranging from natural gas to waste materials.

These atomic pioneers vigorously argued that underground nuclear detonations for peaceful purposes were precisely the kinds of activities that the ISTC should support. They repeatedly proposed—to anyone who would listen—that a nuclear charge could be used to destroy dangerous toxic chemicals. One approach would be to pour liquid chemical wastes into deep wells in the ground and then explode a nuclear device in the midst of the wells. The heat would destroy all toxic properties, or so they claimed. They advanced a related idea to destroy nuclear wastes with underground explosions, despite the inherent unpredictability as to the chain reactions that might result from such untested programs.

An even more alarming Chetek proposal called for collection of all the plutonium and uranium from the nuclear warheads being scrapped as the result of various disarmament agreements, the burial of the nuclear material in underground pits, and then the destruction of the stockpiles using nearby underground nuclear detonations. Proponents contended that the plutonium and uranium would be rendered useless and harmless forever, leaving the material fused together for eternity in a giant molten mine.

Environmentalists shuddered. Budget officials saw dollar signs flying off their charts. Worse yet, arms control specialists pointed out the potential for incorporating the results of these nuclear explosions into improved designs for weapons for the active military stockpiles. The ISTC planning group had little time to devote to such ideas which, politically, had no chance of garnering support from Western or Japanese governments.

With increased international momentum centered on a total cessation of underground nuclear explosions for any purpose, Chetek apparently stopped operating during 1993. Or at least, the enterprise stopped publicly advocating underground nuclear explosions for peaceful purposes.

Maintaining Distance from Military Applications

Shortly after the flurry of publicity in Russia and abroad over Chetek's proposals, a number of research teams from Moscow's rocket-design institutions presented the ISTC planning group with proposals to construct new propulsion systems. They considered their schemes to be of "inestimable value" for space exploration. They had plans for launching new types of rockets from the ground and from aircraft. Again, the budget officials shook their heads in disbelief at the price tags of hundreds of millions of dollars. And the arms control experts pointed out, again and again, the blatant overlap between rockets for space exploration and rockets for delivering nuclear bombs.

In this case, however, our international staff interceded with counterproposals. We urged the rocket scientists to concentrate on adapting existing military systems to space exploration tasks and to forget about developing new types of dual-use rockets.

Then, during a staff visit to a nearby Moscow research institute, we saw a cache of night-vision goggles, binoculars, telescopes, and other devices that had been developed for the battlefield. The experts in infrared technologies were intent on applying their talents to civilian applications, but they were having trouble finding clients for their products. Of course, the police and animal hunters were logical customers for their inventories, but the researchers complained that the Japanese were already distributing very inexpensive products for these markets. Meanwhile, we had considerable difficulty understanding how to prevent new advances in infrared vision enhancement, ostensibly for peaceful applications, from being incorporated back into military systems which had been the impetus for demands for infrared technologies in the first place.[1]

Unlike the situation in the Soviet Union where civilian technologies had contributed little to the military effort, it was commonplace in the United States for technology from civilian R&D to cross over quickly into military systems. The classic example was the development of computer systems by civilian research laboratories. The military services promptly adopted closely related systems for any number of applications.

U.S. government procurement specialists, in the Pentagon and the Department of Commerce, regularly justify their expenditures for development of advanced technologies by citing the dual-market argument. They hasten to emphasize that dual-use technologies can double the returns on investments of taxpayers' dollars in governmental R&D efforts. But the ISTC Secretariat was not eager to promote such feedback loops, which would strengthen the connections leading from

ISTC-supported civilian projects back into Russian military applications.

Many research areas raised questions, and several presented significant problems. Laser research immediately appeared on the list of suspects. But fortunately, lasers for civilian applications often depend on different wavelengths than lasers for military uses. And, as illustrated by Project 29, civilian research on fusion energy is somewhat different from research on fusion weapons. But the development of specialized electronic circuitry, new types of materials such as composites and graphite mixtures, and high-precision manufacturing equipment were frequently legitimate dual-use issues. Also, in another area, the boundaries between research on vaccines and on new biological warfare agents can be very blurred.

A number of the early projects approved by the ISTC Governing Board received special attention in the capitals to ensure that the results would not feed the military sector. The following research efforts, developed within the aerospace industry, were among the projects that caught the eye of specialists concerned with different ways to employ the same technologies; but eventually the projects passed muster in that they posed no serious problems:

No. 92. *Testing a Feed System for Nuclear Propulsion Technology for Exploration of Mars.*

No. 138. *Low-cost Hemispherical Resonator for Small Commercial Navigation Systems.*

No. 199. *New Methods of Laminar Flow Control and Turbulent Drag Reduction in Aircraft.*

Projects in other areas that also warranted careful attention were the following:

No. 15. *Electronics of Organic Materials.*

No. 76. *Atomic and Radiation Processes in Plasmas, Gases, and Solids.*

No. 107. *Generation of Ultrashort, High-Power Laser Pulses for the Investigation of Interactions of Superintense Light Fields with Matter.*

In each case, questions arose about either direct or indirect relationships between the projects and other research activities of potential military interest. But the military impact of the planned research under ISTC auspices was considered quite small and even remote. The benefits of engaging specialists with expertise in these areas in ISTC projects, in terms of reorientation of their careers, seemed clearly to outweigh the risks of enhancing the Russian military effort.

The Secretariat took several precautions during project implementation to reduce the likelihood of significant feedback into military research channels from ISTC-sponsored R&D activities. First, the activities within the ISTC projects were conducted in open areas, physically separated from areas that housed classified military research. Second, funds for ISTC projects went directly into separate bank accounts so as to reduce temptations on the part of the recipient institutes simply to put ISTC projects under the same management structure that controlled funds for projects supported by the defense complex.

Most important, Western and Japanese collaborators regularly participated in ISTC projects. They, together with the ISTC staff members who monitored the projects, served as deterrents to ancillary militarization of ISTC activities; and they were in good positions to help ensure that research efforts would not stray into gray or even black areas.

For the ISTC, dual-use concerns are very real. In dealing with technology the Center has emphasized civilian applications and not development of new enabling technologies that could boomerang back into the military complex. In this way, the Center has tried to avoid both the perception and the reality that ISTC projects would contribute to strengthening Russian military capabilities.

Walls That Isolated Soviet Military R&D

The legacy of Soviet reliance on the military complex to develop almost all the country's advanced technologies, both for civilian and military purposes, is evident throughout the laboratories of Russia. This tradition of locating military and civilian R&D in close organizational proximity to one another should, in principle, have facilitated the transfer of military technologies to civilian applications, and vice versa.

In addition, within Russia there are new financial incentives to break down institutional barriers separating civilian and military technologies. Each institute director is charged with succeeding in both spheres. Consequently, directors should be eager to use their powers in corralling whatever technologies are at their disposal in order to respond both to the continuing demands of military procurement officials and to the potential financial rewards of selling their services to customers on the civilian side.

But in Soviet times, the gulf between military and civilian endeavors was enormous. Even now, institute directors cannot easily overcome the inertia of the past—the rote response to orders from the top, without the least consideration as to whether a customer awaits the anticipated results. Russian managers and scientists have great difficulty accepting the necessity of identifying financially viable customers before taking the initiative to shape research activities from the bottom up.

In the Soviet Union, and most recently in Russia, there never has been an easy flow of information or ideas from the closed facilities into the open facilities and vice versa. It is not uncommon for two researchers working in the same building in nearly adjacent laboratories—one for civilian research and one for military research—barely to know one another.

Further complicating feedback between civilian and military research are the differing perceptions of the purposes and associated technological requirements of research. As cited in a Russian report, the past experiences in combining civilian and military-oriented approaches to new technologies, even when researchers communicated fully between themselves, were not encouraging:

> The transfer of military technologies to the civilian sector proved to be generally impossible, for a number of reasons. First, civilian enterprises lacked funds to purchase the technologies, but even more important is the great technological gap between the civilian and military sectors of industry. Civil enterprises are unprepared to use the results of the R&D organizations of the military sector and the military organizations often have too little understanding of the needs of civilian production, especially in a market economy, because they never were concerned with low production costs; and exploitation of their results was not the main goal of the research projects.[2]

The main deterrent to successful dual-use still remains: civilian and military researchers have always had different mindsets, shaped by different customers and different resources; and the usefulness of regular exchanges of ideas between the two groups is difficult for them to comprehend. These problems are discussed in greater detail in Chapter 7.

At the same time, many Russian weapons specialists spend only part of their workweek on ISTC projects. As they become more certain that their personal fortunes lie in the civilian sector, perhaps they will make the complete transition to civilian research. But in the meantime the feedback circuitry within their heads is not hampered by organizational or philosophical barriers. Thus, the need for vigilance in the selection, and conduct of ISTC projects is obvious.

Plutonium: The Ultimate Pandora's Box

During 1993, the disposal of 100 to 200 tons of plutonium, no longer needed for weapon warheads in Russia or the United States, became an international issue of high priority. American experts advocated the permanent encapsulation of the material so that it could never again be used for any purpose. But the Russians had a different philosophy. They considered the material to be the most valuable energy source ever developed; therefore, they were adamant that nations should use plutonium to resolve their energy needs.

In addition to citing dangers posed by keeping plutonium in a form ready for military use, American specialists estimated that many decades and tens of billions of dollars would be required to develop and construct the nuclear reactors that could use the plutonium for energy generation in accordance with the Russian ideas. The Russians disagreed, noting that the Americans were simply using these inflated estimates as a convenient excuse for opposing Russian competition in the civilian nuclear arena.

In short, Washington argued that while plutonium was a dual-use item, it was too dangerous to handle for peaceful purposes, adding that to use it as an energy source would be too expensive. The Russians contended that this dual-use commodity was manageable and appropriate for civilian purposes. The European governments seemed to be divided on the issue, with France having considerable interest in plutonium as an energy source. The Japanese apparently leaned toward the Russian view, at least to the extent that research should be carried out to determine if the plutonium could be used in an economical and safe manner.

Against this backdrop, in April 1994, a particularly incendiary issue for the members of the ISTC came to light in an article in a Japanese newspaper. The paper reported that the U.S. government had objected to several ISTC projects that involved research on the use of plutonium in power reactors. Russia and Japan both strongly supported the projects, according to the press. The Institute for Power Engineering in Moscow had proposed drawing on the experience of the Russian submarine reactor designers in carrying out the projects.

According to the article, the U.S. opposition succeeded in halting the planned cooperation between Japan and Russia related to utilization of plutonium. The Japanese reportedly argued that the purpose of the ISTC was to employ *plutonium-related* scientists, while the Americans were concerned about careless handling of plutonium in Russia and about plutonium-related projects that conflicted with U.S. nonproliferation policy.[3]

While these projects were indeed before the ISTC board, all discussion of the merits of the proposals was conducted through diplomatic channels in view of the sensitivity of the issue. As of mid-1995, the proposals were still waiting for formal disposition by the board.

But the proposals certainly brought to the fore, within governments and in the press, the widespread concerns over internal Russian procedures for handling plutonium and the questionable desirability of Russia's proceeding with this new type of power reactor. Also, they focused attention on strong American views that the ISTC should not support development of technologies that raised new concerns over proliferation of weapons capabilities.

Exporting Nuclear-Related Technologies

Plutonium is but one ingredient in the ominous recipe of concern to the nuclear nonproliferation experts. Plutonium, along with other fissile material, is of course subject to careful international regulatory scrutiny while also being controlled by individual governments. But other items are not so tightly regulated. Indeed, the scope of dual-use items far less visible than plutonium—and in demand by countries seeking nuclear weapons status—was indicated in a 1994 report of the U.S. General Accounting Office relating to U.S. export licenses for "nuclear-related dual-use" items. The list was impressive, perhaps all the more so for what it did not include. Specifically, many types of electronic components and advanced materials were not subject to licensing because of their existing world-wide availability.[4]

According to this review of export licenses issued by the U.S. government during a seven-year period, the United States approved more than 1,500 licenses for items going to Israel (valued at $193 million), Brazil ($109 million), India ($19.7 million), Argentina ($12.9 million), South Africa ($6.7 million), Iraq ($4.1 million), Pakistan ($2.1 million), and Iran ($0.9 million). This was a small subset of the 336,000 licenses for exports to all destinations for nuclear-related dual-use items, which in total were valued at $264 billion.[5]

About 86 percent of all items licensed worldwide were computer-related. Of course, computers have never been Russia's strong suit. But other items that were included could probably have been provided by Russia, had the customers turned in that direction, including grinding machines for Pakistan and ammonia production equipment related to heavy water production for an Indian research center. Flash X-ray systems and other components to support isotopic separation of nuclear materials, implosion systems, and weapons detonation systems are examples of other items that were licensed.[6]

A second report indicated that Indian missiles can be traced to technologies emanating from a variety of countries, including motors derived from the Russian SA–2 missile along with technologies from France, Germany, the United Kingdom, and the United States. The current Indian shopping list for dual-use technologies that will support their rocket development program (and that should be of interest to Russian suppliers) reportedly includes aluminum alloys with protective coatings, ceramic chip capacitors, FM signal generators, gas field effect transistors and bare semiconductor chips, function generators, oscilloscopes, gear-head DC motors and slewing ring bearings, and torque motors.[7]

A particularly sensitive issue for the United States has been the sale to Israel of advanced supercomputers that could have considerable value in designing nuclear weapons and simulating nuclear testing. U.S. suppliers have shipped advanced Cray and IBM computers to Tel Aviv.[8] A significant number of highly skilled Russian immigrants now reside in that country; but the extent to which these specialists have been brought into the Israeli defense effort, either directly or indirectly, is not known.

That said, the greatest obstacle for most countries seeking nuclear weapons status will continue to be the availability of fissionable materials, either enriched uranium or plutonium. The other technologies cited above will of course contribute in important ways to weapons programs if fissionable material is acquired.

As noted in Chapter 5, the ISTC should play an important, albeit not central, role in reducing the likelihood that highly enriched uranium or plutonium supplies leave Russia. ISTC projects can redirect to well-paying civilian tasks the attention of large numbers of weapons scientists and engineers who are knowledgeable as to the whereabouts and safe handling of such material and might otherwise be singled out by smugglers as potential accomplices. And in some cases, these specialists may even undertake projects that will directly help safeguard dangerous materials within the country.

Proliferation of Other Dual-Use Technologies

The worldwide proliferation of dual-use chemical and biological technologies presents another set of very serious national security problems for many countries.[9] Much of the equipment needed to produce chemical weapons can also be used to produce civilian products. A U.S. government report notes:

> Some agents (e.g., sulfur mustard and the nerve agent tabun) could be produced with widely available chemical industry equipment. The most potent nerve agents (e.g., sarin, soman, VX) involve a process step—the alkylation of phosphorous—that is less common, but that nevertheless is used in a handful of commercial products such as some pesticides and fire retardants.

Turning to biological products, the report states:

> Virtually all the equipment underlying production of biological and toxin agents has civilian applications and has become widely available as fermentation technology. Since militarily significant quantities of biological agents could be produced in a short time in small facilities, they could be used offensively without the need for long-term stockpiles. Crude dissemination of biological agents in an aerosol cloud can be performed with commercially available equipment, such as an agricultural sprayer mounted on a truck, ship, or airplane.[10]

With regard to a still broader range of technologies, many dual-use products of R&D laboratories that have relevance to sophisticated weaponry are now blanketing the globe. Advanced electronic components and, in some cases, opto-electronic components, which can contribute to smart weapons systems have penetrated the markets of almost every country. Lightweight, high-strength metals have found civilian and military applications in even some of the poorest countries. Plastics that can be used both in specialized construction materials and in aircraft and missile systems are becoming common commodities on all continents. Small mechanical and hydraulic systems for controlling industrial processes for both military and civilian activities are widely available.

Most of these technologies are the products of the industrial laboratories of the United States, Europe, and Japan. A significant number had counterpart technologies in the weapons laboratories of the USSR; and looking ahead, the Russian laboratories will probably continue some level of contribution to the worldwide dissemination of high-technology products.

The ISTC programs reflect a new approach to containing dangerous technologies within Russia. While technologies are embodied in products that are traded, as well as in the heads of technical experts, the technical experts remain important in helping organizations with limited experience understand how to use, maintain, and adjust the advanced technologies that they receive for the first time. Indeed, most international sales are package deals that include both hardware and technical consultations. Alternative ISTC programs can be important in reducing the personal incentives for such arrangements.

Regulating the Flow of Dangerous Technologies

What else can be done to encourage peaceful uses of high technology and at the same time deter temptations to use sophisticated skills to support military ambitions of aggressive countries or irresponsible groups? It is clear that even the poorest countries can benefit economically from using some of the advanced technologies with potential military applications. In this regard, a recent report prepared for the U.S. Congress concludes:

> The dissemination of technologies that have at least some relevance to producing weapons of mass destruction might need to be not only tolerated but encouraged if populations in developing nations are to improve their health, environment, and standard of living.[11]

Since the end of World War I, the United States and other Western nations have banded together to attempt to control international transfers of dual-use technologies. For decades, the objective was to deny the Warsaw Pact countries and China technologies that could feed their weapons systems with enhancements that could threaten the West.

Now the international community is shifting gears to prevent the flow of dangerous materials to many other countries, particularly countries with recent histories of territorial ambitions and terrorism. But every day there is an increase in the number of high-tech products that are important for commerce and readily adaptable to military systems.

A joint study of Russian and American experts assembled under the auspices of the National Academy of Sciences and the Russian Academy of Sciences in 1992–93 recommended greater attention to the concept of controlling *choke point* technologies, that is, those technologies without which weapons systems simply will not operate.[12] At one level, a land mine will not explode without activation of a *fuse* by pressure or by an electrical signal. At a higher technology level, a missile will not find its target without a reliable *guidance system*. Given the relatively few choke-point technologies, manageable control systems might be feasible, argued the report.

Choke points have been the focus of some narrowly based control efforts initiated years ago. Perhaps in the long term, a more general approach along these lines will be the only feasible method to inhibit the spread of dangerous dual-purpose technologies. The line between trade for legitimate commercial endeavors and such international transfers for nefarious purposes is too finely drawn for broadly based regulatory controls over all aspects of dual-use technologies to be feasible.

Of course, many countries will continue their own regulatory approaches, individually and collectively choosing technologies of concern. Many of the most dangerous items will inevitably be included.

Most countries have special laws governing the export of sensitive items. The U.S. Congress, for example, has passed laws controlling exports of nuclear, biological, and chemical materials and technologies along with conventional weapons and weapons components. U.S. export laws also control a broad range of dual-use items.

Many international agreements limit exports of these same items. In the past, a number of countries participated in the activities of the now-defunct Coordinating Committee on Multilateral Export Controls (CoCom), which for many years established common standards of enforcement of national export controls among the members. With the demise of the Warsaw Pact, these nations are attempting to reorient their previous East-West orientation to issues of proliferation concern under a new international coalition, called the Waasenaar Arrangement. To this end, additional members, including Russia, are joining the club as the focus shifts to transfers of technology to Third World countries. Also, the United States and other countries frequently enter into bilateral arrangements when there are special issues of concern, including the clarification of the scope of international agreements, such as the recent arrangements between the United States and Russia concerning Russian sales of rocket technology to India.

The regulatory approach interfaces directly with ISTC activities, since regulation of technologies inevitably must address transfers of those technologies through the interactions of people.

Third-World Education and the Profit Line

Much less attention has been given to approaches that will enhance the capabilities of governments of developing countries, where dual-use technologies are produced, traded, or used, to understand the implications of the influx of dangerous technologies. Indeed, an international educational effort—to help responsible leaders in these countries develop sound policies and programs when faced with the prospect of coping with dual-use technologies—is long overdue. Effective controls on imports and exports are not in place in the developing countries, and it is no wonder that uncontrolled high-tech bazaars are commonplace in many countries.

Many dual-use technologies that could pose dangers in the hands of irresponsible parties in these countries are the property of private companies in the United States, Europe, and Japan, as well as under the control of Russian organizations. Nonproliferation experts would like to believe that these companies will take appropriate steps to prevent dangerous technologies from falling into irresponsible hands. Of course, a number of international regimes concerning trade have been in place for some time to help ensure that dual-use technologies are sold only to responsible end users (e.g., regimes devoted to dual-use biological, chemical, nuclear, and missile technologies).

But what incentives are there for American companies, let alone Russian organizations, to be concerned about stricter regulation of dual-use technologies by the developing countries themselves? Shouldn't American companies be concentrating on exploiting all available markets within current legal boundaries instead of being interested in curbing the sales of advanced technologies? Don't American companies better protect the interests of their stockholders if the host countries allow expanded production, for whatever purpose, rather than restrict or regulate foreign high-tech activities?

From the perspectives of individual companies interested in near-term profitability, the answer to these questions is simply: governments and academics should stay out of our way. But in the much broader context of American competitiveness and of national security interests, companies should welcome a better-educated officialdom in developing countries. Specifically,

- Trade specialists often contend that multinational enterprises with roots in countries other than the United States, such as Japan, give higher priority to secrecy and hidden agendas than do most American companies. If this is true, American industry should welcome the shedding of light on the technical details of industrial activities around the world, respecting of course the bounds of industrial proprietorship.
- In the wake of the former East–West CoCom regulations, new international controls to harness some of the most troublesome technologies are evolving. Many more countries will participate in the negotiations related to such controls than participated in earlier East–West deliberations, particularly countries pressing for greater North–South technology transfer. It is in the interest of American industry for the countries participating in the establishment and implementation of such controls to be as well-informed as possible about the technologies that would be the subjects of controls and about the broader technological context for those controls.
- As noted, it will be neither possible nor desirable to subject more than a small fraction of dual-use technologies to international regulatory controls. But in the absence of comprehensive regulations, new types of international approaches for addressing these technologies will surely arise as countries begin to recognize the latent threat of some technologies. The greatest danger lies in a scenario involving poorly informed countries that attain an inac-

curate impression of pending military threats. In haste, they may haphazardly adopt unilateral export controls based on political rhetoric rather than on technical assessments. It is in the interest of U.S. companies to deal with consistent national policies on this issue to the extent possible, or at least to create policies based on a consistent level of technical understanding.

- International terrorism in many forms is on the rise in countries where there are sizable American investments. Terrorists of the present and future will be well aware of the military applications of the technologies produced or used in these countries. Responsible leaders of these countries should be equally aware of such applications so that they will be in a position to ensure the safety of foreign investments in their countries.

- Internal political stability is an important criterion when considering the desirability of foreign investments in developing countries. Such stability is often linked to control of the military wherewithal of a country. The introduction of dual-use technologies by foreign investors may raise new concerns affecting political stability in the host countries. Therefore, the political implications of such investments should be understood by all concerned from the outset.

An analogy to global dual-use concerns might be found in the continuing effort of the world community to resist the establishment of pollution havens abroad. Such protected enclaves enable entrepreneurs and local governments to gain financially from inadequate environmental discharge standards that permit lower-cost production practices. This approach, in turn, often places U.S.-based industry at a disadvantage. The world community should prevent the establishment of secretive dual-use technology havens where realization of hidden agendas could have very worrisome consequences.

As the potential military applications of such technologies become clearer, American industry should gain from an increased worldwide understanding of the challenges of dual-use technologies. Building a worldwide educational initiative in the field of control of dual-use technologies directed toward the leaders of the developing countries is overdue. Such an initiative, spearheaded by the U.S. government, and with active Russian participation, could promote transparency and understanding as an important step toward ensuring responsible ground rules and a level playing field for commerce in advanced technologies with national security implications.

Coping with Pervasive Double-Edged Technologies

As discussed in Chapter 7, industrial conversion from military to civilian activities in Russia is far more complicated than it would appear at first glance. Nevertheless, the charter of the ISTC calls for similar conversion of the scientists and engineers who can stimulate such industrial activities.

Development of dual-use technologies is often a first step in making the adjustment to conversion. Indeed, if the skills of former weapons scientists are to be used most effectively, such an approach seems logical. And the ISTC will undoubtedly continue to be immersed in the dual-use dilemma.

As a final example of this issue, in mid-1995 *The Washington Times* bannered the headline "Russia Uses Pentagon Funds in Constructing New Nukes." Commenting on a report of the General Accounting Office, the article cited ISTC support for the design and testing of a streak camera as an example of a threatening development in the dual-use arena. The report alleged that the camera could be used to measure blasts from nuclear testing as well as pulses from basic physics experiments. As in other cases, however, neither the General Accounting Office nor the newspaper reporter took the time to delve into the details of the project. The response speed of the camera was simply too short to be of use in measuring nuclear test pulses. In addition, the camera was not designed to preserve its imaging capability in the wake of a nuclear blast.[13]

But the issue of dual-use technologies has for many years extended far beyond the confines of the ISTC. Most industrialized countries have been aware of the need to limit the international flow of the most dangerous technologies. In the first instance, as noted earlier, they have relied on the companies that are the wellsprings and the traders of such technologies to exercise good sense in not exacerbating the international scene. At the same time, the countries themselves have often resorted to national and international regulatory methods for coping with the contagion of dangerous technologies.

Now a third approach has been suggested. The advanced countries that have the most experience in trying to separate military and civilian technologies, and increasingly the applications of dual-use technologies, must stay one step ahead of techno-terrorists and troublemakers. The advanced nations should share their experience with leaders on the front lines of decision making in countries with less sophisticated understanding of the implications of dual-use technologies that are interested in reducing the risks from technological chaos that can lead to war and destruction.

Meanwhile, there is no place with a more fragile immune system vulnerable to the activities of techno-terrorists than Russia. And the ISTC is one institution that must continue to be alert to its responsibilities to help thwart this virus.

Chapter 7

Conversion Activities Attract
Few Paying Customers

The objectives of the Center shall be: To give
weapons scientists and engineers . . . opportunities to
redirect their talents to peaceful activities.
Article II of the ISTC Agreement, November 1992

Conversion: From Concept to Reality

"Conversion to nowhere" is how some Russian officials have described the efforts of hundreds of Russian laboratories to adjust to drastic budget cutbacks in defense orders at the research facilities.[1] Blaming the Soviet legacy, they contend:

> Technological spinoff from military activities was almost paralyzed by the lack of incentives and mechanisms for adopting and adapting technologies to civilian production. . . . Although a large share of high-technology civil-oriented goods was produced by defense plants, defense technology was never put to optimal use. . . . Parts and components that were of low quality or defective by military standards were used for civil-oriented runs of production.[2]

Five years before the establishment of the ISTC, the Soviet government had promised a new approach to conversion. The optimistic Soviet rhetoric was promptly adopted by the Russian government as well. It became the great hope of hundreds of thousands of former weapons scientists and engineers in Russia as the route for continuing meaningful R&D programs, in addition to maintaining viable manufacturing activities, at satisfactory wage levels.

In a national effort to redirect many activities from a military to a civilian orientation, soon after coming to office President Yeltsin recruited a personal adviser to concentrate attention on the challenges and opportunities of conversion. A new law on conversion emphasized the creation of "high technologies for products which are competitive on foreign markets." The law also called for tax advantages for conversion research and new budgets for conversion activities in priority areas established by the government.[3] The government established, at least on paper, special funds to support particularly meritorious projects; and foreign bargain hunters from all over the world flew to conversion fairs in Moscow, St. Petersburg, and Nizhny Novgorod. Special conversion databanks and permanent exhibitions of available technologies opened their doors in several cities, and kiosks in Moscow began displaying the new journal *Conversion* on their already overcrowded shelves.

Russian newspapers heralded this new dawning with headlines such as the following: "More Than A-bombs Are Made in Arzamas–16. Equipment for the Production of Cottage Cheese Is Also Manufactured."[4]

The year 1994 witnessed continuing political pronouncements about the importance of conversion, the so-called privatization of some medium-sized enterprises now free to use technologies of their own choosing for improving productivity, and the introduction of less-than-successful voucher systems that would allegedly stimulate an influx of capital to support conversion. On the front lines of the laboratories, however, Russian researchers had given up on the likelihood that they would attract even minimal financial support from within Russia for conversion activities.

Meanwhile, many of the legions of mercenary foreign visitors to Russia, in search of easy money, simply lost interest and disappeared after graciously accepting free banquets, stacks of brochures, and hastily prepared proposals for collaboration.

Still, the scientists and engineers of the R&D institutions of Russia had great difficulty accepting the reality that no one was paying attention to their new civilian-oriented efforts. After all, they had repeatedly been told that they were the elite of the Russian R&D community; and they had "informed the ministry" of their latest achievements.

Also, 1994 was a particularly bad time financially for the former defense research community. Problems in carrying out R&D increased as energy costs moved toward world levels, neglected equipment requiring major maintenance no longer functioned, and overdue bills erased possibilities of additional credit lines. State subsidies continued to evaporate slowly, while unbridled inflation galloped forward. Real wages declined accordingly.

As the salaries of most researchers plunged below the poverty line, many took to the streets to protest. The miners, shipbuilders, nuclear plant operators, and even soldiers were also threatening to strike. Who was listening? A few members of a seemingly powerless Duma, the lower house of the Russian parliament, heard the pleas from the weapons laboratories; but their speeches had little impact within the gridlocked legislative body.[5] Meanwhile, the costs of airline tickets and even telephone service increased dramatically, thus further isolating former defense laboratories in the Urals and Siberia from potential markets in the larger cities.

Russian officials admitted that only 5 percent of their defense institutes could conduct R&D at levels of world standards. They acknowledged that many of their most highly qualified scientists and engineers had left the institutes. They nevertheless believed that portions of many of their large facilities had the wherewithal to compete successfully in an open economic market.[6]

After eight years of highly publicized failures of Soviet technology, beginning with the disaster at Chernobyl in 1986 and followed by misfired space launches, malfunctioning submarines, and fires at nuclear facilities, the weapons R&D community suffered yet another series of discrediting blows. Throughout 1994, Russian science was under assault. The Russian press eagerly revealed the complicity of Russian researchers in the development of nuclear weapons and missile systems in North Korea. Government officials organized public confessionals concerning the details of geological leakages of nuclear wastes after many decades of poorly controlled burial of those wastes in deep wells. Moscow television reported foreign allegations of Russia's cheating on compliance with an international agreement on biological warfare agents. Then in August, when reports of thefts of plutonium and highly enriched uranium from Russia circulated throughout Europe, Russian investigative reporters seized on the inadequacies of measures to protect nuclear materials at research facilities and major storage sites.

Nevertheless, the former weapons R&D community retained a deeply engrained conviction that the technologies that brought the Soviet Union to superpower status would sell on civilian markets, within the country and abroad. They were repeatedly disappointed. Domestically, few production enterprises had funds to finance research activities; they did not even have sufficient investment capital to introduce innovative products or processes from technologies that the R&D community would *give* to them, free of charge.

Thus, the former weaponeers concluded that the only real markets for their conversion products were under the control of foreign governments and foreign companies. But foreign organizations, with a few exceptions, seemed more interested in simply borrowing Russian brains and Russian test facilities to support their own programs, which were rooted abroad, than in supporting serious conversion efforts within the country.

Little Interest in a Hollow Concept

Thus, debates were underway in Russia and abroad as to a realistic definition of the term *conversion*. Indeed, did it have any meaning at all, other than to signify that many previously closed facilities throughout the country were now open for business with new customers yet to be identified?

To some institute directors, conversion simply meant finding alternative sources of funds for the financing that had previously come from the Soviet military-industrial complex. Thus, new projects to develop or support weapons systems for Algeria, India, or Malaysia would qualify as conversion activities.

Other institute directors defined conversion as maintaining maximum employment at the institutes. Some were content with new programs to produce samovars and bicycles, programs that helped meet the payroll. Others gloated in their successes of selling lightweight bulletproof vests and titanium golf clubs.[7]

Still other directors continued to believe that conversion meant developing a wide range of high-tech products that, in their view, the country desperately needed and could surely utilize. But they paid little heed to whether anyone really was prepared to manufacture and market such products. For example, several institutes pressed forward with fiber-optic communication networks for municipalities where city engineers could not even keep the traffic lights operating due to rats chewing up the underground cables. Also, they had new designs for remote nuclear power stations in areas where there was little demand for power.

Almost all directors had established a number of small businesses located on the premises of their institutes, and several tried to privatize portions of their facilities. Some of the new businesses simply served as funnels for contracts to the institutes, since they could avoid many of the overhead charges attendant to bona fide institute contracts. Others allowed institute staff to use facilities during their off-hours. The activities of still others had no relation to the profiles of the institutes: several served as mechanisms for seats on the stock exchanges, some featured clothing workshops, and a significant number sold lumber and consumer goods. One estimate was that in 1993, 10 to 15 percent of the staffs of a large number of institutes were involved in such activities, often increasing their salaries fourfold. And that percentage was probably increasing.[8]

Many Russian observers were skeptical of the sudden interest military institutions took in civilian markets. They insisted that complete abandonment of all military activities at any given facility was essential before discussing conversion at that facility. If a laboratory or production unit continued military activities or maintained its equipment in a state of readiness for such activities, the facility was not engaged in conversion but in *diversification*.[9]

These cynics noted, for example:

> Many non-military goods were needed only for window dressing. Most agricultural machinery plants were established as reserve production facilities for the defense industry. That's why Russian-made tractors weighed as much as Russian tanks.[10]

Young R&D specialists were not interested in philosophical debates about conversion. They only knew that there was no longer sufficient work to go around, that their wage levels were unacceptable, and that their friends working in the commercial sector were doing much better.

Aware that no one really cared whether or not they remained in the laboratories, and indeed that many older colleagues would be pleased to see them leave and thereby reduce pressures on dwindling salary pools, a large number decided to seek their fortunes elsewhere. They were joined in a mass exodus from technological pursuits by many students and potential students of science and engineering who also knew that the wealthiest people in Russia were working in the banking and trading sectors.

Despite this widespread skepticism over the payoff from devoting new careers to converting military activities into peaceful endeavors, hundreds of Russian scientists and engineers nevertheless optimistically prepared proposals (involving thousands of their colleagues) for consideration by the ISTC. They simply had nowhere else to turn. Other international programs were beginning to dribble only very limited funds into Russia; even if ISTC projects simply provided airline tickets to Western Europe or the United States, they would present a useful change of pace and new opportunities for bringing home a few extra per diem dollars, or so reasoned many of the applicants.

Can New R&D Programs Influence Industrial Conversion?

Clearly, R&D conversion activities designed to serve the core requirements of a market economy in Russia must be linked to progress in *industrial conversion*, an equally elusive term, in the former defense plants that so dominate the industrial base of the country.[11] In this regard, American skeptics of Russian efforts frequently point to the following commentary about industrial conversion in the United States to make their case for discouraging such useless activity at the Russian factories.

> Defense conversion attempts have been made, some laughable and in retrospect almost all dismal. . . . The reason for this solid record of failure is simple: defense work has little in common with civilian work. These two areas demand different skills and marketing techniques and have different cultures and organizations. Clearly the defense business, even in the United States, has little to do with free enterprise. Defense contractors have a single customer who directs them from above, rather than many customers who show their preferences in the market below.
>
> Defense contractors lack expertise in mass marketing and in making high volume, low unit-cost items. Their distribution network is, in the commercial sense, nonexistent. Their capitalization is modest. Their product servicing is limited. And the bookkeeping and reporting requirements are staggering. Defense firms know little of consumer tastes, establishing customer credit, or pricing to compete in the commercial marketplace. They know nothing of market research. Much of their work is performed under cost-reimbursable contracts—they are paid whatever costs they incur, which encourages taking huge techno-

logical risks. In a nutshell, defense contractors have adapted to their unique monopsonistic environment in a Darwinian fashion. To further complicate matters, embedded within this monopsony are occasional monopolies, since only a single firm can sell the *customer* a B–2 bomber.[12]

Is this gloomy assessment of the American model relevant in Russia? Of course, it is to some extent. Many of the barriers to success will be even higher in a country built on central planning.

At the same time, the social and economic environment in Russia is much different from that in the United States. When people have no choice but to remain in towns that have single industries which in turn have no investment capital, economic rationality often tumbles aside as the workers make do with what they have. While some of the results of this forced conversion may not be pretty and may not command high prices, the activities often sustain desperate populations for just a little longer. The fact that *there is no one more resourceful than a Russian* has long been conventional wisdom among those who know the Russian culture, and this is ringing true in many activities that are dubbed conversion.

Returning to the Russian weapons laboratories, the nonmilitary activities, despite their many limitations, deserve serious attention for several reasons. First, the livelihood of several million people is directly or indirectly tied to the fate of these laboratories, including many facilities that are the principal employers in towns of up to 100,000 people. Second, if the R&D base of the country is to recover and eventually become a significant force in again serving the needs of a modern industrial state, these relatively well-equipped laboratories should provide an important point of departure for building an R&D infrastructure. Finally, from the national security viewpoint of the West, as well as from the Russian vantage point, the weapons technologies and many of the dual-use technologies embodied in laboratory activities—and in the brains of the associated specialists—should be contained within the borders of Russia. Containment is imperative to avoid the worst fears of proliferation experts.

Also, as civilian activities conducted in former weapons laboratories continue to increase, the warnings both in Russia and in the West about *reconversion* of Russian laboratories—retrofitting back to military R&D activities in response to changes in the political orientation of the country—should not be minimized. Successful foreign collaboration in these activities should reduce the likelihood of reconversion. Indeed, such internationalization of conversion activities may be the most important contribution that the ISTC will make to long-term political stability, within Russia and on the international scene.

There's No Business Like No Business

As noted earlier, for decades military R&D laboratories in the Soviet Union had been heavily engaged in developing civilian products as a part of their *societal responsibilities*. Many Soviet television sets and refrigerators, commercial aircraft and trucks, and motors and turbines had their origins in the military laboratories. For most of these laboratories, the conversion thrust of the early 1990s was considered as more of the same, but expanded into different civilian product lines. This business-as-usual attitude was a principal reason for widespread failures of conversion efforts to generate interest outside the laboratories.[13]

Meaningful conversion could not be just more of the same. Costs were suddenly a critical aspect of product development and manufacturing, and market demand rather than quotas and specifications provided by a central authority had to become the hallmark of successful conversion. Unfortunately, few Russian weaponeers understood these new ground rules.

The largest concentrations of military facilities and researchers that were to be engaged in R&D conversion were associated with the aerospace industry, where the divisions between military and civilian activities had always been blurred. Many of the missile and aircraft design organizations had been well known in the West for several decades, although the extent of their technological strengths remained somewhat clouded.

The conversion interests of Russian aerospace organizations immediately focused on new approaches to space exploration for peaceful purposes, airborne remote sensing for ecological assessments, and new generations of commercial aircraft. Very limited funds were available in Russia to feed the insatiable appetites of Russian researchers capable of providing the world with advanced technologies; and the Russians soon learned that Western aerospace companies were not keen on allowing Russian organizations to compete for contracts or for business in the West.

Finally, in 1994 the Russian Agency for Space Exploration successfully negotiated an agreement with NASA to use Russian talent and facilities. As discussed in Chapter 9, this arrangement called for an infusion into Russia of tens of millions of dollars from the United States to support Russian activities directly linked to joint programs for establishment and maintenance of a space station.

The directors of the principal nuclear weapons laboratories also soon recognized that business as usual was not an approach that would ensure the survival of their excess capacity in the post–Cold War period. Many were located in the Urals region and in Siberia where there was a dearth of other high-tech institutions. The directors promptly floated numerous ideas for technological solutions to overcome problems attendant to geographical remoteness.

Beginning in the late 1980s, the leaders of the nuclear weapons design centers at Arzamas–16 and Chelyabinsk–70 began to expand their contacts with counterparts at Los Alamos, Livermore, and Sandia National Laboratories in the United States. By the early 1990s, almost all nuclear laboratories in Russia were competing in the hunt for flush Western partners with deep pockets.

The American nuclear weapons laboratories had their own funding shortfalls and were also seeking new programs as the development and testing of new types of weapons began to decline.[14]

Spurred on by the Americans, the Russian nuclear laboratories quickly assembled hundreds of proposals for converting their technical wherewithal to civilian purposes. But they had difficulty recognizing that their proposals for conversion would not be taken seriously unless the price tags of the final products were internationally competitive, a new concept for scientists accustomed to monopolistic advantages.

The chemical and biological weapons laboratories, in searching for civilian alternatives, had difficulty seeing beyond the much-advertised conversion programs of the Russian government—programs with touted results that would never materialize. Finally, by 1993 these laboratories began to put on the international table their proposals for conversion programs.

Having been sheltered for decades from the outside world by a plethora of technical and security ministries, laboratory leaders had major problems adjusting to concepts of cost control and marketing. Indeed, five years after receiving instructions to cease R&D on chemical weapons, the major chemical warfare institute had only one well-developed conversion program in place, a program to develop techniques for destroying chemical weapons, with little consideration of cost and no requirement for marketing.[15]

But once the chemical and biological institutes began interacting with Western organizations, their specialists quickly recognized the need to adopt Western approaches to project development and implementation if they were to attract foreign financial support. They defined their approaches in terms of goals and milestones; they calculated budgets on the basis of realistic cost estimates to carry projects through each stage of proposed activities; and they clearly identified the anticipated results of the projects and the likely uses of these results. Now, only if they could find interested customers for their goods and services, they lamented.

The Russian government continued to set forth national conversion priorities as though central planning would continue. One list of R&D priorities published in late 1993 was as follows:

> micro-electronics, opto-electronics, radioelectronics
> high-speed computers, peripherals, and software
> communications technology
> aerospace and new materials
> automated production technology
> medical technologies, food processing technologies, and
>   biotechnologies
> recycling, energy technology, and environmental protection
> surface and water transportation.[16]

Such a listing, while very general, would nevertheless be useful if money were available for supporting activities in the designated areas. But funds were not available, and the list had little value. The institutes paid little heed to such efforts to return to central planning, and they undertook whatever projects they thought would attract funding. They had heard so many false promises from the government about new conversion programs that they listened no longer.

Looking at the list, it is strange that the government did not include nuclear safety as a priority. This is one area for which funds have consistently been available, from both domestic and international sources, for Russian researchers. Indeed, external funding opportunities, including the funds available through the ISTC, soon became far more important in setting Russian priorities than empty lists published by the central authorities.

Reorienting the Research Institutes

An examination of specific civilian R&D projects being pursued by several Russian weapons institutes gives insights as to the Russian responses to the call for conversion. In large measure, their reactions were driven by the particular views of the organizations willing to provide financial support, especially foreign institutions with *real* money. At the same time, in the absence of the interest of a potential customer, much of the R&D degenerated into busywork. Unfortunately, such busywork occupied a large portion of the portfolios of most institutes.

Only a small percentage of the proposals of these or other institutes are likely to attract support in the near future, since *commercialization*—which was to be the measure of success—requires more than technical know-how. In most cases, when proposals command support, foreign institutions recognize the payoff and are quick to become involved. Occasionally, Russian ministries, committees, or enterprises are able to find funds to support favorite projects, or more likely, favored people. Nevertheless, almost all the funds available for the institutes from within Russia are needed to provide even minimal wage payments for staff and for covering the utility costs that must be paid if the institutes are to remain open.

Power Engineering Institute (Moscow)

Following the Chernobyl accident, the Moscow Power Engineering Institute has been continuously under attack by Western critics for its reluctance to recommend a total shutdown, or at least a rapid phase-out, of Chernobyl-type reactors (commonly referred to as *RBMK* reactors, which is the Russian acronym) that provide electricity for several areas of the country and for export.[17] This institute was responsible for many of the design details of RBMK reactors that produced plutonium for the military program as well as essential electricity for the civilian economy. Now, under instructions from the government, the institute devotes much of its effort to improving the safety of the operating reactors, leaving to the ministries the task of determining whether and when the reactors should be closed down. Needless to say, such safety upgrades are popular in the West; the institute has had little difficulty attracting support, particularly from the European Union, for its reactor safety programs, which constitute a small but important portion of the institute's budget.

But as the percentage of the institute's budget provided by the Russian defense program slipped from 75 percent to less than 20 percent, the institute was not content simply to retrofit old reactors. It has also aggressively promoted ideas for new generations of nuclear reactors— in remote areas, on barges, in missile silos, and in other sheltered locations. One favorite design for civilian power stations relies on lead-cooled nuclear reactor technology used in Soviet submarines, as discussed in Chapter 5.

Also, the institute has developed a *technopolis* approach, which is a popular advertising concept, widely adopted in Russia, for clusters of high-tech facilities concentrated in specific geographic areas. The technopolis administrators are trying to market the products of the institute's formerly secret research station near Ekaterinburg in the Urals region. Among the products of research that are for sale are high-strength materials, rare gases required for scientific experiments, and radioisotopes produced for medicine. While some contracts for work in these areas have been signed with institutions in Western Europe, the anticipated revenues will not begin to cover the costs of maintaining this remote site, which now welcomes visitors.

Exemplifying the institute's tilt toward the West, the director has provided space in the facility for a representative of a Western company's nuclear reactor division that is searching for technological opportunities in Russia.

Luberetskoe Scientific Production Association, Soyuz (Dzershinskyi)

About fifty miles south of Moscow, in the town of Dzershinskyi, is a formerly secret research center where solid propellants for Soviet rockets were developed.[18] In 1991, Soyuz began promoting the use of solid rocket fuels to propel objects other than missiles. Their specialists considered that one of their most promising developments was the use of propellants to power large water hoses that could either be mounted in aircraft or used on the ground in battling forest fires. While the institute carried out impressive field tests over the forests and developed a dramatic film showing water cannons extinguishing advancing fire lines, visitors with expertise in fire control were generally unimpressed over the practical utility, and associated costs, of using this technology in operational situations.

Not to be deterred, specialists at the institute then turned their attention to many other items; samples of their products covered a large display room of the institute. Looking to the gas industry as one of Russia's strong assets, the chemists developed new gas generators, explosive devices for gas exploration, and fire extinguishers to combat gas fires. The rocket scientists also became biochemists and polymer chemists as they turned out new pesticides, cleaning agents, construction materials, and even camping and boating gear. Automated production lines became standard fare as the technicians in their large machine shop seemed to be able to make whatever metallic or plastic object attracted a paying customer.

But the customers have been slow in coming. While the name of the director was a household word among the Soviet military brass for thirty years, few foreigners recognize it. Most visitors rather accidentally discover this relatively high level of technology tucked away next to the famous monastery that dominates the village.

Institute of Technical Physics (Snezhinsk)

Farther to the east in the southern end of the Ural Mountains, is the town of Snezhinsk, home of the second nuclear weapons design center established shortly after World War II. At the Institute of Technical Physics in this town, which until recently was known only by the number of its Post Office Box, Chelyabinsk–70, the initial approach to conversion seemed conservative. Basic research efforts in physics such as investigations of special-purpose lasers, new types of X-rays, new sources of neutrons, and innovative plasma accelerators dominated the lists of projects in search of funding partners. The specialists also had many ideas concerning new types of medical diagnostics, but they were uncertain as to the commercial potential of projects in this area.

Then the institute's management turned its attention to the environmental problems that engulf the region. Nearby are the sites of several severe radioactivity releases that began in the 1950s. The scientists from the institute are most comfortable at their computers developing models that will predict how pollution disperses, leaving to others the field work of identifying and cleaning up the chemicals that contaminate the area. Indeed, they have become quite expert in modeling air

**Chelyabinsk–70, July 1994. ISTC staff members and weapons designers
from the Institute of Technical Physics gather beneath a statue of Igor
Kurchatov, organizer of the Soviet nuclear weapons program.**

and groundwater pollution, and even patterns of diseases related to such contamination.

But few scientists at the institute were prepared for 100 percent conversion of themselves and their jobs. They worried that conversion programs might be a passing fad; if they agreed to work full-time on conversion activities, they would have nowhere to go when the projects came to an end. Hence, the scientists typically devoted about one-half of their time to weapons programs to ensure that their permanent places would not be given away; then they turned their efforts to conversion activities on a part-time basis.

In mid-June 1994, with the staff in near revolt because paychecks had not arrived for several months, the institute sent out a wide appeal for the government to provide more funds so that the facilities could survive in a respectable fashion. The old Soviet subsidy mentality was hardly disguised, as this appeal did not once mention how their efforts could help the economy.[19]

At about the same time, my visit to the institute revealed a small team of Chinese specialists in temporary residence arranging cooperative programs that would increase the income of the institute. I was sure that this Chinese connection would soon heighten local sensitivies to the payoff of a new orientation toward marketing the results of research.

State Scientific Center for Virology and Biotechnology, Vector (Koltsovo)

The town of Koltsovo is just fifteen minutes by automobile from the science city of Akademgorodok, near Novosibirsk. For three decades, Akademgorodok had been a showcase of Soviet scientific achievements and had received thousands of foreign visitors. Indeed, in 1964, 1986, and again in 1994, I visited Akademgorodok; and each time I was graciously received at several institutes, including the Budker Institute of Nuclear Physics, which, as we later learned, had housed many weapons scientists. Then, in 1974, highly classified research on biological warfare agents began in the closed town of Koltsovo, unbeknown to the nearby foreign guests.

At that time, the Soviet government established secret R&D institutes in three locations: Koltsovo; Obolensk, south of Moscow; and Libuchanyi, also south of Moscow. Soviet officials contended that the

Novosibirsk (Akademgorodok), September 1994. ISTC visitors tour the Budker Institute of Nuclear Physics, which has found new civilian markets in China for its particle accelerators.

Pentagon was hiding aggressive biological warfare research at Fort Dietrich, Maryland, despite U.S. declarations to the contrary. The Ministry of Health used the classified facilities at Fort Dietrich as the rationale for their own three new research enclaves. Scientists were dispatched from Moscow to several new facilities in Koltsovo to organize research on viral agents with military potential.

The competition with the West in the field of biological warfare is now apparently history. Vector has opened its doors to visitors from around the world.[20]

The workforce of the institute has declined from 6,000 to 2,500, with almost all the departing specialists remaining in the town, where they have established many commercial enterprises. The activities in these enterprises are not well known even to neighbors, and the townspeople are concerned over Koltsovo's growing reputation as a center for launching mafia activity. The research facilities are still in reasonably good shape as the institute moves forward with conversion efforts that to date have been too limited to support even the reduced staff.

Development of new types of vaccines is the centerpiece of the conversion efforts of Vector. Three of the initial candidates are vaccines for measles, hepatitis A, and hepatitis B. Also of interest is a vaccine for hemorrhagic fever. Western specialists have been generally skeptical of the importance of such research given that more advanced R&D has been conducted in the West on related vaccines. In addition, Western specialists have been concerned that the Russian regulatory framework governing research, clinical trials, and production of vaccines may not be adequate by Western standards. An international symposium in Koltsovo in December 1994 on the research activities and Russian regulations governing development, production, and use of vaccines was quite successful in reassuring Western officials that the Russian work could be useful and would be carried out responsibly.[21]

Central Aerohydrodynamics Institute (Zhukovskyi)

Located just a few minutes drive from the eastern boundary of Moscow, this institute is well known as the birthplace of Soviet aviation technology. Richly endowed with dozens of wind tunnels and other large experimental facilities, the institute is trying to adjust to a reduction in defense contracts, that a decade ago supported two-thirds of its activities, to a situation whereby less than 0.2 percent of its 1994 budget came from defense work.[22]

With success in signing seventy-five contracts with foreign partners by the end of 1994, the institute searched for even more. Most of the initial work consisted simply of making available its wind tunnels and other test facilities to foreign aerospace organizations. A few contracts supported genuine R&D efforts, particularly those developed in cooperation with the Boeing Research Center in Moscow, in such areas as the impact of sonic boom related to a new generation of supersonic planes, turbulence encountered by small aircraft crossing the wakes of large aircraft at congested airports, and turbulence on the skin of aircraft at high speeds and varying temperatures. Other areas of interest range from developing a new type of seaplane to building automated greenhouses to selling test stands that help assess truck performance in rough terrain.

But perhaps the most profitable activity of the institute has been the production of parquet flooring. The high-temperature ovens of the institute provide an excellent capability for this successful business with products that appeal to many Russian commercial firms, particularly banks, and to wealthy Russians who are building large new houses.

The institute is the first Russian research organization to establish a permanent office in the United States. A representative of the institute settled in Seattle in late 1994 with immediate access to an American law firm that represents the institute in the United States and to the headquarters of the Boeing Company. He subsequently decided that a Washington, D.C., location, closer to governmental sources of research funding, was more desirable. It is too early to know whether this investment in an overseas office will pay off.

Each Russian institute has its own characteristics, but some aspects are common. Each has cut back its activities because of budgetary limitations, which in turn have resulted in significantly reduced staffs and many inoperative laboratories. Each is searching for contracts abroad. And all are still in a state of shock from losing their special financial arrangements, generous allocations of equipment and supplies, and elite (at least by Soviet standards) consumer product supply lines for their employees.

And each of the institutes hopes that the ISTC will support some of its projects.

Industrial Revitalization and Foreign Investment

Russia will undoubtedly make substantial efforts to regain its status as an industrial power as quickly as possible. One hopes that such status will revolve around production of civilian goods and will not be linked to a return to the Soviet emphasis on military hardware.

If revitalization of industry is to occur in the near term, extensive foreign involvement will be essential both for infusions of capital and for access to modern technology. But the extent to which Russia is willing to mortgage to foreign interests future control over facilities located on its territory in order to accelerate the modernization timetable is, of course, a central issue. The future Russian policies bearing on this question will probably be inconsistent, depending on the political situations surrounding specific decisions.

A related factor is the extent to which Russia is prepared to rely on foreign sources of technology in competition with the products of its own laboratories in meeting domestic industrial requirements for new and improved processes and products. This issue is no less important than foreign control over local assets, although not as obvious to political snipers. Still, the policy winds surrounding technology choices will probably change directions frequently as the Russian government faces specific decisions concerning international cooperation.

In any event, some form of effective R&D infrastructure within the country—regardless of funding sources—will be essential in promoting and sustaining the drive toward industrialization and the development of worldwide technological linkages that have become indispensable for every modern state. At the center of this infrastructure will certainly be some of the existing institutes that for decades served the Soviet military ministries and are now trying to convert their capabilities to civilian activities. Their success will be coupled, at least in part, to the success of many of the more than 2,000 industrial plants that also served the defense authorities.

The successful conversion of the talents of Russian scientists and engineers must encompass not only the rehabilitation of existing facilities but the establishment of new factories and research laboratories as well. One without the other will leave many holes in the future industrial panorama of the country.

The United States has a major stake in participating in Russia's struggle to regain its status as an industrial power. The national security interests associated with joint activities cajoling Russia toward peace and dissuading Russia from military activities are clear. Commercial opportunities for American firms to capitalize on the vast storehouses of natural resources and the large pool of skilled manpower in Russia are manyfold. And projects that enable American scientists and engineers to learn from Russian technical experts about developments that have eluded the United States can pay handsome dividends.

In some areas, Germany and other countries already have a head start in establishing industrial beachheads in Russia. Many Russians would prefer to deal with Americans, however, than with specialists from other nations who carry the historical baggage of the direct involvement of their countrymen in wars on Russian soil. The ISTC provides one mechanism for U.S. specialists to become involved in a very serious way at some of the birthplaces of Russia's technology of the future.

Russian and foreign experts have long lists of steps that should be taken by the Russian government to improve the environment for industrial growth and foreign involvement in the development of the scientific and industrial base of the country.[23] Additional suggestions have been presented in other chapters concerning protection of intellectual property rights (Chapter 3), building confidence throughout the world as to nonmilitary uses of dual-use technologies (Chapter 6), and innovative steps to promote foreign investment in Russia (Chapter 9).

Conversion to Somewhere

Having said all this, we must add that conversion in Russia need not be traveling on a path to nowhere. But the destination of each conversion project must be well defined. In no other area is there more relevance to the age-old maxim, *Be careful: if you don't know where you are going, you may indeed arrive there.*

Soviet military R&D had very specific objectives, carefully defined by the users of the research products. Russian conversion R&D must also have very specific objectives, carefully defined by the end-users, that is, by those customers who are willing to pay for the R&D. And certainly the Russian government must play a key role in establishing an environment that makes it attractive for important end-users to turn to the R&D establishments for help.

The ISTC provides an important international forum, backed by significant financial resources, to consider practical steps that will support steady movement toward the goal of *successful* conversion, which has been so elusive in recent years.

Chapter 8

Can Research and Development Recover in Russia?

Our society no longer sees in science the main source of material and moral values; it no longer deems science to be an honorable or useful activity.

A senior Russian scientist, September 1993

Feeding the Research Base

As we have seen, false starts have plagued conversion efforts at hundreds of research institutes that at one time carried out major R&D programs for the defense establishment. Without foreign intervention, most researchers have either simply marked time while thinking about their futures or have abandoned their laboratories altogether. Foreign financial support and foreign collaborators have brought a few bright spots to the otherwise lackluster conversion efforts. At the same time, many of these institutes continue to pursue dramatically scaled-back weapons programs; others no longer have any financial ties to their earlier benefactors in the defense establishment.

Thousands of institutes and enterprises that had little or no defense role in the past struggle to find their places in the rapidly changing economic scene. They too had been highly subsidized wards of the state, and very few have been able to adjust to the drying up of their annual subventions from a variety of ministries and state committees.

The sudden emphasis on conversion uncovered few, if any, *new* areas of R&D. For example, almost all activities supported by the ISTC are in fields of R&D that had long been within the responsibilities of civilian research organizations of the Soviet Union, and now Russia. Indeed, historically there was hardly an area of science and engineering, however remote from immediate Soviet interests, that did not receive at least token support from the government. This effort to cover every topic susceptible to human inquiry partially reflected the belief of the Soviet leaders that American researchers were undoubtedly covering all these bases. The USSR surely did not want to be surprised or outdone by American discoveries in any field.

To avoid the syndrome of "reinventing the wheel," the ISTC actively promotes cooperation between weapons scientists and engineers and those civilian specialists who have been interested in similar problems for many years. To this end, most ISTC projects include on the project teams not only former weapons experts but also Russian colleagues from the civilian sector. The Western governments believe that such collaboration also will require a high degree of transparency in the civilian activities being undertaken for the first time at the weapons laboratories—and thereby contribute to confidence that ISTC funds are being used appropriately. Also, the integration of weapons specialists into the mainstream of Russian civilian R&D seems essential if a cost-effective infrastructure for supporting economic development of the country is eventually to emerge.

Thus, developments throughout the civilian R&D community—within the Academy of Sciences, the universities, the institutions of the civilian ministries, and the independent laboratories—are of very direct interest to the ISTC. Further, these activities are symptomatic of the challenges that will confront the "born-again" weaponeers suddenly soft-pedaling their roots as weapons experts and now eager to contribute to the science and technology base that should support the revival of the country's new economy in an age of high technology.

Continuing Decline of Research and Development

During 1994, however, a steady stream of eyewitness reports from Russia continued to document the declining state of the civilian and *civilianized* R&D laboratories of the country.[1] More and more laboratories simply were not operating, as researchers spent their time searching elsewhere for ways to augment their low and unreliable salaries. Enormous amounts of obsolete research equipment became mere ornaments taking up floor space. Scavengers stripped large quantities of salable items from the laboratories, the offices, and even the restrooms. The most desirable space of some research facilities had been converted to rental property for banks, commercial shops, foreign organizations, or any group willing to match the dollar outlays of Russian entrepreneurs.

Reflecting the lack of core budgets, entire institutes were closed for days and sometimes weeks to save energy costs, which mounted if the doors were opened. Long holiday weekends became extended vacations. Telephones were disconnected when unpaid bills piled up. Even many of the well-equipped laboratories of the former military-industrial complex were dark.

Institute directors and their deputies were difficult to find, as they spent many weeks abroad searching for funds. Some of these institute leaders had become so entangled in webs of contractual commitments with foreign organizations that questions arose as to who determined the research profiles of their institutes. Many institutes housed small enterprises providing a variety of commercial products and services; these enterprises were established by senior laboratory managers who used them as cash cows to help keep their floundering institutes afloat and at the same time supplement salaries for the managers. For example, sales of men's clothing, newly assembled personal computers, and frozen chickens diverted from foreign aid programs were regular events at the Pulse Technology Institute that housed the ISTC Planning Group and the Prepcom.

Tens of thousands of researchers accurately concluded that no one really cared whether they were at their work sites or not. As the salaries of more than 60 percent of researchers fell below the poverty line established by the Russian government, demonstrations and threatened strikes by scientists at both civilian and defense research institutes continued to receive wide publicity.[2] But these outbursts, which had started several years earlier, had lost their political impact. Other professions had also fallen on hard times, and science appeared to the public more as a skeleton than as a skeleton key with which to unlock future prosperity.

By the end of 1994, the brain drain of active researchers from Russia to the West since 1991 may have reached a total of 2,000 among the 5,000 *scientific* emigrants reported by the Russian government.[3] This level was much less than predicted by Western experts in 1992, when salaries dropped to the equivalent of $25 per month; nevertheless, the exodus resulted in significant erosion of indigenous capabilities within several areas of research (e.g., certain aspects of mathematics and physics).

A cartoon in a popular Russian newspaper captured one important reason why higher predictions of emigration had not come true. In the cartoon, an immigrant is reading a help-wanted advertisement in an American newspaper that says, "Needed: babysitters; prefer nuclear engineers with graduate degrees from Leningrad University and a minimum of twenty years of experience."

Meanwhile, the massive internal brain drain continued as tens of thousands of researchers, particularly young scientists and engineers under the age of thirty-five, sought more lucrative professions in hastily established commercial offices throughout Russia. An estimated 30 percent of all researchers had left for the commercial sector, for retirement, or for other destinations since 1991; another 25 percent retained their affiliations with their institutes only to maintain their medical, retirement, and social benefits while pursuing careers outside those institutes.[4]

Perhaps of greatest concern was the rapid decline in interest of talented students in pursuing scientific and engineering careers—to the dismay of many parents accustomed to a long scientific lineage. In the few years since the failed coup of 1991, the application pressures for admission to some of the best science and engineering faculties of the country had decreased to one-third of previous levels, while the nationwide decline in applicants was about 10 percent per year.[5] Of the graduates in science and engineering from the technical colleges in 1994, more than 80 percent were reportedly seeking their fortunes in the commercial sector or abroad.[6]

Of course, there were many exceptions to the general decline in Russian R&D. For example, excellent research on fullerenes and other new versatile materials was underway in a dusty corner of the otherwise moribund Institute of Graphite. The Institute of Theoretical and Experimental Physics, located in rundown buildings of a former palatial residence, launched an ambitious program for transmutation of dangerous nuclear materials. Young researchers at the Nuclear Safety Institute had little difficulty obtaining contracts for computer modeling of nuclear reactor accidents. The Urals branch of the Russian Academy of Sciences was pouring concrete for a number of buildings in a new science city being built on the edge of Ekaterinburg. The Institute of Catalysis in Novosibirsk had become a money machine by attracting contracts for pollution control technology. Ecological research had reached new heights in the Lake Baikal Basin.

Almost all the success stories in the civilian sector were attributable to one or two enterprising Russian scientific leaders who had convinced foreign organizations to use Russian talent in addressing problems of importance for the West. Indeed, by the end of 1994, probably more than one-half of the significant civilian R&D projects were financed in part by foreign sources.[7]

Slow Boat from Soviet to Russian Science

Many of the traditions of *Soviet* science persist, but the demise of the outmoded Soviet style is quickly approaching. Most researchers long for "the good old days" when financial support from the government was not a survival issue. But they finally understand that a new era is being forced on them as the budgetary spigots continue to close.

Since 1991, the members of the *new* Russian science establishment, from ministers to laboratory technicians, have tried to convince themselves that the one and only solution to the plight of Russian R&D is more money, that the money will eventually appear, and that the current economic crisis will soon be history. Even if money is the needed antidote, the costs are now out of sight for restoring productive activities in even one-half of the R&D facilities built during Soviet times, which include a vast array of institutes of enormous dimensions. According to Russian data, in 1994 the science establishment still employed more than 800,000 researchers in more than 4,500 institutions distributed within four general organizational structures: academies of sciences (16 percent of the institutes and 14 percent of the researchers), educational institutions (10 percent and 7 percent), industrial research institutes (67 percent and 73 percent), and laboratories of the production enterprises (7 percent and 6 percent). While the numbers of institutes and researchers may be overstatements, by any measure the science establishment is awesomely large.[8]

Western observers who study Russian R&D, even casually, quickly conclude that the entire science enterprise must be scaled back drastically, but in a rational way. Substantial downsizing is occurring through attrition as armies of researchers seek more lucrative professions elsewhere and new entrants are a rarity. But those who stay behind are not necessarily the more productive researchers.[9]

Some elements of the Russian government, along with the more progressive Russian scientific leaders, profess to have accepted the necessity to concentrate available funding on only the most meritorious projects and to close unproductive laboratories. But neither the ministries nor the institute directors have much enthusiasm for putting such principles into practice. One of the most enlightened institute directors, and one who is revered in the West, simply states, "My unproductive employees are the victims of the Soviet system, and they should not be penalized by becoming unemployed." A second director, who is also popular in the West, adds, "I could not withstand the wrath of the family of any dismissed employee, even though one-third of the staff is not productive."

The leadership of the Russian Academy of Sciences takes great pride in the fact that the academy is the only institution that was not changed after the collapse of the Soviet Union in 1991. They emphasize that the academy has not *closed* a single one of the more than 300 academy research institutions. This is a rather dubious position, given the financial realities during a time of dramatic transition.

These and other Russian leaders plead for time to develop *humane* solutions to the problems bequeathed by the Soviet era. Unfortunately, time has run out, and the paltry inheritances are now insufficient to support the immediate needs of the Russian population.

Turning to the Soviet legacy, about two-thirds of Soviet R&D supported a military machine that is in desperate need of simple maintenance, rather than the introduction of new systems.[10] Early achievements in the space and nuclear fields are well known, and remarkable technological accomplishments in other areas have now also taken their places in history books.

Another 10 to 12 percent of the Soviet effort was directed to basic research in almost every conceivable field of fundamental science, as noted earlier. In many areas Soviet researchers were international leaders and gained great prestige for the state. However, a significant portion of the effort employed scientists with limited capabilities.[11]

Most of the remainder of Soviet R&D was classified as *applied industrial research*, which overlapped with defense-related R&D. It could be described as a combination of engineering support for manufacturing plants, occasional innovations that significantly enhanced productivity, and efforts to adapt Western approaches (gleaned from published or pilfered reports) to Soviet capabilities. While the R&D institutions were struggling to master new capital-intensive technologies, the manufacturing practices employed in the Soviet Union evolved in an environment that favored labor-intensive and resource-intensive production processes. Then, the applied research that was relevant frequently resulted only in marginal upgrades of obsolete equipment and processes that soon were discarded. Even the most successful applied research seldom found users in more than one or two enterprises because of the compartmentalization of activities throughout the society that stifled diffusion of useful innovations.[12] It was often said within the steel industry, for example, that Soviet innovations spread so rapidly throughout Japan and so slowly in the USSR that within ten years after a new development in the Urals, the average Japanese plant was twenty years ahead of the average Soviet plant.[13]

Aside from concern over the bloated size of the R&D effort, the features of Soviet R&D most criticized by Westerners are the lack of coupling between research and educational activities and the mismatch of R&D and industrial production activities. In the mid-1980s two organizational models developed years earlier to address these problems were finally introduced on a significant scale, but with limited results.

Several dozen *science production associations* brought together conglomerations of manufacturing facilities (typically three or four) and industrial research institutes (often two or three) under central management. This approach was most effective in the military sector, where governmental investment resources were not a problem in introducing innovations of the institutes into manufacturing practices. But, as noted earlier, civilian innovations often languished in the laboratories. In any event, the research institutes of these large complexes are of dwindling relevance as the emerging Russian privatization models rely almost exclusively on foreign, rather than local, sources for technologies.

Also in the 1980s, a large number of *science and education centers* were established to link higher educational institutions with scientific institutes engaged in basic research. This organizational step largely formalized a practice that goes back many decades. R&D specialists in all fields, including institute directors, have enjoyed the educational challenges, the prestige, and the financial benefits of also being professors and lecturers for two or three hours a week; and they have welcomed the opportunity to choose students to work in their laboratories. Overall, however, the number of active researchers seriously involved in education is very small by Western standards, and many institutional barriers continue to insulate mainstream education activities from the R&D community.

As financial accountability became a paramount concern in the beginning of the 1990s, the concept of project budgeting for R&D was introduced on a wide scale by some ministries. Under this system, institutions no longer received lump sums from the government for their operations but received funds earmarked for specific project areas. For example, all governmental funds for one institute of 3,000 employees were divided into seven project areas; the institute lost its past flexibility to shift funds between project areas. State auditors were instructed to check that fund shifting was not taking place. While project budgeting looked good as a way to ensure some degree of accountability for funds, the research institutions quickly developed such broadly defined project areas that much of the former flexibility was retained. Then, with the Russian budget process in chaos at all levels, institutes seemed free to use whatever accounting techniques were necessary to keep the doors open and the paychecks flowing.

Finally, a series of technological failures during the waning years of the Soviet Union (noted in Chapter 7) had a major impact on the problems that soon confronted the Russian government—and greatly degraded international and domestic confidence in Russian technology that does not also carry a Western trademark. The computer revolution in the West in the 1980s, in particular, highlighted the lag in Soviet achievements. Not surprisingly, Russian enterprises soon snubbed the technological achievements of local R&D institutions; and many of these institutions have had more success selling their wares to foreign technology merchants than giving them away to their Russian school chums.

The Russian approach to R&D is being shaped in the wake of a Soviet legacy that emphasized liberal budgets for all comers during several decades of economic growth and then led to an overnight collapse of the R&D system when the funding for military R&D rapidly disappeared.

No longer will the cost of, or the need for, specific R&D projects be secondary considerations to simply keeping the R&D effort moving in general directions. Now Russia must more narrowly define the core of R&D institutions and of the specialists who should be maintained during even the most difficult days, so that the country can indeed retain its status as a modern industrial nation.

The Search for Low-Cost Remedies

Although convinced that money is the dominant missing ingredient for maintaining a viable R&D effort, Russian government officials have for a number of years been trying to find no-cost and low-cost organizational and policy approaches that will help keep as many R&D activities alive as possible. At the same time, officials have such great difficulty delivering on any pronouncements involving money that their innovative policy approaches are of more academic interest to foreigners than of real interest to Russians. Russian researchers associate the government with extended vacations without pay and sharp reductions in the promised amounts of funding for well-established programs, and they consider new policy pronouncements as diversions from addressing the real problems. Indeed, the ministries have become whipping boys for all aspects of the economic crisis.

Nevertheless, a few of the government's policy initiatives deserve attention. They could have direct or indirect impacts on the immediate distribution and use of resources; and in the long run, they will be important determinants of the direction of R&D in the country.

Self-Diagnosis and the People Problem

The Ministry of Science and Technology Policy has documented in detail many of the problems associated with the current approach to R&D. Against a background of underutilized research laboratories that contribute relatively little to science or economic development and of a society beset with so many financial problems that it has lost interest in R&D, in 1993 the ministry distributed to the international community a detailed diagnosis of the situation in Russia. From intellectual property rights, to educational reform, to the climate for investment, the Russian reports provide unusually candid comments both by administrators and scientists on the seemingly intractable problems confronting the nation as a whole and the R&D institutions in particular. Of course, much of the blame has been cast on the legacy handed down from the Soviet Union; this dubious estate has provided grist for far-reaching complaints that have triggered international efforts to try to help Russia salvage the best elements of its past R&D activities.[14]

In 1994, the Science Ministry issued two complementary statistical reports that further rounded out the picture. The first report expanded earlier efforts to provide basic data on the size and character of scientific and engineering activities within the country. It documented the steady decline in the overall R&D budget, which reportedly reached less than 0.5 percent of gross domestic product (GDP) as compared to

1.5 percent to 2.5 percent in most industrialized countries. It presented the downward trend of about 8 percent per year in the number of R&D personnel and at the same time reported that few of the more than 4,500 R&D institutions had any intention of closing their doors. Also, it noted that the number of newly enrolled graduate students in science and engineering was on a steady decline. Finally, the report pointed out that small enterprises engaged in *scientific activities* employed almost 500,000 people, although it failed to note that only a very few of these enterprises carry out significant research.[15]

The second report presented data on the external brain drain of Russian scientists and engineers, including R&D personnel. During the second half of 1992, about 250 researchers emigrated, primarily to the United States, Israel, and Germany. This was a very small percentage of the total number of researchers. More disturbing were data showing that during 1991–92, 508 researchers of the Academy of Sciences emigrated. This represented 0.8 percent of the academy's researchers, who are among the best in the country. Also, by the end of 1992, 1,701 researchers of the academy were abroad either on long-term business trips or working under contract for periods of six months or longer. Of these temporary visitors, 60 percent were under the age of forty.[16]

This hunger of younger scientists for travel to the West was underscored in a poll by a Russian newspaper. The paper reported that 100 percent of the responding young specialists under the age of thirty currently employed in the aerospace and atomic energy fields would welcome the opportunity to spend time working in the West.[17]

Meanwhile, more detailed Russian investigations of the brain drain confirmed the following: The massive flight of scientists and engineers from the institutes to commercial shops and offices, which had far outstripped the limited emigration, was attributable to one simple factor: money.[18]

Fine Tuning the Bureaucracy

As the problems besetting Russian R&D were moving from a state of common knowledge to documented facts, the Ministry of Science and Technology Policy pressed forward with a scheme to establish a large number of State Scientific Centers. By the late 1980s, Evgenyi Velikhov, director of the Kurchatov Institute for Atomic Energy, had become convinced that the Soviet Union, and later Russia, should replicate the system of national laboratories operating in the United States under the patronage of the U.S. Department of Energy. He persuaded the Russian government to designate his institute as a State Scientific Center; the concept was then gradually adopted by the government on a broader scale. By the summer of 1995, more than sixty institutes that were established decades earlier had received designations as State Scientific Centers. Another 400 were waiting in line for such designation.[19]

These centers were to receive preferential financial treatment, both in terms of budget support and tax exemptions. They would become the core of the nation's R&D program and would survive regardless of financial crises facing the nation as a whole.

In principle, the concept of a limited number of centers of R&D excellence seemed sound. The problem is the large size of the designated centers, with some employing more than 5,000 people—many of whom are not very productive. Thus, the implementation of the center concept in effect is contributing to the perpetuation of the very problem it was designed to solve. As the R&D establishment shrinks, only the most productive laboratories should be preserved; the large institutes should close those laboratories with poor track records. Had the centers been limited in size to laboratories of about 200 employees, instead of encompassing entire institutes, the concept would have been very important.

The science ministry could move in an appropriate direction even at this late date by limiting financial support to include no more than 20 percent of the laboratories of any single center, with strict prohibitions on transferring resources from these laboratories to other parts of the centers. Indeed, some of the selected laboratories could then spin off from the institutes.

Another policy that the ministry has aggressively promoted is the adoption of Western-style peer review in deciding which research activities should be supported. For decades, the Soviet government appointed various commissions, subcommissions, and panels of experts that reviewed research programs. In some cases, they were very effective in the selection of the most meritorious proposals for financial support. In other cases, political factors took precedence over national needs and technical merit.

The centerpiece of the *new* approach to peer review, which emphasizes detailed evaluations of R&D proposals by experts considered reasonably objective, is the program of the Russian Foundation for

Fundamental Research. The foundation's budget is supposed to equal 4 percent of the total R&D budget, but in 1994 it was less than 1.2 percent. Nevertheless, the foundation plays an important role in awarding grants of up to the ruble equivalent of $10,000 to individual researchers or small groups of researchers. The foundation deserves high marks for efficiency and fairness. Indeed, Westerners are usually amazed to learn that the foundation does not hesitate to reject poor grant applications from famous Russian academicians.[20]

Believing that there should be a substantial foreign market for Russian technology, most of the Russian ministries have encouraged their R&D institutes to become more aggressive in searching for Western customers. While the government continuously grumbles about the inadequacy of intellectual property laws to protect past R&D investments of the Soviet and Russian governments, the institutes are more interested in meeting their payrolls regardless of the long-term losses from sharing know-how; and they have assumed much greater autonomy during the past several years in making their own business arrangements with foreign organizations for immediate relief. Also in deference to the plight of the institutes, the ministries pay only sporadic attention to exports that might include dual-use technologies that could be used by developing countries for their military efforts as well as for their civilian programs.

In the scramble for foreign funds, groups of Russian experts writing proposals for grants and contracts from the West now thrive; at least two institutes each had more than 100 serious proposals for international support in some stage of preparation during 1994. During our stay in Moscow, one enterprising institute recruited my wife, Carole, to help prepare proposals for international support. Also, in Siberia sixteen institutions of the Academy of Sciences have been dubbed as International Research Centers with almost every one of their project proposals being advertised as a proposal for foreign funding.[21]

Educational reform also became a priority as the government struggled with practical steps to train scientists and engineers who appreciated the demands of a market economy. At the same time, it became necessary to reduce drastically the number of narrowly trained technical specialists who were no longer needed as research and production declined. Several educational institutions began to introduce new courses in management and business practices for scientists and engineers, but these were largely token additions to standardized courses developed during decades of communism when the role of technical personnel was simply to solve well-defined problems placed before them.

Finally, the ministries have tried to ensure loyalty and support from the R&D institutes during this period of financial crisis by giving the directors unprecedented flexibility in all aspects of their operations. The ministries have also tried to assure researchers that all employees will have the opportunity to participate in the selection of their institute directors and will be able to develop their own research proposals for submission to national or international funding agencies as long as the proposals are consistent with the research orientations of the institutes.

In general, the Ministry for Science and Technology Policy has adopted a positive stance as to the future of Russian R&D. It strongly supports the effort of the state Duma to enact an umbrella science and technology law that will focus political attention on the importance of research.[22] The ministry continues to participate in national and international meetings that showcase the best of Russian R&D. It aggressively pursues expansion of tax and customs exemptions that will assist cooperative international programs.

Starting Down the Road to Recovery

As we see in Chapter 9, many U.S. organizations have attempted to accelerate the process of conversion and to assist in the recovery of the Russian R&D base. Some of these efforts are driven by an interest in rapidly downsizing the Russian military establishment. Some spring from a conviction that Russian science should again become a major contributor in pushing back the frontiers of the unknown. Commercial organizations see new opportunities for successful investments and expanded trade. Still other organizations are driven by humanitarian and philanthropic interests.

When the economic crisis in Russia deepened during the early 1990s, desperate Russian officials and scientists pleaded for aid from the West. In several years, however, they became disenchanted with the form in which such aid was delivered, with the ISTC program being one of the few that was truly considered to respond with "cash-in-the-hands-of-the-researchers" to Russian priorities as established by the researchers.

The Russian scientists realized that foreign assistance could be helpful but would never be decisive in preserving and reorienting the R&D

base of the country. In short, they realized that with or without foreign interventions, the Russian government and the Russian R&D community would have to play the key roles in determining the future fate of science in the country.

In some cases, foreign organizations with large resources, such as the World Bank, can encourage Russia to follow certain paths. Indeed, they can make external support conditional on adoption by the Russians of certain policies at governmental or institutional levels. But this foreign influence should not and will not be the pivotal factor that drives the overall R&D effort of the country.

Of course, the future of R&D in Russia is inextricably entwined with the future of the free-market economy, the privatization of industry, the emergence of new forms of social safety nets, the reform of the health and agricultural systems, and the overall budget of the country. At the same time, the R&D community should play a leading role in the quest for new educational approaches, in the restoration of the declining work ethic, and in the continued erosion of the barriers of isolation that for decades separated Soviet society into disconnected groups. Also, the R&D community, with the international traditions of scientific research behind it, should help ensure that Russia will continue to evolve into an open society.

But what can the Russian government do in the immediate future to help preserve the best of the R&D community that is currently being battered by economic stresses? The Russian government could take four important steps:

1. The Russian government should decouple *humanitarian* and *technical aid*, two incompatible concepts combined repeatedly in legal and political documents of the government. Foreign governments have increasing difficulty justifying their programs of cooperation with a technologically advanced country on the basis of *aid*. Further, when assistance mechanisms of the Western countries come into play, the doctor–patient mindset of many foreign assistance providers too often engulfs projects, which are then characterized by an overabundance of Western consultants. Approaches unique to Russia may indeed be the best routes, and they surely are more acceptable than the *models* imported from Pakistan and elsewhere by specialists accustomed to working in developing countries who now find themselves in Russia.

2. The Russian government must give greater attention to its conversion efforts in the weapons laboratories. The efforts of the West are

important but are not sufficient for the large task ahead. Even small amounts of seed money from the government can go a long way in the further development of promising ideas in these relatively well-equipped facilities. Concurrently, the government must be alert to inadequate protection of intellectual property as the laboratories expand their high-technology cooperation into programs not under the ISTC mantle.

3. Central to any recovery of R&D is the future role of the younger generations of scientists and engineers, a role that should rest on a restructured higher educational system. While education has traditionally been a strength of Russia, high marks in technical subjects must now share their places as indicators of achievement with skills in management, economics, and business. Thus, the Ministry of Science and Technology Policy should join Russian education officials in responding to the criticisms of World Bank specialists and others concerning the inappropriateness of the current educational system for a country that is committed to a market economy and for a country that can no longer afford to support half of the world's engineers. The ministry should carry out and publicize a detailed survey of steps that are being taken by the higher educational institutions themselves to realign their departments and curriculums, and the ministry should identify initiatives that seem to be of particular value.

4. While more than 6,000 joint ventures and foreign commercial organizations, including more than 1,100 from the United States, have invested in Russia, relatively little foreign money has been involved. Many of the foreign entities are undoubtedly entrepreneurs who will never make significant investments. A substantial number probably would invest on a larger scale if there were an adequate business infrastructure to help ensure that their funds would not be lost through theft, confiscation, extortion, or excessive taxes. The Russian government needs to give much higher priority to the development and implementation of a business-friendly legal and administrative framework. The future of technology in the country depends on the integration of Russian and Western skills and experience, and this integration will take place only when Western firms feel comfortable doing business in Russia.

The list of proposed remedies could extend for many pages. Indeed, leading Russian scientists have proposed cooperative programs costing $1 billion or more.[23] They are undoubtedly correct in their estimates of the level of resources required to rejuvenate a substantial portion of the

R&D infrastructure. Such funds are not available on the near horizon, however, unless there are unexpected discoveries of readily available high-value natural resources. Also, Western experts have set forth their lists of policy and organizational steps that should be taken. Many of these nonbudgetary recommendations are probably easier to implement.

Such budgetary requirements and policy needs should be kept front and center in Moscow, even though responses are not immediately forthcoming. But in the meantime, a few concrete projects directed at some of the core problems will certainly help in setting the stage for the reemergence of Russian R&D.

A Bottom Line of Tempered Optimism

Having said all of this, can R&D recover in Russia? The answers are all positive, if qualified:

- Yes, but on a time scale that will be determined by the overall economic and social recovery of the nation.
- Yes, but not in its current form, which in too many ways is abstract and disconnected from the real problems of Russia.
- Yes, but only if financial resources from within the country and from abroad are focused on fewer targets.
- Yes, but only if a business infrastructure develops that will encourage meaningful technical innovation.
- Yes, but only if new generations of young Russian scientists and engineers earn their seats at the international tables of science and commerce.

Chapter 9

American Organizations Seek Out Russian Researchers

What is national is no longer science.
Anton Chekov

Help for Russia, or Is It Cooperation?

Since the beginning of glasnost and perestroika in 1985, Western governments and private organizations have greatly expanded their cooperative activities with R&D institutions in Russia.

Initially, most of the motivation in the West for this increased interest was a belief that significant technical benefits could be derived by drawing on past Soviet achievements in science and technology. Foreign commercial firms were looking for technologies that could be incorporated into new processes or products or that could cut the costs of existing ones for both the international and Soviet civilian markets. Also, at least in some areas, Western entrepreneurs knew that the effective use of low-cost but highly skilled Russian manpower could lead to economic payoffs.[1]

The international scientific community emphasized the importance of past contributions of Soviet specialists in expanding the frontiers of knowledge. Foreign researchers sought broader contacts to learn about the latest scientific achievements in the USSR.

At the same time, the U.S., European, and Japanese governments wanted to engage Soviet institutions in projects that were of international importance outside the USSR. This included cooperation in fields such as environmental protection, prevention of nuclear accidents, detection and control of communicable diseases, improved communication and transportation systems, and development of energy resources.

When an independent Russia became a reality, new interests in cooperation arose in the West, together with an intensification of the interests stimulated during the final years of the Soviet era. "The Russian scientific community should play an important role in the struggle for a civil society; and therefore it should be supported during this embryonic stage of democracy," the political experts often argued. "The engineers need to change their ways, which were cast during the days of command and control; and Western change agents can facilitate this essential task in the transformation of Russia to a market economy," was a typical observation of the economists. "We must save the 'schools' of Russian science," clamored the international science community.

While a developing Russian market was whetting the appetites of some foreign producers and traders, a growing apprehension was also emerging that Russia could not, on its own, control its military technologies in times of internal turmoil. Particularly at risk were technologies incorporated in weapons of mass destruction and their delivery systems. The Western military analysts contended, "These technologies could be transferred to countries on not-so-favored lists through the emigration of specialists and through the export or theft of sensitive products."

Of course, this combination of inadequate control over military technologies and the intensification of economic difficulties was the very reason for the original ISTC proposal. But these concerns also triggered other activities, particularly when the sputtering diplomatic process delayed the establishment of the ISTC.

This chapter considers some of the most important cooperative activities orchestrated by American organizations involving Russian institutions, and activities that relate to the R&D base of Russia and therefore are of interest to the ISTC. Organizations in many other countries also play roles in the vast array of international programs in science and technology that involve foreign cooperation with Russia. Nevertheless, the U.S. government is probably the most important player. U.S. companies share the foreign industrial spotlight in Russia with a host of other international firms; but from the Russian perspective, American commercial partners often are the most intriguing, particularly corporations with worldwide reputations.

Still, before addressing U.S. programs, we should recognize that the European countries have very extensive activities that overlap with U.S. interests. For example, a large program of the European Union

(Technical Assistance for the CIS, or TACIS) sends hundreds of consultants in many technical fields to Russia each year; a related program (International Association for the Promotion of Cooperation with Scientists from the Independent States, or INTAS) has provided $25 million to link European institutions with Russian R&D institutions. In 1992 and 1993 the British government provided substantial resources to the Royal Society to expand its programs of cooperation with many research institutes in Russia, particularly institutes of the Russian Academy of Sciences. A number of German, French, and Dutch agencies also promote cooperation in higher education, basic research, environmental protection, and other fields. The Center for European Nuclear Research (CERN) and the European space and atomic energy agencies continue their long-standing interests in Russia.

As for industry, German firms, along with American companies, have been the most aggressive in seeking out profitable arrangements. But the private-sector activities of the French, Italians, Swedes, Japanese, South Koreans, and many others are also important; and the scope and size of their technology-related trade and investment portfolios are growing.

Turning to the international organizations, many UN agencies have programs in Russia (e.g., seminars, technical advisory services, training programs, equipment grants) that involve local research, educational, and industrial organizations.[2] The World Bank and the European Bank for Reconstruction and Development have launched major loan activities that cut across many social, educational, and industrial sectors. NATO sponsors arms control and technical seminars in several regions of Russia. Finally, nongovernmental organizations of many kinds are constantly sending representatives to Moscow and St. Petersburg in search of Russian scientists and engineers interested in being contact points for all sorts of projects.

In sum, tens of thousands of foreigners living in Russia or regularly visiting the country are engaged in a wide variety of intergovernmental, commercial, and private activities that are so numerous that even the Russian authorities cannot keep track of them.

Some activities complement the programs of the ISTC; others depend on the same limited pool of Russian specialists to lead their efforts; and, in effect, compete with ISTC programs. Ominously, a few, such as those of interest to international terrorist organizations, can directly challenge the objectives of the ISTC.

Politicizing Cooperation at the Highest Levels

In early December 1993, Carole and I attended a reception for Vice President and Mrs. Al Gore at the American ambassador's residence, Spaso House. The Gores, together with Prime Minister Chernomyrdin and his wife, were presiding at a celebration capping yet another round of signatures sealing bilateral cooperative agreements, primarily in science and technology.

The speech of the prime minister, and his many subsequent toasts, brought back memories of similar ceremonies I had attended in Spaso House thirty years earlier when the initial wave of bilateral space, atomic energy, health, agriculture, construction technology, and geology agreements were signed by senior officials of the U.S. and Soviet governments. Indeed, the overaged and overweight Russians in attendance in 1993 projected a nearly identical image to their Soviet predecessors, and their rhetoric about specialists from the two countries working together rang a familiar bell.

But there were two differences.

The Russians were speaking with a degree of sincerity that had been absent, both in emotion and deeds, thirty years earlier. When Chernomyrdin spoke of embracing the many new opportunities for mutually beneficial relationships, he was dramatically understating the situation that had resulted from the new Westward orientation of the country.

The second difference was Al Gore. The youthful vice president appeared to be half the age of his Russian counterparts, and he spoke with a vibrance and enthusiasm about the future that was seldom heard in Moscow. "Naive optimism," scorned the old Soviet/Russia hands. But Gore truly believed that the new bilateral agreements that had just been signed would change the way of doing business in Russia, and he didn't hesitate to let his feelings ring out.

Two months later, President and Mrs. Clinton also visited Moscow. The president's agenda emphasized arms control measures, including the Russian relationship with Ukraine. But he also presided over the signing of several other cooperative agreements as the portfolio of bilateral agreements grew to include about two dozen programs in science and technology. Among the many fields of interest were biomedical sciences, radiation health research, geological investigations, environmental protection, energy conservation, nuclear-waste remediation, and high-energy physics.

In the early 1960s, the United States and the USSR signed a half-dozen agreements in science and technology. In the early 1970s, a dozen were signed. Now, two decades later, two dozen agreements are on the books. I doubt that there are many more areas of science and technology still to consider. Is it any wonder that the vice president employed several full-time assistants trying to keep track of what was happening under these agreements?[3]

Why Wait for the ISTC?

In late 1993, the U.S. Department of Energy released a list of more than 100 Russian research institutes that had abandoned some of their military programs for more promising cooperative arrangements in civilian-oriented R&D with nineteen American organizations, including six of the national laboratories that operate under the mantle of the department. Most of these international contacts had begun as exploratory exchange visits of technical personnel to identify problems of mutual interest. Then as new economic and political realities unfolded in Russia, much of the cooperation quickly centered on conversion programs at Russian nuclear institutes. A few activities involved other types of Russian weapons specialists as well, including experts in chemical explosion technologies and advanced materials for rocket systems.[4]

From 1992 to 1995, many hundreds of officials and specialists traveled to Russia on behalf of the Department of Energy to establish cooperative programs. Dozens of Russians visited the United States. One group of researchers from Los Alamos Laboratory visited Arzamas–16 on six occasions over a period of two years to participate in joint experiments. Such frequent access to sensitive facilities in Russia was unusual; and Arzamas–16 was one of the most tightly controlled closed cities in the country.

To increase the interest of Russian laboratories in collaboration, the American partners frequently provided funds for Russian air travel to the United States, as well as for lodging and meals. As these liaisons developed, the American institutions began awarding funds to Russian institutes to cover additional costs of their participation, including the costs of salaries and materials. A typical award (or more accurately, a *fixed-price contract*) during the initial days was about $50,000; but some contracts grew into hundreds of thousands of dollars. With these financial incentives, a number of senior officials from the Russian institutes became regular visitors to the United States in search of more work for their laboratories.

The U.S. government expenditures for R&D contracts in Russia soon reached into the millions of dollars, amounts that triggered the panic buttons of American skeptics convinced that the programs were simply feeding the Russian military establishment. In response, U.S. officials felt compelled to emphasize repeatedly the rationale underlying the activities. First, the officials underscored that bargains could be found in Russian laboratories—with labor costs often only 10 percent of the costs of comparable work in the United States. Of course, imports of sophisticated equipment for experiments had increased costs in Russia, 20 percent or more higher than in Europe or the United States, and therefore labor-intensive projects received priority. A second justification for the activities was the importance of engaging Russian weapons scientists in civilian endeavors lest they be tempted to sell their knowledge to countries of proliferation concern. Finally, insights gained about Russian capabilities would contribute to better informed U.S. political, economic, and exchange policies involving Russia, or so the program advocates predicted.

On the way to Arzamas–16 during the early summer of 1994, I encountered the director of Los Alamos Laboratory, who was also traveling to that city. He told me that he viewed his laboratory programs as jump-starts for the ISTC, since their objectives were essentially the same as ISTC objectives. He shared my concern over possible competition between the two organizations for the limited number of senior Russian managers entrusted with leading international projects. For example, both the ISTC and his laboratory were developing projects in environmental protection, nuclear reactor safety, and medical applications of radioisotopes. He noted, however, that the U.S. laboratories, including the Los Alamos Laboratory, would quickly phase out their lab-to-lab programs as soon as the ISTC became operational, and their activities would then be brought under the umbrella of the ISTC.

The U.S. Congress, encouraged by the staffs of Los Alamos and other national laboratories, had different ideas. In 1994, the Department of Energy received $35 million from a congressional appropriation to promote U.S. business interests in cooperation with Russian institutes. The national laboratories were to serve as matchmakers in bringing together Russian researchers with American industry. With this financial boost, cooperative programs increased in number and size, although some American business and industry leaders were reluctant to participate in the Department of Energy initiative. Many companies had already established direct contacts with Russian researchers, and other companies relied on commercial technology brokers who have been matchmaking for almost a decade. The jury is still out as to the degree that this new governmental matchmaking will enhance American business interests.[5]

In any event, the Department of Energy seems destined to play an important role in cooperative activities involving the nuclear weapons laboratories in Russia. Of special importance will be the support provided by the national laboratories to their Russian counterpart institutions in the development of programs for safeguarding Russian nuclear materials, particularly highly enriched uranium and plutonium. The national laboratories have much to contribute in this area, an area of cooperation seemingly more appropriate than their efforts to try to broker arrangements involving U.S. industry.

Together Flying High

In 1994, another major U.S. initiative involving Russian defense specialists came on line as NASA earmarked $400 million for cooperation with Russian technical organizations in supporting the development and operation of the International Space Station Program. The leaders of NASA used some of the same arguments as their Department of Energy counterparts in justifying expenditures in Russia at a time when the agency was laying off technical personnel at its facilities around the United States. "The bargains in Russia are simply too great to resist," stated the NASA administrator before the U.S. Congress.

NASA committed to purchase hardware and services from the Russian space agency and its subcontractors for approximately $100 million per year through 1997 in support of a joint program involving the American Shuttle and the Russian Mir station. Among the specific activities were Russian provision of flight-proven docking mechanisms, joint development of more efficient ways to generate electrical power in space, demonstration of joint operations for extravehicular activity, and commitment of American astronauts to spend up to twenty-four months on board the Russian Mir station. Spending U.S. funds abroad while NASA was downsizing in the United States was repeatedly justified on the basis of the *unique* capabilities offered in Russia.[6]

Within the NASA program, a competitive grants component of $20 million was established for Russian specialists who proposed to conduct R&D activities in support of the Mir Station agenda. The fields of interest identified by NASA were life sciences, space biotechnology, astronomy, geophysics, material sciences, and environmental monitoring. The funds were to be provided to the Russian space agency, which in turn would set up a peer-review program to assess applications and would administer the distribution of the funds.[7]

The Russian aerospace industry desperately needed such a financial boost, since most of their other conversion plans had failed to materialize. A few projects had been initiated with contractors of the U.S. Department of Defense, including McDonnell Douglas, Lockheed, and Rockwell. Overall, however, there were far more plans than action.

Inconsistent Foreign Assistance

In mid-1993 I received an urgent telephone call from an American "industrial expert" who had moved to Nizhny Novgorod for a one-year stint under the auspices of the Agency for International Development (AID). He was the first of several retired American business executives recruited to advise Russian firms on how to go about the process of conversion. He had been in Nizhny Novgorod for several months and had come upon a project that was being developed by Russian submarine experts for the ISTC. The purpose of his call was to urge us to provide the money as soon as possible. He was not interested in the details of the project; he simply assumed that since an American firm was involved, it must be a good project.[8]

A few days later, a second retired business executive called. He was trying to promote conversion in the Moscow area, but he did not know where to start. He had made a few telephone calls to Russian defense-related laboratories offering his expertise, but the Russians were too busy to meet with him. A few months later, yet another group of recently retired business executives who had come to Moscow to help with converting Russian enterprises from military to civilian endeavors contacted us with the same question, "What should we do?"

The ISTC staff was undermanned, and we needed help. These volunteers with impressive credentials could provide us with a new outreach to weapons specialists who might wish to participate in ISTC programs. Therefore, we invited the retirees to visit our offices so that the staff could inform them about our activities, perhaps help open otherwise closed doors for them, and elicit their assistance in our efforts to reach out to as broad a community as possible.

This approach never worked. The volunteers were taking their directions from constantly changing U.S. government officials in Moscow who had little interest in the ISTC, and the business executives were instructed to strike out on their own. The well-intentioned volunteers, new to Russia, finally realized that they were trying to blaze the same trails into the forests that we had already penetrated; they could ride piggyback on our efforts. But by then their tours of duty were over; and they were heading home.

In short, this abbreviated foreign aid effort to use volunteers to make a significant impact on conversion programs in Russia had little payoff. But we learned an important lesson. Conversion is a long-term undertaking, and short-term advisers in an unfamiliar environment have little chance of making much of a difference.

Two related conversion programs of AID were more successful. Both were directed toward offering training opportunities in Western practices for Russians in the United States instead of providing American experts to consult with them on their home turf.

The National Academy of Sciences/National Academy of Engineering has for some time conducted annual competitions for American scientists and engineers who propose to host Russian colleagues, for up to one academic year, at American universities and research centers. Under an AID program, priority has been given to applications from American hosts for Russian specialists who had been working for the military complex.

The visitors carry out individual projects in applied research, particularly in fields with near-term applications. Academy experts hope that channeling the specialists' energies and sharpening their priorities in the civilian sphere will create direct benefits not only to them but eventually to the Russian economy, after they return home to apply their new techniques. A second phase of the program included a seminar in Russia where the exchange participants discussed with American experts the practical problems they were encountering in using the lessons they learned in the United States and steps that might be taken to overcome these problems.

The initial applicant pools for the program were very rich in terms of the high quality of talent and the creative ideas for applied research. The level of the research activities conducted by the Russian scientists in U.S. university and laboratory settings was generally quite high. Of course, the applicability of these experiences in Russia is still being tested. Also, there is always the lingering concern that some of the participants will opt to emigrate from Russia for permanent opportunities in the West.[9]

The Department of Commerce administers a second program involving former weapons specialists, as well as other industrially oriented scientists and engineers. This program places Russian specialists in American companies for shorter time periods, usually no more than several months. Geared heavily toward the projected practicalities of Russian privatization efforts, the program emphasizes Western management and business practices. Again, the transferability of the training experiences to the local scene—and the commitment of the participants to continue to live and work in Russia—are still being tested.[10]

These conversion *exchange* programs have been minor, indeed almost insignificant, components of the AID portfolio of projects in Russia, which in their entirety cost hundreds of millions of dollars each year. The agency's much more extensive activities in the fields of energy and environment could have been of great interest to the ISTC, but there was essentially no connection between the efforts of the two organizations. While AID was not interested in providing direct support to the research activities of those scientists and engineers of concern to the ISTC, a better-coordinated effort could have resulted in greater AID sensitivity to opportunities for developing markets for the products of Russian R&D laboratories, particularly when American technologies proved to be too expensive.

But the more important consideration was that AID's programs were cast in terms of *assistance*, a concept that quickly lost its popularity in Russia—and a label that the ISTC tried to avoid. Russian political leaders were not enthusiastic about being portrayed as beggars, and the general population had difficulty seeing any tangible benefits from assistance. Instead, they watched television and read newspaper accounts angrily reporting the large numbers of highly paid Western consultants charging hundreds of dollars per night to their expense accounts while residing for extended periods at four-star hotels in Moscow.[11]

Russians at all levels were often desperate for money, and they would accept help when it was proferred. But they simply did not want their relationships with the West to be characterized as charity. The time to replace programs of foreign assistance with programs of mutually beneficial cooperation is long overdue.

In brief, the ISTC approach has differed from the AID approach in two significant ways: Russian institutions, not Western consultants, have prepared all documents concerning their ISTC projects; and the Russians managed those projects—including the money—once they were approved. Second, project proposals to the ISTC were not approved unless they offered benefits to the foreign party funding the project.

As discussed in chapter 10, the ISTC approach seemed to offer more models for future programs in Russia than did the AID approach.

Energizing American Companies

A number of American companies that were not simply U.S. government contractors have also played important roles in interacting with Russian weapons laboratories. The U.S. government began sending trade missions to the USSR decades ago. But in the early 1990s, the Department of Commerce intensified its activities to help U.S. businesses identify investment opportunities, with special attention to the latent capabilities of the military-industrial complex for serving both the domestic and foreign markets.[12] The department established trade development offices and American Business Centers in a number of cities. Peace Corps volunteers and American consultants were on location to help identify U.S. sources of goods and services and to assist Russians with the preparation of bankable business plans. Several other government agencies and newly established enterprise funds even offered direct financial support to potential American investors.

Every trade mission reported a litany of reasons why American businesses were not enthusiastic over risking funds in Russia. The list included the absence of laws governing ownership of property, the ever-changing tax requirements, the vague financial regulations, uncertain Russian employment practices affecting expatriates residing in Russia, a vulnerability to confiscation of property and money, rampant crime, and graft and corruption within the government.[13]

In many cases, American companies simply walked away from opportunities to participate in commercial activities in Russia. For example, Merck decided against involvement in vaccine production, even after accepting substantial U.S. government funds for a feasibility study of production opportunities at former biological weapons sites. The company apparently decided that the marketing opportunities and the advantages from the low labor costs in producing vaccines in Russia did not warrant the necessary investment. Also contributing to the decision to forego operations in Russia was the underlying concern that involvement at former biological warfare facilities might result in some retroactive responsibility for past environmental contamination problems that could still linger in the area.

At the same time, a few American companies decided to invest considerable resources in working with Russian weapons experts. For example, Sun Microsystems involved some of the leading Russian defense scientists as computer programmers for their new software. The General Electric Company began working with Russian aerospace experts in the development and production of helicopter engines. The Boeing Company sponsors a number of computer modeling efforts carried out by Russian aerodynamic specialists at its research center in Moscow. The Digital Equipment Corporation initiated a sizable program to provide higher educational institutions, including institutions that had been the breeding grounds for military research specialists, with modern equipment, which could excite interest for further purchases of their products.

Also, as noted earlier, a number of technology middlemen in Russia and abroad have been trying for many years to matchmake Russian technology offerings with foreign commercial opportunities. Of course, many of the larger American firms are already in direct contact with potential sources of technology in Russia and do not need middlemen. But smaller American firms usually lack personnel who can concentrate on the Russian market, and several American consulting organizations have been active technology brokers for them with mixed records of success.[14]

Increasingly, additional American firms are turning to the former weapons community of the USSR as a source of technical manpower to support their programs in Russia. They hire a few of the best and brightest to work in their corporate outposts there. They contract with others who can facilitate access to Russian technological wherewithal and can help circumvent the bureaucratic barriers to doing business in the country.

Occasionally, they encourage Russian specialists to seek financial support from the ISTC to carry out projects of interest to their companies. More often, however, they consider their own financing of counterparts to be cheaper in the long run than waiting out the uncertainty of the ISTC approval process. In any event, they seem more interested in using well-honed Russian skills and proven test facilities than risking their investment capital in exploring new research areas.

The day will come when the ISTC closes its doors. The most likely replacement, at least in the near term, will be an aggregate of increased Russian support for civilian R&D activities at the weapons laboratories and a wider range of foreign investors in Russia who are ready to use the products of such laboratories. But both halves of this combination are still in the incubator stage. More convincing proof is required before the Russian Ministry of Finance will be persuaded that the payoff from R&D warrants major increases in funding. And before many foreign investors will be comfortable committing to Russian technologies, the risks posed by chaotic legal and business practices must be dramatically reduced.

Improving the Prospects for Survival of Russian Research

The leaders of almost every industrialized country recognize the long-term importance of maintaining an active program of *basic* research. They believe that basic research can contribute to educational efforts to provide the needed manpower of the future. Basic research can provide windows into the scientific and technological advances of other countries and can occasionally produce unexpected discoveries that have a major social or economic payoff. Of course, the central issues are "How much research?" and "Which areas of research?"

Several American programs have contributed to maintaining the remnants of a basic research infrastructure within Russia. In particular, for many years the National Science Foundation and the National Institutes of Health have supported cooperation in a range of the basic sciences. Recently, the Soros Foundation provided temporary relief for thousands of impoverished basic scientists who were literally cut adrift in the downsizing of the economy. Most recently, the Howard Hughes Medical Institute has initiated a program of research grants for biomedical scientists in Russia and other countries of the former Soviet

Union. The initial thirty-two awards for Russians averaged about $125,000 over five-year periods. Several American professional groups, and particularly societies of physicists, mathematicians, and astronomers, have raised funds to support colleagues in Russia. These private efforts have been important; and a significant portion of the current basic research effort in the country has been tied to these programs.[15]

Thus, considering support of both basic research and technology-oriented activities, the American involvement in Russian R&D activities since 1991 has been very extensive. In the short run, this involvement has helped maintain enthusiasm and momentum within the Russian R&D community. Indeed, without the involvement of Americans and other foreigners, most Russian R&D would have come to a halt.

In the long run, however, the foreign inundation of Russian R&D efforts could also have negative effects. Specifically, when the Soros-financed program ends, the Russian basic research community will surely feel let down; and the brain drain may increase. Similarly, if substantial programs of cooperation do not fill the void when U.S. foreign assistance programs end, exchange activities will rapidly disappear. Interest in working in Russian R&D institutes without foreign umbilical cords will decline accordingly.

A New Course for the United States

The arguments for a continued high level of U.S. involvement in science and technology developments in Russia are persuasive. The United States clearly has strong national interests in participating in the evolution of a new Russia—a Russia that provides access to vast untapped storehouses of natural resources; a Russia that has a highly educated and skilled population that has made countless contributions to the worlds of science and culture; and a Russia that must shed the legacies of the Cold War and become a responsible member of the international community.

The United States still remains a preferred partner over a number of countries, including Germany and Japan, in the eyes of many Russians, and has unique opportunities to influence the course of developments in Russia—politically, economically, militarily, and technologically. Similarly, U.S. governmental, commercial, and scientific organizations can benefit substantially from Russia's experience and achievements in many areas of common interest.

But two cautions are offered. First, some American organizations are simply trying too hard to participate in too many aspects of Russian R&D. The number of Russian officials and scientific leaders who are available even to talk with visitors, let alone lead joint projects, is limited; and the lines of foreign consultants waiting to propose new initiatives to the same cast of Russians reflect the overloading of a system that has not yet shed all the barnacles of the past era of central control.

Second, cooperative programs involving American scientists and engineers are important if the United States is to stay abreast of Russian achievements. Such cooperation also provides opportunitites to remind Russian researchers continuously that somebody really cares about their activities and that someone is waiting for the next experimental report. But, politicizing these activities often causes false expectations. The Russian and American governments would be wise to reduce their fascination with press releases that announce the latest R&D agreement. Their specialists need the freedom to cooperate on their own time schedules in a sustained and quiet manner. Collaborative goals are better served by projects of three to five years than by the many short-term, quick-fix efforts that are politically appealing but seldom have a lasting impact.

Finally, several new programmatic efforts are suggested. At the top of the list, as AID phases out its programs of assistance in Russia, foreign assistance funds should be used for establishing a program for the next five to ten years that will support important applied R&D efforts in Russia of interest also to U.S. institutions. Precedents for such *foreign assistance departure programs* exist in other parts of the world. Two examples are the business-oriented promotional program initiated in the early 1990s on the eve of AID's departure from Thailand and the support of the Korean Advanced Institute of Science as AID withdrew from South Korea twenty years ago. Also, the experience of an American-Israeli binational foundation in supporting industrial research in Israel that was established by the two governments provides useful insights as to how such a program can become self-sustaining using commercial profits from investments in research.

Also, the World Bank has become a major force on the financial scene in Moscow. The U.S. government should ensure that the bank adds the development of the R&D infrastructure to its portfolio of activities in Russia. Given the long lead times required to develop programs within the bank, starting now could help the Ministry of Science and Technology Policy develop approaches that would be supportable by the international lending community at a later date, when the course of the Russian economy and the support to be played by the scientific community is clearer.

Finally, while the defense and industrial enterprise funds established for Russia by the United States are a step toward increasing U.S. investments, more ambitious programs should be considered. For example, one group of American economists has prepared a program of government guarantees whereby American companies would recoup most of their investments in technology-intensive industrial facilities if the efforts collapsed. This initiative could help offset German and Japanese efforts to skim the best of Russian technological wherewithal for commercial benefit. The investments would be used largely to purchase goods and services in the United States, with each investor committed to an effort of at least five years. If, and only if, the investments do not bear fruit to cover their investments after five years of sustained effort would the American companies be eligible for reimbursement of portions of their original investments.[16]

Another bold initiative, the establishment of a Technology Commercialization Fund, is presented in Chapter 10.

Reinforcing Russian Initiatives

While this chapter has emphasized steps that have been and can be taken by American institutions to participate constructively in Russian R&D, especially in downsizing the military R&D effort, such steps are not nearly as important as the measures adopted by the Russian government and Russian institutions. U.S. government agencies need frequent reminding that cooperative programs can be most effective if they are designed to support Russian initiatives, rather than simply promote Western initiatives.

One innovative Russian effort was attempted several years ago. The Russian Academy of Sciences set up a joint company with American partners in Washington, D.C., to market the products of the research laboratories of the academy.[17] Several Russian scientists had previously attempted such an arrangement in Geneva. Neither effort has been very successful. But it is encouraging that at least a few Russians are reaching out for new approaches that will actively engage Americans, instead of simply waiting for American businessmen to knock on their doors with proposed deals of dubious benefit to the Russian partners.

The hallmark of U.S. activities intended to benefit Russia should be efforts that reinforce, not lead, those programs developed by Russian individuals and institutions, programs that are consistent with American perceptions of the future of the country. Of course, most U.S. programs have dual objectives of helping American as well as Russian institutions. In practice, the real challenge is to develop projects *jointly*, with neither side trying to dominate the arrangement.

Chapter 10

Replicating the ISTC Model

Model: set an example, set the pace, lead the way.
Roget's International Thesaurus, Fifth Edition, 1992

The Closing Political Window in Russia

During a visit to Washington in early 1995, a senior Russian official who had been instrumental in the establishment of the ISTC stated, "Because of rising nationalist sentiment throughout the country, Russia will never be able to negotiate that kind of agreement again." He added, "We had better take full advantage of the ISTC now that we have it."

This diplomat clearly believed that the Russian government had made unusual *concessions* in exchange for the financial contributions of the foreign parties to the ISTC Agreement. In his eyes, it would no longer be possible to agree anew on the provisions of the ISTC Agreement relating to tax exemptions, customs waivers, and diplomatic privileges for persons associated with the Center's activities, nor to agree on the provisions of the ISTC Statute concerning intellectual property rights and access to closed facilities.

These issues had dominated debates in the Supreme Soviet. Then the state Duma wrestled with ratification of such concessions. "Even if ratification is achieved, this should not be considered a precedent for other agreements," warned the diplomat.

In both the old and new parliaments, loud voices have opposed foreign infringement on the internal affairs of Russia. To many Russian politicians, the continuing economic crisis within the country and the ever-growing restlessness of scientists are less and less important in comparison with the legislators' publicly popular outcries to defend sovereign rights and prevent foreign influence on national security decisions. In any event, continued political bickering among the many

Russian political factions suggest that the Duma will probably have great difficulty in coming to any consensus in the near future on a topic that intermingles critical financial, security, foreign policy, and internal sovereignty issues.

The ISTC exists and will continue to function unless the Duma takes action to dismantle it. And the size of the Center's constituency of local advocates increases with the signing of each project agreement. Indeed, some members of the Duma have even begun lobbying for their favorite projects. As long as the ISTC member states and the Secretariat do not abuse their prerogatives, both the growing corps of Russia's investigative reporters and the opponents of the Center concept will have difficulty finding fault. Most important, as long as the funds keep flowing and the weapons specialists remain content, the ISTC has a good chance of surviving all but the most violent political turmoil within Russia.

A Report Card for the ISTC

In March 1995, U.S. officials in the White House Office of Science and Technology Policy asked me to prepare an evaluation of the progress of the ISTC and to report my findings at a seminar in Washington two weeks later. Fortuitously, I had planned to visit Moscow during the week following this request. Therefore, while in Russia I met with the staff of the ISTC and with a number of other ISTC-watchers, and I prepared a report card on the Center. I then asked a senior Russian official who was very knowledgeable about the detailed workings of the ISTC to prepare his own report card, and we compared our results.

Our evaluations centered on the following questions:

- Had important Russian specialists of proliferation concern become engaged in ISTC projects?
- Were the financial and technical rewards of working on ISTC projects sufficient to offset financial enticements that might be proferred by others interested in obtaining weapons know-how from the project participants?
- Did the projects encourage weapons specialists to switch their careers to peaceful endeavors?
- Were the projects contributing to the transition within Russia to a market-based economy through changes in management ap-

proaches, changes in financial approaches, and/or efforts to commercialize research products?

- Were the projects contributing to a revitalized civilian science base of the country?
- Did the projects effectively link weapons and civilian specialists in common peaceful endeavors?
- Did the projects bring weapons scientists into the mainstream of international civilian science?
- Were the projects encouraging openness in formerly closed facilities?
- Was the ISTC effectively coordinating Western and Japanese efforts directed to common objectives?
- Did the Center respond to Russian conversion priorities?
- Were the administrative procedures of the ISTC effective and efficient?
- Were the Center's financial operations efficient and fiscally sound?

In all categories, the ISTC was performing amazingly well. Using the Russian system of scoring 5 for outstanding and 1 for poor, I gave the Center an overall 4+. My Russian colleague, who independently scored the Center, came out with a 5–.

We both gave very high marks to the speed and efficiency with which the Center had committed the initial $50 million that would employ 6,000 scientists and engineers. (Within six months, these numbers climbed to commitments of $75 million and 10,500 participating specialists.)

We both were mightily impressed with the management and financial accounting changes that had been implanted in the institutions where ISTC projects were located. For the first time, project managers below the levels of institute directors and deputy directors were given full responsibility for ensuring that large projects were carried out in a way determined by the researchers themselves and that all funds associated with the projects were carefully guarded from diversions.

We strongly differed on one important point. I felt that too large a portion of the projects was devoted to basic research; thus, the Center would have little impact on the economic development of the country. My colleague argued that the ISTC had not been structured to accommodate technology commercialization activities and therefore should not be criticized in this regard. He quickly added that this vacuum area needed prompt attention.

We also had different perspectives on the impact of the Center in encouraging weapons specialists to switch from military to civilian research careers. I noted that most of the participants in ISTC projects committed only 50–75 percent of their time to the projects, each apparently keeping a foot in the weapons area as well. My Russian colleague responded that many former weaponeers maintained a toehold in other activities of the institutes lest they lose the social and retirement benefits that were not covered by the ISTC. In any event, we both agreed that the longer the ISTC is in business, the more meaningful will be the incentives for career switching.

Of course, I could hardly be classified as a fully objective evaluator of ISTC activities, having had a personal hand in almost every aspect of the management systems established and in all the projects approved during the early days. Obviously, I felt very pleased when the parties to the ISTC Agreement formally characterized the ISTC as "very successful" at about the same time as my own evaluation of it—six months after I had left Moscow.[1]

Learning Lessons from the Diplomats and Scientists

What have been the diplomatic lessons learned in establishing an organization in Russia that apparently works without harassment, without graft or corruption, with a minimal staff, but with a sizable budget? What can be gleaned from examining the many breadcrumbs on the path from diplomatic handshakes to program action? What can be learned from the practical experiences in changing bearers of high-tech swords into inventors of high-tech plowshares?

Most important, can the strengths of the ISTC approach be replicated for other programs, in Russia, in other states of the former Soviet Union, in more distant countries? Can the approaches to harnessing weapons specialists be transferred to encouraging other specialists to channel their energies in desirable directions? Can some components of the diplomatic framework for multilateral governance be replicated in other settings involving the same or other governments?

The concept of a small, special-purpose international organization directed to a narrow task is not new. Such organizations have been spawned by larger international bodies, particularly the United Nations. In these cases, however, the organizations have been closely linked to the parental bodies.

Also, in recent years several special-purpose organizations, independent of any organizational parent, have been established in fields closely related to the interests of the ISTC. For example, a large number of countries are setting up a new organization to monitor the implementation of an international agreement banning chemical warfare activities. In addition, the United States, the European Union, Japan, and Russia have established a new organization to implement the International Thermonuclear Experimental Reactor Program, which is dedicated to international action that should bring fusion energy closer to reality.

But in one significant respect, the ISTC is unique. This international organization focuses its attention on supporting specific kinds of individuals. The contents of the projects are obviously important; but the overriding aspect is the backgrounds of individuals who participate in the projects, name by name and speciality by speciality. No other international organization, or indeed national organization, is so heavily focused on the backgrounds and roles of so many individual participants in projects funded from abroad.

The Principal Pillars of the ISTC Approach

The experience of the ISTC in nurturing highly qualified specialists, especially experienced scientists and engineers, is one of the most significant contributions to the international community of the ISTC model. This attention to brainpower began when the diplomats considered the character of ISTC projects. But most important, this *focus on people* spreads throughout all aspects of the organization's activities— with continued attention to the details of who participates in projects, the roles of individual participants, and how participants are to be rewarded. These three strands—sometimes referred to as "detailed minutiae" by Russian institute directors not accustomed to outsiders prying into how they manage their staffs—are at the core of the ISTC concept.

Another principle of broad international applicability, particularly in the foreign assistance arena, has been the Center's insistence that *project proposals and project workplans genuinely reflect the interests of the Russian scientists and engineers who will carry them out.* The

Center welcomes the reactions of foreign experts to the proposals of the Russians. Indeed, the Russian institutions themselves are interested in such views and seriously consider foreign reactions and suggestions concerning their ideas. But Russian institutions prepare all project documents to be considered by the Center, and these documents are defended by Russian specialists, not foreign experts. Also, groups of specialists in Russian institutions, not foreign middlemen, have the technical responsibility and financial accountability for carrying out the projects. In short, foreign collaborators reinforce, but do not lead, the efforts.

Many American organizations, particularly those that have had large foreign assistance contracts for work in Russia or elsewhere, challenge this faith in Russian capabilities. They apparently are convinced that Russians cannot, on their own, design or carry out sophisticated projects—Western style. And Russians clearly could not responsibly handle the money, argue the cynics. Of course, this same attitude is frequently encountered in developing countries where expatriates regularly bemoan the inadequacies of available manpower for designing and carrying out projects.

But the ISTC experience shows that, at least in Russia, the capabilities of the scientists and engineers, and even their accountants, to adjust to Western standards are regularly underestimated. Sometimes the Russians themselves underestimate their abilities.

A third major lesson from the ISTC effort is *the importance of careful and detailed planning of the policy framework*, carried out jointly by all concerned governments. The results of that planning were codifed in about a dozen *agreed* documents ranging from a formal international agreement to administrative procedures within the Secretariat. Once this legal-financial-adminstrative framework was established, the Secretariat avoided many of the problems that beset start-up operations, particularly activities within new multilateral institutions. In Russia, it is crystal clear that a slow start onto a fast track has many long-term advantages over a fast getaway into a swamp.

The key triad of considerations extracted from the ISTC experience in corralling weaponeers into peaceful arenas might be called a high-tech people focus based on local initiative within an agreed management framework, or a PLA approach. As discussed later, the PLA approach would seem applicable to a variety of technical cooperation, foreign assistance, and counterproliferation efforts.

Opening the International Umbrella for Other Programs

Of course, the easiest way to diffuse the ISTC experience is simply to bring other programs into the ISTC tent. From the beginning of the negotiation of the ISTC Agreement, the diplomats considered the possibility of using the legal, policy, and organizational framework of the Center as an umbrella for programs and projects that might be of interest but could not be predicted at the outset. Article Ten of the Agreement states:

> Although nothing in this Agreement limits the rights of the Parties to pursue projects without resort to the Center, the Parties shall make their best efforts to use the Center when pursuing projects of character and objectives appropriate to the Center.

Keeping in mind the observations of the Russian official that the adoption of the ISTC Agreement was a one-time event, we should not be surprised that the parties to the Agreement have considered the possibility of bringing bilateral projects under the ISTC umbrella.

As stated in the Agreement, the key consideration is the compatibility with the objectives of the ISTC of a new program that might take refuge from the tax inspector by moving under the mantle of the Center and/or might focus multilateral attention on an approach that one party considers to have been neglected by the other parties in the past.

Specific policy issues will undoubtedly arise if the reach of the ISTC is to expand. For example, the initial ISTC projects have been almost exclusively oriented toward engaging large numbers of scientists and engineers with expertise related to weapons of mass destruction. Should this criterion be broadened to accommodate projects of interest to one party that emphasize support of specialists who are experts in conventional weaponry? Could projects that engage only a small percentage of weaponeers and larger numbers of civilian specialists be included?

As a second area of potential interest, the initial ISTC projects called for transferring cash to the Russian participants. Could projects that provide equipment but not cash for the Russian participants be included within the ISTC framework?

Other questions relate to the details of the project approval and project implementation process for special programs to be funded only by one country. For example, should the Governing Board assume an additional burden of approving each individual bilateral project, no matter how small, coming into the framework of the ISTC, or could the board simply approve the overall parameters of the new program? Could board members request that specialists from their countries participate in new bilateral projects being developed and funded by others? Should there be any relaxation of the rights and obligations of the Secretariat in ensuring that a bilateral project is carried out in a responsible fashion?

A final concern is whether the Secretariat has the necessary administrative wherewithal to accept expanded responsibilities for new types of projects. The Center is still in its embryonic stage. The Secretariat staff is small and often overextended. The risk of financial scandals in the absence of constant vigilance cannot be dismissed. Placing an additional burden, particularly a new type of burden, on an unprepared Secretariat could lead to neglect of the core set of ISTC activities.

These questions have probably been raised more than once in Washington, Tokyo, Brussels, and Moscow. The answers will determine whether the ISTC continues to pursue a modest but tightly controlled and predictable program, sharply focused on a well-identified group of specialists. The alternative is for the Center to take on a broader responsibility of providing an administrative framework for a more diverse set of activities that reach other groups of Russian specialists and provide larger financial resources.

Broadening the Program's Reach to Use Technology

The parties to the ISTC Agreement should be thinking more boldly by addressing the central issues of industrial conversion and economic development that are facing Russia, instead of expending a great deal of political energy simply turning the ISTC into a Christmas tree with more lightweight basic research ornaments.

During our stay in Russia from 1992 to 1994, I witnessed a continuing decline in productivity of all sectors—in the institutes, in the factories, and in the fields. Surely, this decline would have to bottom out soon, for there was little additional free-fall space, or so we thought.

Then in March 1995, I learned that within the military-industrial complex, production of military goods had declined by an additional 36 percent and production of civilian goods by 21 percent during 1994.

Such statistics could have dire consequences for the proliferation of advanced technologies. First, within the enterprises are thousands of the "dangerous" people of interest to the ISTC. Second, the enterprises of the military-industrial complex have been customers for Russian R&D institutions; as their production potential shrinks even further, their interest in supporting civilian R&D activities dwindles accordingly. Finally, should the civilianized weapons researchers develop commercially interesting products, they increasingly face the atrophy of the manufacturing capabilities that could provide a basis for commercialization of their inventions.

While a continuing slump in the military-industrial complex may be good news for those nonproliferation experts concerned about Russia's exports of military hardware, for others concerned about the exports of technologies, a sick military-industrial complex could have very negative implications.

As discussed in Chapter 7, for the past five years many Western countries have been interested in the conversion of Russian enterprises. The conventional wisdom in the West has been that the only way conversion will work is for Western firms to move in and establish partnerships with Russian counterparts, since the Russians don't know how to do it alone. In short, the foreigners should bring the management know-how, while the Russians contribute the skilled manpower and facilities.

But who provides the money? He who pays the piper calls the tune. And the Russians have been unable to provide funds even to pay salaries, let alone invest in new types of production. Thus, in some cases, the Russians are more than ready to follow the foreign pipers; in others, they are not.

Hundreds of trade missions have visited Russia in search of investment opportunities attractive to the West. While there have been some success stories, a large industrial potential remains idle. Meanwhile, because of a lack of capital, Russian enterprises have had very little opportunity to demonstrate what they can do on their own in the technical and managerial arenas.

Given the substantial untapped capabilities in the military-industrial complex together with the experience of the ISTC showing that Russian technologists can indeed develop solid projects if there is real money available, I suggest that a new Technology Commercialization Fund be established within the framework of the ISTC. The fund would support its own set of projects while having all the legal and diplomatic benefits associated with the ISTC.

Specifically, a fund with an initial capitalization of $100 million dedicated to supporting the introduction into commercial production of particularly promising technological ideas of the highly talented Russian workforce could be an important factor in the conversion of significant components of the military-industrial complex.

For example, the city of Samara needs new energy sources. A nearby defense plant has developed very relevant gas turbine technologies. With investment capital of about $3 million, the city could have a new power station that could be amortized over a few years; a number of dangerous engineers would be employed in the civilian sector; and a portion of an important production facility would be civilianized.

Another example concerns the oil industry. Russian and foreign oil companies import steel pipe from the West. The manufacturers of Russian pipe that served the military industry have been handicapped in procurement competitions because they do not produce pipe with threads and other features that meet Western specifications. With a modest investment, these former defense plants could become competitive in a highly lucrative domestic market.

Two additional examples can be found at the Moscow enterprise that designed and produced Russia's antimissile missile. The specialists are ready to produce 10,000 radio telephones for the rapidly emerging markets throughout the country. They contend that all they need is a *loan* of $1.5 million for this initial production run and for the relay stations. They estimate that they will recoup the investment costs within two years. Also, this enterprise is seeking about one-half that sum to support the initial production of devices for scanning human livers suspected of being diseased. They claim that these devices are more sensitive than Western devices that sell for three times the estimated Russian price. While the viability of each of these proposals needs to be investigated more thoroughly, such investigations will not occur without the stimulus of real money for those who can make persuasive techno-economic arguments.

Projects supported by the new fund would differ considerably from the current ISTC projects, although the philosophy of direct funding of the Russian institutions and participants would not change. Specifically, each project would be directly linked to commercialization and could include limited construction of needed manufacturing facilities, the upgrading of production equipment, and pilot production runs.

Probably a smaller portion of the overall costs of the projects would be available for payments to the specialists for their participation than in other ISTC projects.

Consideration could be given to the new fund requiring repayment upon successful commercialization activities. Sensitivity on this issue is necessary, however, lest opponents of the ISTC in the Duma, who could be involved in the eventual ratification of the ISTC Agreement, misinterpret such a scheme as an effort on the part of the Center to become a *commercial* organization.

While the efforts of many countries to support their own companies as they seek a place in the Russian military-industrial complex will continue, a complementary ISTC Technology Commercialization Fund could become an important incentive for Russian military-industrial enterprises that espouse civilian ambitions to "get with the program."

Multilateral or Bilateral Programs?

The U.S. and other governments will undoubtedly continue to carry out a variety of science and technology programs outside the framework of the ISTC. In considering the applicability of the ISTC experience to these programs, the three PLA pillars of the ISTC concept discussed earlier can be important signposts. In addition, some diplomatic and operational experiences of the ISTC may also provide important lessons learned.

Beginning with the frequent debate as to when multilateral approaches should be pursued in lieu of bilateral programs, the ISTC experience has brought into sharp focus the advantages, as well as the liabilities, of Western countries and Japan acting multilaterally, in concert with Russia. In a nutshell, the advantages of the multilateral approach have been the following:

- Additional political clout in applying pressure on a sluggish and sometimes hesitant Russian bureaucracy for promised actions, clout that the ISTC has exercised through coordinated demarches of its members, through the collective deliberations of the board, and through the pressure of the Secretariat on Russian officials.
- A high degree of intergovernmental coordination of program activities from inception of an idea to completion of an activity.
- Substantial insulation of program activities from the political va-

garies of bilateral political relations between Russia and the other member countries, particularly the United States.

- A reduction in the number of staff members needed to carry out complementary programs supported by different parties, since the Secretariat serves the needs of all members.

Of course, the major drawback of decision making by consensus has been the longer lead times needed, first to move the Center concept forward and then to launch individual projects. Whatever the advantages of operating through the Center or establishing or using other multilateral mechanisms for other programs, each country will want to retain the flexibility, speed, and political trappings associated with acting bilaterally with the Russian government.

For example, programs in Russia of the U.S. Departments of Defense and Energy and of NASA involve the active participation of substantial numbers of former Russian weapons scientists and engineers who are exploring civilian pursuits. Indeed, in certain cases, the same Russian specialists participate part-time in these bilateral programs and part-time in ISTC projects.

These bilateral programs are carried out under the diplomatic protection of the U.S. Embassy in Moscow, and therefore they are able to circumvent certain taxes and custom charges that plague many private efforts. But these programs do not enjoy the personal income tax waivers for Russian participants and the rights of foreign access to project sites set forth in the ISTC Agreement and Statute. Further, the ISTC intellectual property ground rules do not apply.

Turning to foreign assistance in Russia, the U.S. programs have the administrative advantage of being considered as humanitarian aid, even though the bilateral agreement governing U.S. assistance efforts in Russia is very vague.[1] Also, the embassy provides a diplomatic conduit for many AID activities.

Nevertheless, AID could well take a leaf from the ISTC diary, particularly the one related to the transfer of funds into and within Russia, and refine their procedures as appropriate. Indeed, AID often justifies its practice of transferring funds to American organizations and not directly to Russian organizations on the grounds that it has no way to keep track of funds given to Russian entities. The ISTC philosophy is just the opposite: provide the funds earmarked for Russia to Russians and not to middlemen.

AID also points to the Russian reputation for mismanagement to buttress its philosophy that Russian institutions want and need advisers more than they need money. Of course, given the choice between advisers or nothing, Russian institutions take advisers with the hope that they will lead to money. In some cases, such as establishing stock markets, American expertise can be important. But Russian institutions are sufficiently sophisticated to know when they truly need advice and not simply the next American consultant off the plane because he comes free of charge.

Finally, many U.S. agencies carrying out programs of scientific and technical collaboration are encountering some of the same problems that the ISTC spent many months resolving. These problems relate to payments to Russian institutions, to procurement of equipment and warranties in Russia, to hiring local consultants, to arranging customs clearances, to organizing local communication networks, to arranging for space, and to auditing and monitoring project activities. The experience of the ISTC is very relevant and should help other U.S. governmental activities in the country.

Thus, it seems that the ISTC experience provides valuable lessons for other programs that have been or will be established in Russia. But are these experiences relevant in other political and technical settings?

An ISTC Clone in Ukraine

Originally, the diplomats negotiating the ISTC Agreement had planned for the Center to provide financial support to weapons specialists from all interested states of the CIS. In late 1992, however, the United States, joined by Sweden and Canada, decided for political reasons that a separate center should be established in Ukraine. Japan subsequently agreed to this plan.

The establishment of an independent center in Kiev does not mean that Ukraine cannot also be a member of the ISTC; for more than eighteen months after the political agreement that a separate center would be appropriate, the Ukrainian government actively explored how it might also join the ISTC.

Two reasons for such membership in the Moscow center in addition to membership in an independent center in Kiev became apparent. First, EU funds would be available only through the ISTC in Moscow, since the European Union was not scheduled to become a member of the Ukraine center. Second, ISTC membership would be important if joint projects involving Russia were undertaken, such as projects related to the effects of the Chernobyl reactor accident, which contaminated lands in Russia and Belarus as well as in Ukraine.

But the center in Kiev, named the International Science Center of Ukraine (ISCU), will presumably be the principal international mechanism for financing the conversion efforts of former weapons specialists in Ukraine. The R&D specialists were involved primarily in the development of rocket technology, with an estimated 11 percent of the Soviet effort in rocketry having been concentrated in Ukraine. Only a handful of nuclear, biological, and chemical scientists and engineers were in the mainstream of Soviet weapons development, although a substantial number had worked pursuant to defense contracts on the periphery of mainstream activities.

Despite the limited number of specialists in Ukraine of proliferation concern, the diplomats conceived ISCU as a full-service organization with its approach patterned after the approach of the ISTC. The underlying international agreement and statute are quite similar to the ISTC documents, and other management documents of the ICSU draw heavily on the ISTC experience.

The establishment of the ICSU encountered many of the same problems that had emerged in Moscow. The political delay within the Ukrainian government extended over many months. Once an agreement was formally adopted by Ukraine, the United States, Canada, and Sweden, further delays with the Ukrainian government arose before the first projects could be undertaken. A facility for the Secretariat was a problem. The Ukrainian Foreign Ministry was slow in according the promised diplomatic privileges to the staff and other participants in ISCU activities, and the tax inspectors in Ukraine were no more enthusiastic about exemptions than their colleagues in Russia.

Finally, by late 1995, the Governing Board of the ISCU had scheduled its first meeting. The process of developing and approving project proposals began in a serious way.

The initial financial commitments to the ISCU were less than $15 million. Nevertheless, in comparison with commitments to the ISTC that serve a much larger number of weaponeers posing proliferation dangers, the budget is reasonable and indeed relatively large. At the same time, an administrative apparatus rivaling in complexity the apparatus in Moscow will be required if the same procedures are followed. Thus, there is a great incentive to streamline procedures in Kiev, lest much of the available funding be swallowed up in administrative overhead.

While the ISCU is not an identical twin of the ISTC, it comes close to being a fraternal twin.

Redirecting Weaponeers in North Korea

"Tell me more," was the reaction of a senior U.S. official when I set forth the proposition that an ISTC-type approach might be useful in keeping high-tech North Korean scientists out of trouble.

I proceeded to make the following points:

- A program to engage North Korean scientists and engineers in international collaborative activities would introduce a new dimension of openness into that country.
- If North Korean specialists were involved in peaceful endeavors, they would have less time to devote to dangerous activities. Their country, as well as the participants in the program, would benefit.
- Since the standard of living in North Korea is low, the costs of providing salaries to attract very good specialists to civilian projects would not be a major hurdle.
- The future of North Korea is of vital regional importance to South Korea and Japan, and these two countries would eagerly participate in such an arrangement. Perhaps even China and Russia would be interested.

With a cautious nod, my acquaintance said, "You're right. It is all a matter of time. Our relations with North Korea need to be sufficiently well developed to introduce such a concept."

I left this informal meeting determined to try to help accelerate the timetable for improved relations with North Korea. I hope that in the not too distant future, serious consideration will be given to an ISTC-type approach to cooperation between that country and several other countries with deeply rooted interests in developments on the Korean peninsula.

Rebuilding the Intellectual Capacity of
Bosnia, Croatia, and Serbia

The relevance of the ISTC model is not limited to the nuclear and rocket arenas. Serbia, Croatia, and to a lesser extent Bosnia had well-developed scientific, agriculture, health, and higher educational institutions before the war. While many were controlled by persons selected on the basis of political loyalties rather than merit, the institutions nevertheless housed an impressive number of very capable specialists. Now the institutions are almost all in poor condition. Some have been destroyed or badly damaged. Others are run down and in a state of disrepair. Almost all the staffs are seriously depleted, demoralized, or both.

Once the fighting ceases, the United States and the European Union probably will make significant funding available for humanitarian relief and assistance in reviving the economies and rebuilding the nations of the region. An ISTC-type approach could help ensure that funds available for rebuilding scientific, higher educational, agricultural, and medical institutions are used wisely and expeditiously. This model also would ensure that officials of the interested donors are directly involved in overseeing projects in the region, in preference to the customary approach of placing implementation responsibilities in the hands of Western intermediary organizations such as Western universities or relief agencies.

The ISTC model does not seem appropriate for humanitarian relief, economic stabilization, or reconstruction of the transportation, communication, power, or water infrastructures of the countries. These important activities will need large transfers of credits, goods, and services from the West, as contrasted to supporting the rebuilding of the intellectual capability of local institutions, which is a *people problem*. The ISTC was designed to solve people problems.

In the absence of a new international mechanism (discussed below), the United States and the European Union have several choices in confronting the people problem. They could transfer funds to the three counterpart governments in mutually agreed priority areas with these governments responsible for defining the projects and handling the funds themselves. But few specialists who have lived in the former Yugoslavia have any confidence that the governments would distribute the funds on the basis of merit or indeed on the basis of any objective criteria.

Alternatively, the Western donors could rely on intermediary non-governmental organizations (NGOs) with strong ties in the region that could channel funds to the most worthy recipients as decided by the NGOs themselves or in partnership with the governments involved. In addition to the costs of supporting the NGOs, such a proposal invites unnecessary competition and confusion among many Western organizations, establishes multiple approval levels within the NGOs and the governments, creates an accounting nightmare, and opens the possibility of favoritism through "old boy" networks.

Lastly, the financing countries could work through a UN agency that would either collect and distribute funds or simply serve as a coordinator for either of the first two approaches. Unfortunately, there usually is little value added from interposing a role, and a new layer of authority, for a bureaucratically inflated UN organization.

My proposal calls for establishment of a special-purpose intergovernmental Development Center for a period of approximately five years. One Center could be set up to service all three countries (Bosnia, Croatia, Serbia); or, if absolutely necessary for political reasons, three Centers with nearly identical structures and served by the same Secretariat could be set up to keep the activities within Bosnia, Croatia, and Serbia politically separate.

Drawing on the Moscow experience, the United States and the European Union, and Japan and Russia if politically desirable, in concert with the local governments, would establish this new Development Center headquartered in the region. It would be under the supervision of an intergovernmental Governing Board and the directorship of a Western executive director supported by a small multinational staff. The Center would operate pursuant to an international agreement and statute and would develop standards for project proposals and contractual agreements with recipients of funds. It would ensure timely review of proposals by experts and governments, and it would provide an international pledging forum for officials to decide which projects should be funded by which governments. The Center's Secretariat would serve as the vehicle for transferring funds from the donor countries to the selected project recipients, for monitoring and auditing project activities, and for receiving and disseminating reports on the projects. (Sound familiar?)

As with the ISTC, the Center would have several important characteristics. First, staff members would be seconded to the Secretariat by the participating countries, with no need for a new personnel system. Second, program funds made available through the center would be used only to cover the costs of local specialists and institutions, with the expenses of foreign partners in the projects covered by other funding mechanisms established as necessary in each donor country.

Most important, pursuant to the ISTC model of a two-step approval/funding process, all projects would be approved by a consensus vote of the Governing Board; then the members of the board would pledge the funds to support those approved projects of special interest to the respective countries. This consensus reduces the likelihood of unnecessary overlaps with other projects of the individual countries and discourages the support of projects that do not measure up. Project funds from the donors would not be pooled, but each government would retain control of its project funds until releasing them to the Center on a project-by-project basis for supporting those projects selected by that government.

After funds are released by the donors for specific projects, the donors can remain directly involved, to the extent desired, in all aspects of implementation. After all, the International Development Center would be an intergovernmental organization working under the direction of a board composed of the representatives of the donors.

There are several advantages:

- The Center, reflecting the interests of the donors as well as the local governments, would provide one-stop shopping for local specialists and institutions in search of financial support.
- Local specialists, not foreign experts, would generate the project proposals that are truly of interest to them, with the foreign governments having review and approval rights.
- All project funds transferred by donors to the Center would end up in the hands of local specialists and institutions, not in the hands of consultants.
- The on-the-ground presence of a Secretariat, under the direction of the participating governments, would ensure a responsiveness to real needs and a high level of confidence in ensuring technical and financial performance by project recipients.
- The solid legal basis for the Center would avoid many problems related to the status of projects and the handling of funds.

A big concern is not to create an unwieldy international bureaucracy. The Moscow experience indicates that a lean and effective Center can be established from ground zero even in a difficult operating
environment, and with a minimum of delay. Indeed, creating the organization anew is a great advantage in avoiding the accretion of dead
wood that plagues almost all well-established international organizations. The concerned governments are already well up on the learning
curve for establishing such a special-purpose international organization
as a result of the Moscow experience, which addressed many complicated management, administrative, and program issues.

If the ISTC model can improve performance in the field of international development assistance, in the former Yugoslavia or elsewhere,
it will make a contribution to the international community with a potentially large multiplier effect.

Other Beneficiaries of the ISTC Experience

Let us now turn to other areas of the world where financial energizing,
drawing on the PLA approach, could encourage more intensive efforts
of scientists and engineers to work for economic development.

One example is in the Middle East, where efforts to improve the quality of life of the Palestinians have been woefully ineffective. The number
of well-trained Palestinian scientists and engineers is impressive, and the
amount of money that countries are willing to commit to the region seems
unlimited. Yet the track record of existing mechanisms for effectively
using the funds in building a viable nation is not very encouraging.

More attention to individuals, more reliance on local initiatives, and
a better consensus on the program framework and legal basis for project activities might provide a much-needed boost for foreign intervention in that region. If considered an equal partner in the undertaking,
the PLO would probably welcome the PLA.

Returning to concerns over the spread of nuclear weapons and
rockets, the time lag for drawing on the experiences of ISTC and the
PLA approach in attracting weapons scientists to peaceful endeavors
in other countries will probably be much longer than in the foreign
assistance area. Perhaps during the next decade, more and more countries will accept the importance of their active involvement in collective security arrangements, particularly with regard to the role of
weapons of mass destruction.

The need to downsize all arsenals of the world should become a popular theme that begins to have an impact on many nations. At the same time, the United States and other nations concerned with proliferation will probably link international security concerns more tightly to international economic issues as the global markets continue to expand in many directions. And, as discussed in Chapter 6, it is important that the proliferation of dual-use technologies should become a more significant determinant of the foreign policies of developing as well as developed countries.

As the security architecture of the world redesigns itself to fit with the new political and economic landscapes, three countries with dangerous weapons capabilities and volatile economic development problems might also be appropriate settings for the PLA approach. The necessary changes will not take place overnight, but they may well be under way during the late 1990s.

First, many countries hope for the early downsizing of the Chinese weapons effort. But what are the incentives for the Chinese to redirect resources from military efforts that enhance political stature to economic priorities that can raise the standard of living?

As the leadership changes, two possible incentives could eventually emerge that would enhance the relevance of the ISTC experience. First, the bait of financial inducements for some weapons specialists to work collaboratively on high-tech projects of broad international interest, perhaps initially on a part-time basis, might be attractive. Second, international pressure for China to become a part of the worldwide effort in *threat reduction*, linked to China's search for global trade markets, might provide an opening. If such an opening develops for the PLA scenario, China would probably have some initial difficulty accepting the focus on people and surely would insist on local initiative and the need for crystal-clear ground rules.

In addition, the troublesome growth of Indian and Pakistani nuclear capabilities might also be targets for the PLA approach. In these two cases, the merits of a focus on people, as well as the importance of local control of projects and clear ground rules, would be more easily understood. The need for economic relief is clear. But acceptance of foreign intrusion into their military programs will depend on progress in diffusing the perceived and actual threats of the buildups across their borders. Perhaps a regional ISTC would not be entirely out of the question.

The ISTC Story Continues to Unfold

We are still in the early days of the ISTC experiment. One hopes that the institution will continue to receive strong support within and outside Russia and the other CIS countries. In the worst case, it could be snuffed out overnight. But in the best case, it could continue to grow in importance as a contributor not only to the conversion of people who can make significant contributions to the scientific backbones of their countries but also to the conversion of industrial facilities producing goods that rely on the efforts of a reoriented workforce.

As an experiment, the ISTC has already been an unequivocal success. It has provided enough data relevant to problems that will be faced in Russia, in other CIS countries, and around the globe to have more than repaid the expenditure of resources and diplomatic energy that has been directed to its operations.

This book has been a first attempt to capture and evaluate the performance data from the ISTC experiment. Now the challenge is to package the conclusions in appropriate security, political, and economic envelopes. The objective must be to help policymakers use the best of the ISTC experiences in addressing the future problems of cooperation with the CIS countries, in supporting conversion at many levels in Russia, in countering the proliferation of weapons of mass destruction and their delivery systems, and in improving approaches to fostering economic development throughout the world.

Meanwhile, the programs of the ISTC offer civilian outplacement services to large numbers of weaponeers from the Soviet era who might otherwise be tempted to accept jobs in areas of their former expertise.

Epilogue

I never think of the future. It comes soon enough.

Albert Einstein

A Difficult Road Home

Our chaotic departure from Moscow was a telling allegory for the bigger canvas that would continue to unfold in Russia. As Carole and I waited for a driver and car to take us to Sheremetevo Airport on the final day of our tour in Moscow, we were torn between our attachment to the Russian people and our desire to resume a more predictable life in northern Virginia. Of course, we felt a certain satisfaction knowing that the flags were flying in the vestibule of the ISTC facility and that several thousand former weapons specialists were beginning to receive steady paychecks. Also, we were relieved to have escaped mishaps and injuries while careening along the icy sidewalks, plunging into the wild traffic and dangerous potholes, and simply living in the midst of burgeoning criminal elements. On the personal side, however, we already sensed a psychological letdown, suspecting that the future chapters of our lives would never match the excitement of the Moscow adventure.

On a deeper level, we were haunted by the uncertainties we were leaving behind—and there implications for the Russian people and indeed for the world.

Several Russian friends had gathered with us to exchange farewells amid a small mountain of suitcases on the sidewalk in front of our apartment building. Even our Chechen neighbor walked by, smiled, and gave a nod.

Despite the many positive forces at work, including the ISTC, the life stories of each of our Russian friends reflected the strains of economic shortfalls and unsettling apprehensions of the future. Each of them cared deeply about how the transition was affecting their fami-

213

lies, especially the safety of their children, and how the next generation of Russians could live with pride and dignity. Also, we could sense that each of them genuinely appreciated the concern in the United States over developments in Russia, a concern that had sent us to their country.

As valuable time passed, the driver we had reserved through the American Embassy simply did not show up; and no one was manning the embassy's emergency telephone number. We had become accustomed to the collapse of well-planned events in Moscow, but we had naively assumed that surely on our day of departure the American Embassy would not let us down. They never had before. Finally, after thirty minutes of nervous pacing, we gave up on our request for transportation, which I had confirmed earlier in the week with three separate telephone calls to the embassy.

Fortunately, one of the former weapons scientists seeing us off had driven to our apartment complex in his small Zhiguli. We gratefully accepted his offer of a lift to the airport, since it was too late to contact a Russian car service and taxis no longer cruised outside the center of the city. Somehow we squeezed our possessions and ourselves into his vehicle. Although it was Saturday morning and traffic was light, the impatient drivers around us insisted as always in driving down the sidewalks whenever such a tactic would let them avoid a momentary delay on the streets—a common sign of freedom run amok.

As we sputtered along the wide boulevard leading from the center of the city to the airport, the gasoline in a rusty can on the shelf of the back seat just behind Carole's head began sloshing about. Soon the car was filled with fumes. But this was not necessarily bad news. The can obviously was not empty, and the car's gas gauge was registering below the scale.

We kept checking the time. Our friend at the wheel tried to soothe our anxieties by recklessly dodging between larger cars to make up for the delay out of the starting blocks. Unfortunately, the hostile driver of one of these oversized vehicles did not appreciate our small bug crowding him. He roared around us and immediately slammed on his brakes, waiting to hear the crunching of our radiator. Miraculously, our brakes worked perfectly; we did not ram the back of the sleek tank in our path. Even the gasoline can cooperated, bouncing harmlessly off Carole's head as she jolted back and forth.

The last straw of our final day in Russia's contemporary version of the Wild West was the debris of a major accident blocking the high-way just two miles from the airport. *Too far to walk and not much time to fret* were my thoughts as we sat motionless on the highway that looked and felt more like a crowded parking lot. But then we experienced the second Russian miracle of the day. The traffic parted, and we darted to the terminal.

Watching through the airplane window the vast landscape of Russia shrinking into the mist, we wondered how much impact the ISTC would ultimately have there. In what directions would the political and economic forces press the people, and just what path would Russia as a nation take as it marched (or was jolted) into the twenty-first century?

Soon we were home in the United States. Both personally and professionally our future lives were uncertain. But compared to our Russian friends, we had few worries; the roads ahead of us were far less treacherous than those we had left behind.

Reorienting the Russian R&D Bear

Within a few days, one of the leaders of Russian science came to my office in Washington seeking support for his proposal for positioning Russia to request more than $1 billion from Western governments for collaborative science projects with the West. He noted that the Western countries had so far provided over $24 billion of *assistance* to Russia. Yet very little had been directed to science, the discipline he naturally considered to be the greatest hope for the future of the country.

My colleague was one of the first Russians who had successfully pursued a dual career, initiated in the secret military laboratories and then expanded into open laboratories well known throughout the world. Thus he knew that the futures of underemployed weapons scientists and engineers were directly linked to the revival, indeed the survival, of the overall R&D establishment of the country. He knew that in the civilian sector, only the laboratories with international connections were functioning. And he knew that the costs of maintaining even a handful of the best laboratories would be enormous.

His specific proposition was to identify the 10,000 Russian scientists without whom Russian research would come to a halt. The $1 billion would be placed in an anti-brain drain fund that would be a temporary safety net for this august group. The funds would provide salary guarantees and much-needed laboratory equipment for the

10,000 and for their key young protégés to ensure that Russian science would survive the economic crisis of the next few years.

Although having just returned to Washington, I was sure his $1 billion request was simply off the Washington screen. At the same time, his estimate was far too low if the idea was to ensure that Russian R&D remained on the forefront of international efforts in a variety of important fields.

Russian R&D is in shambles. Massive equipment purchases are needed. Indeed, $10 billion would have been a more realistic estimate. And of course this proposed sum would not address problems that are not strictly research, such as environmental cleanup, bringing the operating nuclear reactors up to international safety standards, and reducing the huge wastes in the energy distribution system. But at least he did not shy from large numbers that discouraged almost everyone else, and he recognized the importance of supporting the next generation of leaders of science as well as the academicians who too often hope to live on their past reputations.

No less important than money, a nationwide rehabilitation of work habits is clearly a precondition for meaningful R&D, whether R&D is funded at a level of tens of millions, hundreds of millions, or even billions of dollars. Most researchers have understandably lost interest in spending much time in stagnant workplaces. They have become entangled in such complex webs of so many personal obligations and financial dealings that even large paychecks have difficulty pulling them back to the laboratories on a full-time basis.

A second but related precondition is a new approach to defining meaningful research goals, not only in lofty speeches and in broad policy statements, but at the laboratory and bench levels. Most researchers have become calloused to false promises and new proposals that have gone into circular files. Their enthusiasm for research must become rekindled—but an interest in research that will make a difference in a country now beset with busywork.

Just as the early bomb designers knew that their efforts would someday be rewarded with the sight of a mushroom cloud hovering above their experimental test, the reoriented weaponeers and their civilian counterparts must now be able to envisage what they can contribute to the blank canvas behind the parting clouds of despondency and lost hope. Nintendo games and clean air for their children? Reliable transportation and communication systems for themselves? Adequate health care for their retired parents? Well, these approaches would represent a start. Are useful and tangible products of science and technology too much to ask?

We know that Russian researchers can change the world. American disarmament experts witnessed their destruction of missiles by firing them down range, and the Americans reported that each one of them hit the bull's eye. With a comparable effort, Russian scientists and engineers should be able to hit the targets of economic needs; we surely do not want them to return to the missile range.

I was optimistic when I left Moscow that the ever-deteriorating situation in Russian R&D could be reversed, and I pursued an optimistic course when I hit the ground in Washington.

Climbing Out of a Deep Cave

As time passed, I was beseiged with a steady stream of discouraged Russian visitors and pessimistic reports about the continuing decline of Russian R&D capability. No journals, no supplies, no functioning equipment, and sometimes no salaries routinely topped the inventories of the status of Russian research.

Perhaps Carole and I had been too close for too long to the actual situation in Russia. Perhaps we had lost our perspective as to the seriousness of the scientific decay as we became numbed by more mundane scenes: restrooms that had been stripped of their fixtures, holes in buildings where bricks had been removed for personal use, and burned-out light bulbs that had been substituted for functioning bulbs in order to disguise the theft of the good ones.

From my new, distant vantage point in Washington, the situation seemed even more desperate than when viewed up close. Nevertheless, I still held to my conviction that more money is not the only needed antidote for reinvigorating R&D activities. Indeed, the dreadful state of material well-being of Russian researchers is inevitably entwined with a pervasive attitude that their new inventions of any type are *by definition* desirable; therefore they should be supported. Indeed, Russians are preaching their faith in technology wherever they go. A recent example reflects a common attitude of former weaponeers.

In early 1995, a scientist from St. Petersburg came to my Washington office and asked for help. He had spent many years designing goggles for the Soviet Air Force, goggles that would filter out the bright glare of the sun and the scanning strokes of laser beams. With these goggles, pilots would never be blinded from natural or man-made optical rays during combat. His idea was to adapt this technology for use by welders.

Spurred on in good faith by academics at Colorado University, he had succeeded in developing a new welder's face shield, using liquid crystallography techniques. Now he was searching for funds that would allow him to refine the technique, produce a few samples, and explore the market for the product. The Achilles heel of his otherwise solid product appeared when he unveiled the price: each shield would cost about $10,000. Though he was aware that welders could buy shields made from other materials for several hundred dollars, he offered a serious but unconvincing case that his shield was more advanced.

I dutifully referred the visitor to two American welding experts. I was sure they would set him straight. He would learn the pitfalls of blindly assuming that the interests of academics coincided with business realities while arriving at the cruel truth that he had been wasting his time for two years.

Thus the Russian R&D establishment faces a double challenge. It must replace its elaborate but obsolete physical infrastructure for carrying out R&D. At the same time, care must be taken to design R&D programs that will produce results that someone actually wants while scrapping those nonviable activities that are of interest only to the researchers.

This is a monumental challenge in an environment where for seventy-five years R&D was conducted for its own sake. No idea was too obscure, no price too outrageous, and no quality too poor for the civilian market.

The Western Stake in Russian R&D

At the end of the day, does it really matter to the West whether Russian R&D continues in any form? Only a handful of recent Russian innovations have stirred interest by the West, and some of them have been cataloged in earlier chapters. The country itself increasingly relies on Western technology whenever possible. It is unlikely that local R&D will make substantial inroads into this pattern in the next few years.

Current contributions of Russian laboratories to scientific and technical advances of interest to the United States are also limited, and some of them are being captured in the projects of the ISTC. An entire generation of potential scientific leaders has largely deserted the laboratories for commercial shops, which suggests that a quick recovery is not in sight, even if unlimited financial resources were to be available. Meanwhile, the older researchers simply hang on to their positions, spending less and less time in the laboratories.

Even the long-standing argument that the West should support the Russian scientific elite because this elite provides important impetus for political and economic reform has lost much of its meaning. The buyers of television time, the wealthy businessmen, the professors of economics and management in the new university departments, and, yes, the government bureaucrats are the engines of change, albeit often engines without steering columns. The scientific elite, if there is such a class today, will have an impact on the history books for their very important earlier contributions to reforming the Soviet Union, rather than reforming Russia. The academicians and the clubs of professors simply do not command the attention that they attracted a few years ago.

Despite these dismal realities, it is of vital interest to the United States—and to the West—that Russian *civilian* R&D survives, for the reasons cited below. Of course, military R&D will continue at a reduced level in the Soviet tradition and will survive whether we like it or not.

1. For many years to come, tens of thousands of underemployed Russian scientists and engineers with potentially dangerous weapons expertise will live in Russia. While their weapons skills may become rusty, they will not be so rusty as not to be of interest to terrorists and renegade states. Thus it is important that as many of these specialists as possible be kept busy, with or without the programs of the ISTC; and the Russian government should be encouraged to provide opportunities for their continued pursuit of peaceful objectives.

2. The historical wisdom that a stable Russia is better than an unstable one still pertains, and the traditions of scientific objectivity can contribute to stability. A relevant corollary notes that a well-fed Russian bear is less dangerous than a hungry bear, and the protein kits of scientists can help. Russia will always devote some of its resources to scientific research in the belief that society will eventually benefit. The West should encourage R&D targets and funding levels that will help lift the standard of living in Russia. Some benefits of increased pros-

perity will surely reach the people, and the political environment of the country should improve accordingly.

3. A strong and disciplined cadre of nuclear researchers can play an important role in securing dangerous material. Science can offer approaches that will reduce the likelihood of another Chernobyl. Also, active researchers should be in the vanguard of designing improved systems for safeguarding nuclear material from diversion or theft to rogue states.

4. Only in fourth place is the argument that the United States will benefit directly from Russian R&D. In some areas, such as geological surveys, environmental studies, and investigations of polar regions, such benefits are certainly very important. But in many other fields we continue to benefit from Russian expertise, not because Russian laboratories are functioning, but because the experts are working in foreign laboratories on temporary or permanent assignments. The principal exception to this rather pessimistic appraisal of Russian wherewithal is in the area of space exploration, where momentum built up during Soviet times continues to push researchers in Russian laboratories along the frontiers of knowledge.

In the longer term in all fields, however, the Russian R&D system will need a major infusion of technical expertise with young blood before the country again becomes a major wellspring of scientific discoveries of truly international dimensions.

The Importance of R&D for Russia

Russian scientists, like everyone else in the society, are having enormous difficulty convincing their own government that their activities must be strongly supported during a time of economic crisis. In my view, there are five compelling reasons why a new type of R&D that focuses on fewer target areas can be critically important for Russia.

1. Russia should be no less concerned than the Western countries and Japan about the transfer of Russian weapons know-how abroad. The many unpredictable neighbors on Russia's southern flank are reason enough to provide employment alternatives for vulnerable weapons R&D specialists.

2. The Soviet Union had an educational system that produced well-trained scientists and engineers suited for a command economy. The demand for technical specialists may fluctuate, but it will never disap-

pear. Now the scientists and engineers of the new Russia need less theory and more hands-on experience in the laboratories, as well as preparation in economics, marketing, and management techniques that characterize a market economy. A stronger research component within the educational system can be of great value in supporting a new emphasis on applications and on a recognition of the initiative that must be pursued by successful scientific entrepreneurs.

3. For the next decade, Western technology will continue to gain preeminence on the Russian scene. A strong R&D base can help Russia ensure that its institutions participate in applying this influx of Western technologies to local conditions instead of simply being bystanders who may occasionally be consulted by foreign interests.

4. While Russian research institutions may not thrive as sources of modern technologies in the near future, their specialists can play crucial roles in helping Russian enterprises and agencies select and effectively use Western technologies that are available.

5. Health and environmental problems increasingly threaten the lives of Russians. The widely publicized fact that the longevity of the Russian male has dropped to age fifty-nine is all the evidence needed to support that claim. A solid research base in these fields seems essential in the development of effective programs for mitigating the effects of decades of neglect of the environmental and health needs of a passive population.

Yes, Russia surely needs an R&D base of activities. The size and type are the central questions, questions that must be addressed by the Russian government in the technical and economic context of the needs of the next century and not in the comfort zone of the nostalgia of decades past.

The Next Five Years

The unpredictable political and economic caldron of Russia's future will be pockmarked with unanticipated surprises. The tug-of-war between nationalist ambitions and reform imperatives, instincts shared to varying degrees by most Russian leaders and pretenders, will be evident at many levels of government and within many circles of Russian society. This clash of desires will characterize the Moscow drama for the remainder of the century.

Russia's relations with its near neighbors and with the more distant countries of the world will continue to be controversial at home and abroad. The political debates over Russia's relationship to NATO will be important; and its role as a European state will be frequently tested by unpleasant incidents on its Western borders. And, of course, the broader questions relating to the future role of the Russian military forces will be central to the Russian position on the international scene.

Nevertheless, several aspects of the future of the country are clear; and this outlook goes to the heart of the ISTC program. Russia will retain a sizable nuclear military establishment to deter adversaries and gain recognition at the tables of power throughout the world. The stockpiles of nuclear weapons and materials throughout the country will not disappear, and their safe and reliable storage will cause concern around the world for decades. Russia will continue to pursue space exploration objectives, using hardware systems that could easily be turned into military weaponry. Russian chemists and biologists will continue to carry out research that, if misdirected, could produce agents with killing power unlimited.

In the immediate future the ISTC should provide a rallying point, a demilitarized zone (DMZ) in Moscow, for those Russian weapons specialists who want to contribute to the development of their country and for governments that believe that investing in the future of these specialists is an investment in the future of collective security and a safer world.

Indeed, the United States has only limited tools for influencing Russia's quest for trading partners with questionable motivations. For example, Iran's development of expanded nuclear reactor capabilities, North Korea's search for satellite launching systems, and China's enthusiasm for becoming a major producer of dual-use technologies are entwined with the commercial interests of Russia.

The ISTC is one of the tools of moderation that is now available. And it can also be the birthplace of related approaches that could help determine the future of international peace and security.

Notes

Prologue

1. Glenn E. Schweitzer, *Techno-diplomacy, U.S.-Soviet Confrontations in Science and Technology* (New York: Plenum, 1989), 89–90.

2. Margaret Shapiro, "Russian Agency Said to Accuse Americans of Spying," *The Washington Post*, January 14, 1995. This article cites a newspaper account in *Nezavisimaia Gazeta* reporting that Russia's Federal Counterintelligence Service has asserted that American research centers, institutes, and aid organizations are spying and working to undermine Russia as a competitor with the United States. See also Igor Abramenko, "Intelligence Against Science," *Novaia Ezhednevnaia Gazeta*, January 26, 1995; and "Chekists Again Want to Teach the Scientists," *Izvestiia*, December 28, 1994.

3. Benjamin S. Lambeth, "Russia's Wounded Military," *Foreign Affairs*, March/April 1995, 86–98. During early 1995, Russian television stations and newspapers daily berated the poor performance of the Russian Army in Chechnya. A particularly scathing article about the lack of "technological" preparedness was written by an engineer, Aleksandr Andrievskii, "We Are Exchanging Tanks for Bananas," *Rossiiskaia Gazeta*, March 16, 1995, 3.

Chapter 1. Fear of a Weapons Brain Drain
Stirs International Action

1. George J. Church, "Who Else Will Have the Bomb?," *Time*, December 16, 1991, 42, 47–48. A more up-to-date assessment of nuclear proliferation concerns is included in Leonard S. Spector, Mark G. McDonough, with Evan S. Medeiros, *Tracking Nuclear Proliferation, A Guide in Maps and Charts, 1995* (Washington, D.C.: Carnegie Endowment for International Peace, 1995).

2. *Reorientation of the Research Capability of the Former Soviet Union: A Report to the Assistant to the President for Science and Technology* (Washington, D.C.: National Academy Press, 1992). The report presents the views of 120 leaders of the U.S. science and engineeering community, brought together at the National Academy of Sciences on March 3, 1992, at the request of the White House. Their charge was: "To consider how to preserve the basic science capability of the former Soviet Union." Also see David P. Hamilton, "Piecemeal Rescue for Soviet Science," *Science*, March 27, 1992, 1623–33; and Kim A. McDonald, "Russia Is Struggling to Salvage Science, New Academy Formed," *The Chronicle of Higher Education*, January 8, 1992, A44–45.

3. William J. Broad, "In Russia, Secret Labs Struggle to Survive," *The New York Times*, January 14, 1992, C1.

4. As to the technologies involved, see S. Rosenthal, "Iraq's Bomb, Chip by Chip," *The New York Times*, April 24, 1992, A35.

5. "Genscher's Forebodings," *Wirtschaftswoche*, August 26, 1994. The Germans continue to claim credit for the ISTC proposal, even though Germany passed to the European Union the responsibility for representing Europe in the undertaking. In July 1992, Evgenyi Velikhov, director of the Kurchatov Institute of Atomic Energy, informed the author that several years earlier he initiated a World Laboratory Program at several institutes in Russia, with umbilical cords to a secretariat in Switzerland, as a means to attract weapons scientists to peaceful endeavors at participating Russian laboratories and at the same time reduce customs and tax problems. As noted in Chapter 4, in August 1994 Georgian President Shevardnadze informed the author that he had discussed the ISTC concept in 1990 and 1991 with colleagues in Europe. Also, in late 1991, Russian Foreign Minister Kozyrev talked about a similar program during travels in Europe. Meanwhile, the early discussions in the United States between American and Soviet scientists centered on bilateral programs. While Genscher's idea for an international program may not have been entirely new, he nevertheless deserves credit for taking the initial steps to translate an idea into action.

6. U.S. Department of State, *Joint Statement on the Establishment of the International Science and Technology Center*, released February 17, 1992. See also Thomas L. Friedman, "U.S. to Offer Plan to Keep Scientists at Work in Russia," *The New York Times*, February 8, 1992, 1; and Thomas W. Lippman, "Russian Scientist Aid Is Developing," *The Washington Post*, April 24, 1992, A10.

7. "Do They Value Us?" *Poisk*, July 4–10, 1992, 13. This publication of the Russian Academy of Sciences reported that the wages ranged from the equivalent of $10 to $18 per month for a junior scientist to $17 to $32 for a leading scientist to $36 to $44 for an institute director to $133 for the president of the academy.

8. *Decree of the President of the Russian Federation on the Establishment in Russia of an International Center for Supporting Scientists and Specialists*, No. 258, March 18, 1992.

9. U.S. Embassy, Lisbon, *Declaration upon the Initialling of the Agreement on the International Science and Technology Center*, May 24, 1992.

10. "Problems Delay Emergence of Moscow Research Center," *Nature*, July 23, 1992, 270. This report about the difficulties in finding a location for the Center's premises provides a partial explanation of the developments that led to its location at the Pulse Institute.

11. "Center for Reversing the Nuclear Brain Drain from Russia Will Begin to Work Already in October," ITAR-TASS, as reported in *Delovoi Mir*, October 10, 1992.

12. International Science and Technology Center, *Statute*, adopted on March 17, 1994, Article XIII.

13. Ibid., Articles X and XVI.

14. Ibid., Articles VI and VIII.

15. *Science, Technology, and Innovation Policies, Federation of Russia, Background Report*, prepared by Ministry of Science and Technology Policy for

the Organization for Economic Cooperation and Development, Paris, September 2, 1993.

16. *Statute*, Article X. A standard overhead of 10 percent on direct costs other than travel and equipment was established, which meant that for most projects about 7 percent of the total budget was available for overhead.

17. *Statute*. See Appendix C.

18. *Order of the President of the Russian Federation on the Signing of an Agreement on Establishing an International Science and Technology Center*, No. 662-rp, November 8, 1992.

19. *Agreement on Establishing an International Science and Technology Center*, signed in Moscow on November 27, 1992, by representatives of the European Atomic Energy Commission, the European Economic Community, the United States of America, Japan, and the Russian Federation; and *Statement upon Signature of the Agreement Establishing the International Science and Technology Center*, issued in Moscow on November 27, 1992, on behalf of the signatories. This Agreement refers to the Vienna Convention on Diplomatic Relations, April 18, 1961, with regard to the privileges and immunities of persons traveling in connection with activities of the Center.

20. Russian Ministry of Foreign Affairs, *Terms of Reference of the ISTC Preparatory Committee*, Moscow, January 10, 1993.

Chapter 2. Planning Proceeds Despite a Recalcitrant Parliament

1. International Science and Technology Center, *Instructions for Preparing Proposals*, revised version adopted by Governing Board on September 22, 1994.

2. The three key deputies involved were Chairman of the International Relations Committee Evgenyi Arshakovich Ambartsumov, who was favorably disposed to the ISTC Agreement; Mikhail Nikitich Tolstoi, the military physicist from St. Petersburg, who was the chief advocate; and Evgenyi Konstantinovich Pudovkin, the submarine captain from St. Petersburg, who was the chief opponent. Other interested participants included Iona Ionovich Andronov, a former foreign corespondent for *Literaturnaia Gazeta*, who opposed the Agreement; Aleksandr Sergeevich Dzasokhov, former secretary of the Communist Party of the USSR, who was generally supportive; and Vitalyi Ivanovich Sevastianov, a cosmonaut, who was not enthusiastic about the Agreement. Perhaps the strongest supporter was Chairman of the Science Committee Shorin, who did not play much of a role.

3. "How Much Do You Cost, Dear André?" report prepared by the Analytical Center of *Den, Den*, March 15, 1993.

4. Andrei Edemskii, "Parliamentary Opposition Guards Nuclear Secrets," *Kommersant*, March 19, 1993.

5. See *Agreement on Establishing an International Science and Technology Center*, November 27, 1992.

6. Of special relevance to our visit were the activities described in *Department of Burning and Explosions*, brochure of the Institute of Chemical Physics in Chernogolovka, 1991.

7. As background, we were provided with *Micron: Leadership, Stability, Traditions*, brochure of the Enterprise Micron in Zelenograd, 1993.

8. H. Sorokin and J. Gonnov, *Problems of Science in Atomic Industry; Adaptation of Large-Size Scientific and Technical Centers to Market Conditions*, report prepared for International Conference on Science, Technology, and Innovation Policies in Russia, sponsored by the Organization for Economic Cooperation and Development, Moscow, September 21–23, 1993. This report presents a good overview of conditions and activities in Obninsk.

9. Celestine Bohlen, "Amid Nuclear Transition, Russia's Scientific Elite Loses Its Security," *The New York Times*, July 4, 1993, 12.

10. In late June and July 1993, a flood of articles appeared in all the major newspapers in Moscow reporting on threatened strikes at Arzamas–16. Particularly telling was a commentary in *Rossiiskaia Gazeta* reported by Mark Trevelyan, in "Nuclear Scientists Warn of Falling Standards," *The Moscow Times*, June 22, 1993, 5. It stated, "The science cities have all come to the end of the line in their role of strengthening the country's defensive capacity. Their new role is as yet unclear." Finally, a delegation of scientists from Arzamas–16 met with a number of deputies of the Supreme Soviet to air their complaints as reported in "Fate of the Nuclear Centers," *Rossiiskaia Gazeta*, July 27, 1993, 5. Rumblings of discontent continued at Arzamas–16 into 1995. See, for example, Charles Hecker, "Payment Crisis Hits Elite Nuclear Center," *The Moscow Times*, June 16, 1995. Also, for an interesting commentary on the internal political dynamics of the city, see Kimberly Marten Zisk, "Arzamas 16—Economics and Security in a Closed Nuclear City," *Post-Soviet Affairs*, 1995, 11, 1, 57–60.

Chapter 3. Diplomatic Dodges Around the Parliament

1. *Agreement on Establishing an International Science and Technology Center*, Article XVIII, November 27, 1992.

2. President of the Russian Federation, "Decree," *Rossiiskaia Gazeta*, October 9, 1993, 1.

3. *Protocol on the Provisional Application of the Agreement on Establishing an International Science and Technology Center*, which was signed in Moscow, December 27, 1993.

4. *Order of the President of the Russian Federation on Provisional Application of the Agreement Establishing an International Science and Technology Center*, No. 767rp, December 17, 1993.

5. Alexander Gordeyev, "Out of Work, Can Build Chemical Weapons," *The Moscow Times*, June 3, 1994, 5. This article describes conditions at the Shikhanyi Branch on the Volga River of the State Research Institute of Organic Chemistry and Chemical Technology, which has its main offices and laboratories in Moscow.

6. Three former biological warfare R&D institutes that were very interested in the activities of the ISTC were the Institute of Molecular Biology "Vector," located in Koltsovo and specializing in viruses; the State Research Institute of Applied Microbiology, located in Obolensk and specializing in bacteria; and the Institute of Immunology in Libuchanyi.

7. Sergei Agafonov, "160 Russian Nuclear and Rocket Specialists Helped North Korea Build a Nuclear Bomb," *Izvestiia*, January 27, 1994, 1. This was one

of a continuing series of press reports about Russian participation in the weapons programs of North Korea. This article reported that seventeen rocket specialists were in North Korea under unofficial auspices, including some who had changed their names. Clearly, many earlier exchanges had been formally organized by the Soviet government; there was great confusion as to what was official and what was not. It is not surprising that the specialists from Miass were caught in the middle of these uncertain episodes.

Chapter 4. The International Center Goes into Fast Forward

1. *Agreement on Establishing an International Science and Technology Center*, Article IV, November 27, 1992; *Statute*, Article IV, International Science and Technology Center, March 17, 1992.

2. International Science and Technology Center, *Joint Press Statement on the International Science and Technology Center*, released in Moscow, March 18, 1994.

3. See the five documents, each entitled *Joint Press Statement on the International Science and Technology Center*, released by the International Science and Technology Center in Moscow on June 18, September 23, and December 9, 1994, and on March 30, and June 30, 1995.

4. *Joint Press Statement on the International Science and Technology Center*, June 30, 1995.

5. Tax-exempt status for grants is set forth in a "Letter of the State Tax Service of the Russian Federation No. YuU-4-06/88N and the Ministry of Finance of the Russian Federation No. 04-06-01 of June 11, 1993" entitled "On the Procedure for Considering Taxation of Grants Received from Foreign *Charitable* Organizations, as Registered with the Ministry of Justice on June 1993, No. 282." The Ministry of Science and Technology Policy interepreted the Russian word *blagotvoritelnyi* to mean "nonprofit," which in its view would include the ISTC, although others prefer the word "charitable," which might not include the ISTC. In any event, with regard to the VAT, the exclusion from VAT of grants of the type provided by ISTC seemed to be clearly stated in "Changes and Additions No. 4 of the Instructions," State Tax Service of the Russian Federation of December 9, 1991, No. 1 "On the Procedure for Calculating and Paying Tax on Added Value," *Finansovaia Gazeta*, no. 16 (124), 1994. Of course, tax exemptions are clearly stated in the ISTC Agreement, with the exception that an exemption for VAT is not explicitly provided for purchases of services whereas an exemption for purchases of goods is explicit.

6. International Science and Technology Center, *Model Project Agreement*, September 22, 1994.

7. *Statute*, Articles X and XVI, March 27, 1994.

8. State Customs Committee of the Russian Federation, "On Freeing the International Science and Technology Center from Payment of Custom Duties," *Ukazanie*, March 9, 1994, No. 01-12/157. This document was used to clear items through customs, although other problems often arose; such as, the necessity to pay storage fees covering the time from when the item arrived until it was picked up, inconsistencies between the bill of lading and the list of goods presented by the Secretariat, and that were lost in transit.

9. See, for example, Ellen Barry, "Recycling Nuclear Scientists," *The Moscow Times*, May 11, 1994, 9; Vladimir Pokrovskii, "ISTC Has Overcome Formalities," *Nauka i biznes*, May 1994, 1; Jim Vail, "US Gives More Money to Russian Scientists," *The Moscow Tribune*, September 24, 1994; Fred Hiatt, "U.S. Paying Millions to Russian Scientists Not to Sell A-Secrets," *The Washington Post*, September 24, 1994; and Carole Dorsch, "1992 'KGB' Brain Child Finally Stops Nuclear Brain Drain," *Business World Weekly*, October 5, 1994, 1.

Chapter 5. Putting the Weaponeers to Work

1. The estimate of 200 was cited by American weapons experts at a seminar at the Brookings Institution in Washington, D.C., in March 1992, shortly after the ISTC was proposed, and was repeated at a meeting at the University of Maryland in April 1992. An earlier estimate of 2,000 was offered informally by the director of the CIA, as reported in R. Jeffrey Smith, "Gates Fears Soviet 'Brain Drain,' " *The Washington Post*, January 16, 1992; and in Gerald F. Seib and John J. Fialka, "Scientists of Former Soviet Union Find the U.S. Slow in Putting Out the Welcome Mat for Them," *The Wall Street Journal*, February 3, 1992, A14. Shortly after I arrived in Moscow in July 1992, I again heard the number 200 used, but always by very senior Russian weapons scientists who would consider themselves within such a limited *elite* group.

2. See for example, Thomas Land, "Stopping the Russian Nuclear Brain Drain," *Nature*, February 13, 1992, 576; K.S. Jayaraman, "Russians Look to India for Jobs," *Nature*, March 19, 1992; Thomas Kann, "South America Polishes Its Sales Pitch in Drive to Attract Eastern Europeans," *The Wall Street Journal*, March 20, 1992; "Real Rocket Science Comes to High Finance—YES in Israel," *Business Week*, January 17, 1994, 71–72.

3. Foreign Intelligence Service of the Russian Federation, "New Conclusions after the 'Cold War'; Proliferation of Weapons of Mass Destruction," Moscow, 1993.

4. Michael Mandelbaum, "Lessons of the Next Nuclear War," *Foreign Affairs*, March/April 1995, 22–37.

5. Over the years, many reports have circulated about a female Iraqi microbiologist referred to as Dr. Germ who has attempted to use Western technologies in fashioning a biological weapons capability in Iraq. See, for update, R. Jeffrey Smith, "Iraq Had Program for Germ Warfare," *The Washington Post*, July 6, 1995, A1.

6. "New Conclusions after the 'Cold War,' " 43.

7. Russian estimates reported in the press and at meetings in Moscow during 1992–93 and estimates I inferred from Russian statistics indicated a wide range of opinion as to the number of Soviet specialists involved in the development of weapons of mass destruction and their delivery systems—from 600,000 to 1.5 million. My estimate of the Russian scientists, engineers, and technicians with significant experience in high-tech R&D is about 1.3 million, including about 1 million with experience related to some aspect of weapons of mass destruction and their delivery systems. Of the 1.3 million, about 125,000 were associated with MINATOM, 1 million with the other military branch industries; 25,000 with the

Ministry of Defense; 30,000 with the Academy of Sciences; 20,000 with the Ministry of Health, and 100,000 with educational institutions and other organizations of the country.

8. The now well-known ten atomic cities were first discussed publicly in 1991, and numerous reports have been prepared about them, individually and collectively. Their old and new names are as follows:

Arzamas–16: Sarov
Chelyabinsk–65: Ozersk
Chelyabinsk–70: Snezhinsk
Krasnoyarsk–26: Zheleznogorsk
Krasnoyarsk–45: Zelenogorsk
Penza–19: Zarechnyi (at Kuznetsk)
Sverdlovsk–44: Novouralsk
Sverdlovsk–45: Lesnoi (at Nizhnaia Tura)
Tomsk–7: Seversk
Zlatoust: Trekhgornyi (at Uruzan)

A good summary of their activities is included in Pavel Felgenhauer, "Nuclear Cities' Secrets Revealed," *The Moscow Times*, August 25, 1994, 3. Some Western analysts question whether hidden cities still remain. There is confusion among some scholars because a number of cities have more than one institute. Also, many other closed cities were in the secret category; but they were not classified as atomic *R&D* cities, which apparently is a criterion to be on the list of ten. At the end of 1992, the Russian press published a list of MINATOM institutions that would be exempted from privatization laws, and there were no surprises on the list. Also, the 1992 Ministry for Atomic Energy of the Russian Federation report, *MINATOM of Russia*, was more revealing than any of its predecessor reports, and it also did not include any surprises. An elaboration of this document was presented in "Russia's Nuclear Complex Opens Itself to the Country and the West," Special Issue, *International Affairs*, Ministry of Foreign Affairs, Moscow 1994. This is not to say that there could not be additional atomic cities yet to be uncovered, but the probability of such deception is not high simply because Western experts can account for all the elements of the nuclear fuel cycle within the ten cities and within other declared cities. At the same time, there probably are Ministry of Defense cities that have nuclear activities and remain in the *secret* category.

9. An early report of the activities of the ISTC was included in *Background Document, International Science and Technology Center*, prepared for a Workshop on *Overcoming Obstacles to Cooperation* held under the auspices of the OECD and the European Union (INTAS) in Brussels, September 8–9, 1994. Also see *First Annual Report, the International Science and Technology Center, March–December 1994*, Moscow, September 1995.

10. See seven ISTC reports, each of which is entitled *Projects Approved for Funding by the Governing Board*, International Science and Technology Center, March 18, June 18, September 23, and December 9, 1994, and March 30, June 30, and September 26, 1995.

11. For a general overview of Mayak, see *Association Production Mayak, 45 Years*, brochure released by Mayak, December 6, 1993. For discussions of envi-

ronmental problems, see three undated brochures distributed by Mayak: *Ecological Consequences of Activities of Mayak, Liquidation of the Karachai Lake—First Priority Task of Mayak*, and *Eastern Urals Radioactive Footprint*.

12. Office of the President of the Russian Federation, *Facts and Problems Related to Radioactive Waste Disposal in Seas Adjacent to the Territory of the Russian Federation*, materials for a report by the Government Commission on Matters Related to Radioactive Waste Disposal at Sea, Created by Decree No. 613 of the Russian Federation President, October 24, 1992, 1993. This well-known early report on Arctic and Far Eastern marine pollution remains a good point of departure for consideration of the radioactive waste problems in these areas.

13. A simple but effective graphic depiction of some of the major radioactive contamination problems was presented in James O. Jackson, "Nuclear Time Bombs," *Time*, December 7, 1992, 45. Murray Feshbach, *Ecological Disaster*, a Twentieth Century Fund Report (New York: The Twentieth Century Fund Press, 1995), provides a discussion of environmental problems in Russia. The references in the publication are helpful in leading the researcher to interesting source material.

14. Lev Ryabev, "Program for Increasing the Safety of Nuclear Reactors and Conceptual Development of Nuclear Energy in the Russian Federation. The Possibilities for International Collaboration," paper presented at a seminar in Los Alamos, New Mexico, June 15, 1993.

15. "Twenty-one Planned New Reactors," as set forth in Government Decree No. 1026, December 12, 1992. This list does not seem to have changed significantly during the past several years, although the schedules probably have slipped. Four of the reactors were more than 60 percent complete in 1992, and work had begun on three others.

16. "Appeal of the Directors of Atomic Stations and Enterprises of the Nuclear Power Complex to the President of Russia and to the Chairman of the Council of Ministers of Russia," Press Service *Nekosa*, August 5, 1993.

17. Richard Boudreaux, "Watchdog Counts 20,000 Nuclear Violations," *The Moscow Times*, February 15, 1994.

18. Among the commonly cited diversions of fissile materials were (*a*) October 1992, a Russian was apprehended in Podolsk with 1.5 kilograms of highly enriched uranium; (*b*) May 1993, twenty-seven crates containing four tons of beryllium and a small amount of highly enriched uranium were discoverd in a bank vault in Vilnius, Lithuania; (*c*) February 9, 1994, St. Petersburg butcher was apprehended attempting to sell three kilograms of highly enriched uranium stolen from a facility at Electrostal; (*d*) August 10, 1994, German authorities intercepted 0.5 kilograms of a mixture of different grades of plutonium on arrival in Munich from Moscow; (*e*) December 14, 1994, Czech authorities seized three kilograms of highly enriched uranium. More details are provided in T. Cochran, "U.S. Assistance to Improve Physical Security and Accounting of Fissile Materials in Russia," conference on Nuclear Non-Proliferation in 1995; *Renewal, Transition, or Decline*, Washington, D.C., January 31, 1995. Also see Carnegie Endowment for International Peace, *Nuclear Successor States of the Soviet Union*, Washington, D.C., 1994, for examples of illicit exports.

19. Center for East-West Trade Policy, *The Monitor: Nonproliferation, Demilitarization, and Arms Control*, University of Georgia, February 1995.

20. Leonid Bershidsky, "Federal Agents Peddled Uranium, Paper Says," *The

Moscow Times, August 31, 1994, 3. This article reports on a story in *Moskovskii Komsomolets*.

Chapter 6. Harnessing Hostile Technologies for Peaceful Purposes

1. Scientific Technical Center Informtekhnika, *Production of NPO Orion for Civilian Equipment and National Economy*, Moscow 1993.

2. *Background Report, Science, Technology, and Innovation Policies, Federation of Russia*, prepared by the Ministry of Science and Technology Policy for the Organization for Economic Cooperation and Development, Paris, September 2, 1993, 183.

3. *Nikkei*, Tokyo, April 25, 1994. This paper carried an article and an editorial item on the plutonium issue according to telexes received in Moscow from Japanese trading companies.

4. General Accounting Office, *Export Licensing Procedures for Dual-Use Items Need To Be Strengthened*, report to Senator John Glenn, GAO/NSIAD–94–119, April 1994.

5. Ibid.

6. Ibid.

7. "The Risk Report," Wisconsin Project on Nuclear Arms Control, University of Wisconsin, January–February 1995, 8–9.

8. Ibid., 1.

9. The activities of Dr. Germ are reported in William Safire, "Iraq's Threat, Biological Weapons," *The New York Times*, February 16, 1995, A27.

10. Office of Technology Assessment, U.S. Congress, *Proliferation of Weapons of Mass Destruction, Assessing the Risks*, August 1993, 6.

11. Ibid., 5.

12. National Research Council, *Dual-Use Technologies and Export Control in the Post-Cold War Era* (Washington, D.C.: National Academy Press, 1994).

13. Bill Getz, "Russia Uses Pentagon Funds in Constructing New Nukes," *The Washington Times*, May 23, 1995; and Bill Getz, "Hearings to Probe U.S. Financing of Russian Arms Work," *The Washington Times*, May 24, 1995. Also see Thomas E. Ricks, "Draft Report Says U.S. May Be Aiding Russian Nuclear-Arms, Nerve-Gas Work," *The Wall Street Journal*, May 22, 1995.

Chapter 7. Conversion Activities Attract Few Paying Customers

Portions of this chapter were previously published in Glenn E. Schweitzer, "Conversion Activities in the Russian Weapon Laboratories," *Technology in Society*, Vol. 17, No. 3, pp. 239–261, 1995. Permission for use granted by Elsevier Science Ltd., Pergamon Imprint, the Boulevard, Langford Lane, Kidlington OX5 1GB, U.K.

1. Useful overviews of conversion in the Russian weapons laboratories are presented in L. Kosals, *Defense R&D Institutes in Changing Russia*, Working Document No. 5, International Conference on Science, Technology, and Innova-

tion Policies in Russia, OECD, Moscow, September 21–23; *Science, Technology, and Innovation Policies, Federation of Russia, Background Report*, prepared by Ministry of Science and Technology Policy for the Organization for Economic Cooperation and Development, Paris, September 2, 1993, 182–98; and David Bernstein, ed. *Defense Industry Restructuring in Russia: Case Studies and Analysis*, (Stanford: Center for International Security and Arms Control, Stanford University, December 1994).

2. *Background Report*, 183.

3. House of Soviets of Russia, *Russian Federation Act: On Conversion of Defense Industry in the Russian Federation*, No. 2552–1, Moscow, March 20, 1992.

4. "More than A-Bombs Are Made in Arzamas–16," *Business World Weekly*, Moscow, April 15, 1993, 1.

5. "Fate of Nuclear Centers," *Rossiiskaia Gazeta*, July 27, 1993, 5, reports on an intensive discussion session between members of the Supreme Soviet and scientists from Arzamas–16. These discussions and roundtables involving members of the state Duma continued during 1994 and were widely reported on Russian television.

6. Kosals, *Defense R&D Institutes*, 11.

7. Paul Abercrombie, "Now It's the 9-Iron Curtain," *The Washington Post*, July 28, 1993, D9; and "Foreign Businessmen Visit Arzamas–16," ITAR-TASS Release, November 23, 1992.

8. Kosals, *Defense R&D Institutes*, 13.

9. Y. Tumanov, chief engineer at Arzamas–16, in February 1994 interview reported on Russian television.

10. "Myths about Defense Industry Hinder Conversion," *Business World Weekly*, Moscow, No. 44/89, 1993, 10.

11. A common estimate in Russia is that one-third of the population of Russia is economically dependent on the fate of defense-related enterprises. While the percentage is changing, it is nevertheless very high. Of special concern are activities in the 70 "military cities" (which include the ten "atomic cities") where defense enterprises are the principal employers.

12. Kenneth Adelman and Norman Augustine, "Defense Conversion," *Foreign Affairs*, Spring 1992, 11–12.

13. *Background Report*, 183.

14. See, for example, Christopher Anderson, "Weapons Labs in a New World," *Science*, October 8, 1993; and S. Hecker, "Retargeting the Weapons Laboratories," *Issues in Science and Technology*, Spring 1994, 44–51.

15. Activities at State Research Institute for Organic Chemistry and Chemical Technology, Moscow, as of mid-1994.

16. *Background Report*, 194.

17. Research and Development Institute of Power Engineering, *Conversion*, Moscow, 1994.

18. *Key Projects of Conversion Products Manufacture*, Luberetskoe Nauchno-Proizvodstvennoe Obedinenie, Soyuz (*sic*), 1994.

19. Yuri Bersenov, "Nuclear Weapons Complex of the Country in Serious Situation," *Nezavisimaia Gazeta*, June 28, 1994.

20. State Scientific Center for Virology and Biotechnology, (Vector), *Results of Scientific Investigations, Information Material*, Koltsovo, 1994.

21. International Science and Technology Center, *The Report of the Vector Symposium*, Moscow, December 14, 1994.

22. Central Aerohydrodynamics Institute, *List of TsAGI's Conversion Projects*, and *Advanced Methods and Facilities Ensuring Mechanical Strength, Reliability, and Long Service of Mechanical Engineering Structures*, Moscow, undated, available June 1994.

23. See, for example, *Evaluation Report: Science, Technology, and Innovation Policies of Russia*, DSTI/STP (93) 22, September 7, 1993, prepared for International Conference on Science, Technology, and Innovation Policies of Russia, OECD, September 21–23, 1993, Moscow.

Chapter 8. Can Research and Development Recover in Russia?

Portions of this chapter were previously published in Glenn E. Schweitzer, "Can Research and Development Recover in Russia?" *Technology in Society*, Vol. 17, No. 2, pp. 121–142, 1995. Permission for use granted by Elsevier Science Ltd., Pergamon Imprint, the Boulevard, Langford Lane, Kidlington OX5 1GB, U.K.

1. Two interesting background reports are "Storm Clouds over Russian Science," *Science*, Special Report, May 27, 1994; and "The Life and Death of Russian Science and Technology," *Popular Science*, Special Issue, August 1994.

2. Vladimir Zakharov and Vladimir Fortov, "Science Is Already in a Coma," *Izvestiia*, November 2, 1994. They report that 83 percent of scientists are paid below the poverty line. This assertion is more extreme than many other reports in the Russian press. Accurate information is difficult to compile as the official poverty line and the salary levels change at least monthly due to inflation. See also I. Tsanenko and A. Urevich, "Science Is Killed," *Mirovaia Ekonomika and Mezhdunarodnie Otnosheniia*, February 1995, 37–44.

3. The Russian Ministry of Science and Technology Policy announced at an OECD Meeting in St. Petersburg in November 1994 that 5,000 *scientists* had emigrated from Russia, presumably since 1991. (In Russian, the word for scientists usually includes engineers engaged in research.) Russian newspaper reports and government analyses of emigration indicate that on the order of 40 percent of scientists who leave are active researchers, and thus the estimate of 2,000. As indicated in note 18, during the second half of 1992 about 250 researchers left. This estimate also suggests that 2,000 is a reasonable number for the four-year period from 1991 to 1994 given that there was no obvious evidence of dramatic changes in the patterns during that time. A significant number of the departures were from institutes of the Russian Academy of Sciences, with most of the departing scientists categorized as *researchers*. Within this group were undoubtedly a significant number of scientists who could not be considered as *active researchers*. Even if the estimate of 2,000 is off the mark by 50 percent, it is very clear that the number of departures has been a very small percentage of the R&D workforce.

4. E. Nekipelova, L. Gokhberg, and L. Mindelli, *Emigration of Scientists: Problems, Real Estimations*, prepared for Center for Science Research and Statistics, Moscow, 1994. On page 11 they report that 25 percent of researchers left defense institutions from 1989 to 1992. Also see, *Science, Technology, and Inno-*

vation Policies, Federation of Russia, Background Report, prepared by the Ministry of Science and Technology Policy for the Organization for Economic Cooperation and Development, Paris, September 2, 1993. On page 199, information relevant to the 30 percent is presented. Some reports indicate that 10–15 percent of departures from Russian institutes are *involuntary*; however, the difference between *involuntary* and *voluntary* is often unclear.

5. Data obtained from the State Committee for Higher Education in January 1995.

6. Zakharov and Fortov, "Science Is Already in a Coma."

7. In July 1994, the science and technology minister publicly stated in Moscow that one-third of the nation's research budget was provided from foreign sources. Presumably he was speaking about civilian R&D. After that time, the number of foreign-supported activities significantly increased (e.g., Soros Foundation, ISTC, INTAS), and the number of domestically funded activities decreased. The recent situation differs sharply from the funding patterns in 1992 when 92 percent was from the Russian state budget according to Center for Science Research and Statistics, *Russian Science and Technology at a Glance, 1993*, Moscow, 1994, 36. Efforts to obtain better estimates of the foreign contributions are hampered by the reluctance of institutes to divulge their foreign income lest their domestic subsidies be reduced accordingly or the tax inspectors become more aggressive.

8. *Background Report 41–91; Russian Science and Technology at a Glance, 1993*, 9, 23.

9. *Evaluation Report: Science, Technology, and Innovation Policies of Russia*, DSTI/STP (93) 22, September 7, 1993, prepared for International Conference on Science, Technology, and Innovation Policies of Russia, OECD, September 21–13, 1993. Page 6 states, "The research system should perhaps be reduced by half."

10. Sometimes the level of 75–80 percent is cited as the percentage of R&D directed to military programs. These estimates seem high. They apparently include some R&D activities in space exploration and nuclear energy development that should be considered as civilian R&D, and they do not seem to recognize that most military laboratories for many years had some efforts directed to civilian spinoff applications.

11. While 10–12 percent is usually the percentage attributed to basic research, these estimates may underestimate the extent of basic research conducted in the military laboratories. Of course, arguments can arise as to whether any research financed by the military-industrial complex should be considered as basic research.

12. *Background Report*, 31–33.

13. Glenn E. Schweitzer, *Techno-diplomacy, US-Soviet Confrontations in Science and Technology*, (New York: Plenum, 1989), 63–100.

14. *Evaluation Report*, presents the OECD assessment of the situation and that organization's list of remedies.

15. *Russian Science and Technology at a Glance, 1993*.

16. Nekipelova, Gokhberg, and Mindelli, *Emigration of Scientists*, 33–35, 46. It is assumed that about 75 percent of the emigrants from the R&D institutes are active researchers, which may be a high estimate.

17. "Share of People Willing to Work Abroad," *Nezavisimaia Gazeta*, Sep-

tember 15, 1994. While this poll was probably not scientifically based, it reflects the attitude of young researchers encountered throughout the country that much of their future rests with international contacts.

18. Nekipelova, Gokhberg, and Mindeli, *Emigration of Scientists*, 33–35. Also, Galina Kitova, *Study on Research Mobility in Russia*, report being prepared for Analytical Center of the Ministry of Science and Technology Policy, Moscow, in progress as of September 1994.

19. Ministry of Science and Technology Policy, *Listing of State Scientific Centers of the Russian Federation*, September 30, 1994. Forty-two centers are included. According to Ministry officials, an additional 20 centers were approved in early 1995 with another 400 waiting in line for approval. As to the legal basis, see "Decree on State Scientific Centers," *Rossiiskie Vesti*, June 29, 1993, 5; and Council of Ministers, *Decree on the Initial Measures to Ensure the Activities of the State Scientific Centers*, Decree No. 1347, December 25, 1993.

20. *Russian Foundation for Basic Research (RFBR)*, Moscow, November 22, 1993. This short brochure summarizes the approach of the foundation.

21. "START Starts in Siberia," Siberian Department of Russian Academy of Sciences, Novosibirsk, undated, published in 1992, 12. This report describes the activities of some of the sixteen international centers.

22. "Rivals for Power Lay Down the Law," *Science*, November 18, 1994, 1153. While this article emphasizes the differing opinions on the details of the three draft laws, it does not give adequate credit to the several years of effort of the Ministry of Science and Technology Policy to put in place some type of law, however imperfect. The law may be of greater symbolic importance than practical significance, since many other laws (e.g., laws affecting branch ministries, laws on taxes and customs) will probably be more important for the future of Russian R&D. One of the controversial aspects of the law is whether the Russian Academy of Sciences will *own* its buildings or whether they will remain the property of the state and thereby be subject to all regulations concerning state property.

23. Zakharov and Fortov, "Science Is Already in a Coma."

Chapter 9: American Organizations Seek Out Russian Researchers

1. Early U.S. interest in Soviet technology is reported by one of the pioneers in searching Russian institutions for interesting innovations. See John W. Kiser III, "What the Russians Could Teach Us," *The Washington Post*, December 22, 1991. U.S. government hesistancy in entering into technology exchange arrangements with Russian weapon institutions was reflected in three articles by William J. Broad in *The New York Times*: "U.S. Bars Americans Buying Soviet Technology," March 1, 1992; "Genius for Hire: The Soviet's Best, At Bargain Rates," March 15, 1992, and "White House Drops Barrier to Buying Soviet Technology," March 28, 1992. An update on more current interest of U.S. technology-oriented firms is included in Andrei Baev, Matthew J. Von Bencke, David Bernstein, Jeffrey Lehrer, and Elaine Naugle, "American Ventures in Russia," Report of a Workshop, Center for International Security and Arms Control, Stanford University, May 1995.

2. UNESCO was one of the first UN agencies to take action, albeit on a very

small scale. See, "UNESCO Launches Fund to Support Russian Fundamental Sciences," press release in Moscow by UNESCOPRESSE, March 5, 1992.

3. For a discussion of the earlier bilateral science and technology agreements, see Glenn E. Schweitzer, *Techno-diplomacy, U.S.-Soviet Confrontations in Science and Technology* (New York: Plenum, 1989), ch. 6.

4. U.S. Department of Energy, Technology Management Group, Office of Defense Programs, *Industrial Partnering with the Newly Independent States of the Former Soviet Union*, Washington, D.C., November 1993.

5. "Partnering with the United States Industry Coalition," New Mexico Engineering Research Institute, Albuquerque, released in 1994. The source of funds is identified as Section 575 of the Foreign Operations Appropriations Act of 1994.

6. "NASA and Russian Space Agency Sign Space Station Interim Agreement and $400 Million Contract," NASA release 94–101, June 23, 1994.

7. "$20 Million Support of Russian Scientific Community under $400 Million NASA/RSA Contract," NASA release, December 1994.

8. *Defense Industry Conversion Program*, brochure issued by International Executive Service Corps, Stamford, Conn., July 1992.

9. "Cooperation in Applied Science and Technology," 1995–96 program announcement, National Research Council, Washington, D.C., December 1994.

10. U.S. Department of Commerce, International Trade Administration, *Special American Business Intern Training Program for Managers of the Independent States of the Former Soviet Union*, brochure issued 1993.

11. See, for example, "Western Aid, Promises and Reality," *Business World Weekly*, Moscow, July 30, 1993.

12. A centerpiece of the effort was reflected in *Russian Defense Business Directory*, prepared by U.S.-Russia Business Development Committee, Defense Conversion Subcommittee, 1993. Updated in 1994 and 1995.

13. For example, U.S. Department of Commerce, International Trade Administration, *Obstacles to Trade and Development in the New Republics of the Former Soviet Union*, March 1992; and Margaret Chapman and Kathryn Wittenben, "American Business Involvement in Defense Conversion in the Former Soviet Union: Opportunities, Constraints, and Recommendations," American Committee on U.S.-CIS Relations, December 1992. As to financing difficulties on the Russian side, the entire issue of *Mir, Nauka, Tekhniki, Obrazovaniia*, Russian Academy of Engineering, 1–2, 1994, was devoted to the integration of banking and industrial capital. Of particular interest in this publication are the practical problems of mobilizing capital set forth in A.P. Kuznetsov, "Aviation Industry: Investments and Conversion and Production Development."

14. See, for example, Sabra Charetrand, "Russia, with Red Tape; a Technology Boom," *The New York Times*, August 8, 1993.

15. Christopher Anderson, "Russian Science Aid Falls Short," *Science*, September 10, 1992. This was the first of a series of reports in this journal about cooperation with Russia in science and technology. Unfortunately, most of the reports published by *Science* have concentrated on only a few of the many efforts of American scientists and have given a somewhat limited presentation of the organizations involved. But the basic point of the early *Science* article that the assistance was very small was, and continues to be, accurate. A more up-to-date review of the Soros-financed program, referred to in the article, is included in

International Science Foundation, "International Science Foundation, 1994 Annual Report" (including the Supplement), Washington, D.C. 1995. Also, "HHMI Awards Major New Series of Grants to Assist Outstanding Biomedical Scientists in Eastern Europe and Former Soviet Union," Howard Hughes Medical Institute, Bethesda, Md., July 1995. As for a more critical review of assistance efforts in general and a proposed new approach that emphasizes cooperation rather than aid, see R.E. Butler and Alexey Alexeyev, "Charting a New Course for U.S.-Russia Cooperation," *Business World Weekly*, Moscow, March 20–26, 1995, 2.

16. National Research Council, *Redeploying Assets of the Russian Defense Sector to the Civilian Economy*, (Washington, D.C., National Academy Press, 1993).

17. Kim A. McDonald, "Russia's Science Academy Forms U.S. Firm to Solicit Commercial Research Contracts," *The Chronicle of Higher Education*, June 10, 1992.

Chapter 10. Replicating the ISTC Model

1. "Joint Press Statement on the International Technology Center," released by the International Technology Center in Moscow on March 30, 1995.

Appendix A

Chronology of Significant Events Leading to Establishment of ISTC

1992

February 17	Tripartite Statement by Andrei Kozyrev, Hans-Dietrich Genscher, and James Baker calling for the establishment of ISTC
February–April	Three four-party negotiating sessions in Brussels and Moscow
March 3	Yeltsin Decree to establish ISTC
March 11	Joint Statement by representatives of European Community, United States, Russia, and Japan to promote establishment of ISTC
May 24	Text of ISTC Agreement initialed by four parties in Lisbon
June 1–5	Four-party negotiations in Moscow
June	International staff begins to arrive in Moscow
July–October	Three meetings of International Planning Group for ISTC in Moscow
September	Four parties reach agreement on consistency of text of ISTC Agreement in eleven languages
November 8	Yeltsin Order approves ISTC Agreement
November 27	ISTC Agreement signed by four parties in Moscow
December	Two consultation sessions among four parties in Moscow

1993

January	Russian government submits ISTC Agreement to Supreme Soviet for ratification

January 10	Preparatory Committee (Prepcom) for ISTC established
January–February	Hearings of Supreme Soviet
February 8–12	Meeting of Prepcom in Moscow
May 25	Commission of Supreme Soviet representing five committees considers ISTC agreement
July 15	Prepcom staff meets with deputies of Supreme Soviet
September	Yeltsin disbands Supreme Soviet
October–November	Many four-party negotiating sessions in Moscow to develop provisional ISTC Protocol
December 17	Yeltsin Order accepts ISTC Protocol following previous acceptance by United States and European Union
December 24	Japanese Cabinet approves ISTC Protocol
December 27	ISTC Protocol signed by four parties in Moscow

1994

January	United States, Russia, and Japan complete internal approval procedures necessary for entry into force of Protocol
March 2	European Union completes internal approval procedures following positive decision by European Parliament
March 2	ISTC established
March 15–16	Meeting of Prepcom in Moscow
March 17–18	First meeting of ISTC Governing Board in Moscow

Appendix B

Agreement Establishing an International Science and Technology Center

The European Atomic Energy Community and European Economic Community, acting as one party, and the United States of America, Japan, and the Russian Federation;

Reaffirming the need to prevent the proliferation of technologies and expertise related to weapons of mass destruction—nuclear, chemical, and biological weapons;

Taking note of the present critical period in the states of the Commonwealth of Independent States (hereinafter referred to as "CIS") and Georgia, a period that includes the transition to a market economy, the developing process of disarmament, and the conversion of industrial-technical potential from military to peaceful endeavors;

Recognizing, in this context, the need to create an International Science and Technology Center that would minimize incentives to engage in activities that could result in such proliferation, by supporting and assisting the activities for peaceful purposes of weapons scientists and engineers in the Russian Federation and, if interested, in other states of the CIS and Georgia;

Recognizing the need to contribute, through the Center's projects and activities, to the transition of the states of the CIS and Georgia to market-based economies and to support research and development for peaceful purposes;

Desiring that Center projects provide impetus and support to participating scientists and engineers in developing long-term career opportunities, which will strengthen the scientific research and development capacity of the states of the CIS and Georgia; and

Realizing that the success of the Center will require strong support from governments, foundations, academic and scientific institutions, and other inter-governmental and non-governmental organizations;

Have agreed as follows:

ARTICLE I

There is hereby established the International Science and Technology Center (hereinafter referred to as the "Center") as an inter-governmental organization. Each Party shall facilitate, in its territory, the activities of the Center. In order to achieve its objectives, the Center shall have, in accordance with the laws and regulations of the Parties, the legal capacity to contract, to acquire and dispose of immovable and movable property, and to institute and respond to legal proceedings.

ARTICLE II

(A) The Center shall develop, approve, finance, and monitor science and technology projects for peaceful purposes, which are to be carried out primarily at institutions and facilities located in the Russian Federation and, if interested, in other states of the CIS and Georgia.

(B) The objectives of the Center shall be:

(i) To give weapons scientists and engineers, particularly those who possess knowledge and skills related to weapons of mass destruction or missile delivery systems, in the Russian Federation and, if interested, in other states of the CIS and Georgia, opportunities to redirect their talents to peaceful activities; and (ii) to contribute thereby through its projects and activities: to the solution of national or international technical problems; and to the wider goals of reinforcing the transition to market-based economies responsive to civil needs, of supporting basic and applied research and technology development, inter alia, in the fields of environmental protection, energy production, and nuclear safety, and of promoting the future integration of scientists of the states of the CIS and Georgia into the international scientific community.

ARTICLE III

In order to achieve its objectives, the Center is authorized to:

(i) Promote and support, by use of funds or otherwise, science and technology projects in accordance with Article II of this Agreement;
(ii) Monitor and audit Center projects in accordance with Article VIII of this Agreement;
(iii) Establish appropriate forms of cooperation with governments, inter-

governmental organizations, non-governmental organizations (which shall, for the purposes of this Agreement, include the private sector), and programs;

(iv) Receive funds or donations from governments, inter-governmental organizations, and non-governmental organizations;

(v) Establish branch offices as appropriate in interested states of the CIS and Georgia; and

(vi) Engage in other activities as may be agreed upon by all the Parties.

ARTICLE IV

(A) The Center shall have a Governing Board and a Secretariat, consisting of an Executive Director, Deputy Executive Directors, and such other staff as may be necessary, in accordance with the Statute of the Center;

(B) The Governing Board shall be responsible for:

(i) Determining the Center's policy and its own rules of procedure;

(ii) Providing overall guidance and direction to the Secretariat;

(iii) Approving the Center's operating budget;

(iv) Governing the financial and other affairs of the Center, including approving procedures for the preparation of the Center's budget, drawing up of accounts, and auditing thereof;

(v) Formulating general criteria and priorities for the approval of projects;

(vi) Approving projects in accordance with Article VI;

(vii) Adopting the Statute and other implementing arrangements as necessary; and

(viii) Other functions assigned to it by this Agreement or necessary for the implementation of this Agreement.

Decisions of the Governing Board shall be by consensus of all Parties on the Board, subject to the conditions and terms determined pursuant to Article V, except as provided otherwise in this Agreement.

(C) Each of the four Signatory Parties shall be represented by a single vote on the Governing Board. Each shall appoint no more than two representatives to the Governing Board within seven (7) days after entry into force of this Agreement.

(D) The Parties shall establish a Scientific Advisory Committee, made up of representatives to be nominated by the Parties, to give to the Board expert scientific and other necessary professional advice within forty-five (45) days of every project proposal's submission to the Center; to advise the Board on the fields of research to be encouraged; and to provide any other advice that may be required by the Board.

(E) The Governing Board shall adopt a Statute in implementation of this Agreement. The Statute shall establish:

(i) The structure of the Secretariat;

(ii) The process for selecting, developing, approving, financing, carrying out, and monitoring projects;

(iii) Procedures for the preparation of the Center's budget, drawing up of accounts, and auditing thereof;

(iv) Appropriate guidelines on intellectual property rights resulting from Center projects and on the dissemination of project results;

(v) Procedures governing the participation of governments, inter-governmental organizations, and non-governmental organizations in Center projects;

(vi) Personnel policies; and

(vii) Other arrangements necessary for the implementation of this Agreement.

ARTICLE V

The Governing Board shall have the discretion and exclusive power to expand its membership to include representatives appointed by Parties that may accede to this Agreement, on such conditions and terms as the Board may determine. Parties not represented on the Governing Board and inter-governmental and non-governmental organizations may be invited to participate in Board deliberations, in a non-voting capacity.

ARTICLE VI

Each project submitted for approval by the Governing Board shall be accompanied by the written concurrence of the state or states in which the work is to be carried out. In addition to the prior agreement of that state or those states, the approval of projects shall require the consensus of Parties on the Governing Board, subject to the conditions and terms determined pursuant to Article V, other than such Parties that are states of the CIS and Georgia.

ARTICLE VII

(A) Projects approved by the Governing Board may be financed or supported by the Center, or by governments, inter-governmental organizations, or non-governmental organizations, directly or through the Center. Such financing and support of approved projects shall be provided on terms and conditions specified by those providing it, which terms and conditions shall be consistent with this Agreement.

(B) Representatives of the Parties on the Board and personnel of the Center Secretariat shall be ineligible for project grants and may not directly benefit from any project grant.

ARTICLE VIII

(A) The Center shall have the right, within the Russian Federation and other interested states of the CIS and Georgia in which the work is to be carried out:

(i) To examine on-site Center project activities, materials, supplies, use of funds, and project-related services, upon its notification or, in addition, as specified in a project agreement;

(ii) To inspect or audit, upon its request, any records or other documentation in connection with Center project activities and use of funds, wherever such records or documentation are located, during the period in which the Center provides the financing, and for a period thereafter as determined in a project agreement.

The written concurrence required in Article VI shall include the agreement, of both the state or states of the CIS or Georgia in which the work is to be carried out and the recipient institution, to provide the Center with access necessary for auditing and monitoring the project, as required by this paragraph.

(B) Any Party represented on the Governing Board shall also have the rights described in paragraph (A), coordinated through the Center, with regard to projects it finances in whole or in part, either directly or through the Center.

(C) If it is determined that the terms and conditions of a project have not been respected, the Center or a financing government or organization may, having informed the Board of its reasons, terminate the project and take appropriate steps in accordance with the terms of the project agreement.

ARTICLE IX

(A) The Headquarters of the Center shall be located in the Russian Federation.

(B) By way of providing material support to the Center, the Government of the Russian Federation shall provide at its own expense a facility suitable for use by the Center, along with maintenance, utilities, and security for the facility.

(C) In the Russian Federation, the Center shall have the status of a legal person and, in that capacity, shall be entitled to contract, to acquire and dispose of immovable and movable property, and to institute and respond to legal proceedings.

ARTICLE X

In the Russian Federation:

(i) (a) In determining profits of the Center subject to taxation, funds received by the Center from its founders and sponsors—governments, inter-governmental organizations, and non-governmental organizations—and any interest arising from keeping those funds in banks in the Russian Federation, shall be excluded;

(b) The Center, or any branch thereof, shall not be subject to any taxation on property that is subject to taxation under the tax laws of the Russian Federation;

(c) Commodities, supplies, and other property provided or utilized in connection with the Center, and its projects and activities may be imported into, exported from, or used in the Russian Federation free from any tariffs, dues, customs duties, import taxes, and other similar taxes or charges imposed by the Russian Federation;

(d) Personnel of the Center who are not Russian nationals shall be exempt from payment of the income tax in the Russian Federation for physical persons;

(e) Funds received by legal entities, including Russian scientific organizations, in connection with the Center's projects and activities, shall be excluded in determining the profits of these organizations for the purpose of tax liability;

(f) Funds received by persons, in particular scientists or specialists, in connection with the Center's projects or activities, shall not be included in those persons' taxable incomes;

(ii) (a) The Center, governments, inter-governmental organizations, and non-governmental organizations shall have the right to move funds related to the Center and its projects or activities, other than Russian currency, into or out of the Russian Federation without restriction. Each shall have the right to so move only amounts not exceeding the total amount it moved into the Russian Federation.

(b) To finance the Center and its projects and activities, the Center shall be entitled, for itself and on behalf of the entities referred to in subparagraph (ii)(a), to sell foreign currency on the internal currency market of the Russian Federation.

(iii) Personnel of non-Russian organizations taking part in any Center project or activity and who are not Russian nationals shall be exempt from the payment of any customs duties and charges upon personal or household goods imported into, exported from, or used in the Russian Federation for the personal use of such personnel or members of their families.

ARTICLE XI

(A) The Parties shall closely cooperate in order to facilitate the settlement of legal proceedings and claims under this Article.

(B) Unless otherwise agreed, the Government of the Russian Federation shall, in respect of legal proceedings and claims by Russian nationals or organizations, other than contractual claims arising out of the acts or omissions of the Center or its personnel done in the performance of the Center's activities:

(i) Not bring any legal proceedings against the Center and its personnel;

(ii) Assume responsibility for dealing with legal proceedings and claims brought by the aforementioned against the Center and its personnel;

(iii) Hold the Center and its personnel harmless in respect of legal proceedings and claims referred to in subparagraph (ii) above.

(C) The provisions of this Article shall not prevent compensation or indemnity available under applicable international agreements or national law of any state.

(D) Nothing in paragraph (B) shall be construed to prevent legal proceedings or claims against Russian nationals or permanent residents of the Russian Federation.

ARTICLE XII

(A) Personnel of the Governments of the States or the European Communities that are Parties present in the Russian Federation in connection with the Center or its projects and activities shall be accorded, by the Government of the Russian Federation, status equivalent to that accorded to administrative and technical staff under the Vienna Convention on Diplomatic Relations of 18 April 1961.

(B) Personnel of the Center shall be accorded, by the Government of the Russian Federation, the privileges and immunities usually accorded to officials of international organizations, namely:

(i) Immunity from arrest, detention, and legal process, including criminal, civil, and administrative jurisdiction, in respect of words spoken or written and all acts performed by them in their official capacity;

(ii) Exemption from any income, social security, or other taxation, duties, or other charges, except those that are normally incorporated in the price of goods or paid for services rendered;

(iii) Immunity from social security provisions;

(iv) Immunity from immigration restrictions and from alien registration; and

(v) Right to import their furniture and effects, at the time of first taking up their post, free of any Russian tariffs, dues, customs duties, import taxes, and other similar taxes or charges.

(C) Any Party may notify the Executive Director of any person, other than those in paragraphs (A) and (D), who will be in the Russian Federation in connection with the Center's projects and activities. A Party making such a notification shall inform such persons of their duty to respect the laws and regulations of the Russian Federation. The Executive Director shall notify the Government of the Russian Federation, which shall accord to such persons the benefits in subparagraph (B)(ii)–(v) and a status adequate for carrying out the project or activity.

(D) Representatives of the Parties on the Governing Board shall be accorded by the Government of the Russian Federation, in addition to the privileges and immunities listed in paragraphs (A) and (B) of this Article, the privileges, immunities, exemptions, and facilities generally accorded to the representatives of members and executive heads of international organizations in accordance with international law.

(E) Nothing in this Article shall require the Government of the Russian Federation to provide the privileges and immunities provided in paragraphs (A), (B), and (D) of this Article to its nationals or its permanent residents.

(F) Without prejudice to the privileges, immunities, and other benefits provided above, it is the duty of all persons enjoying privileges, immunities, and benefits under this article to respect the laws and regulations of the Russian Federation.

(G) Nothing in this Agreement shall be construed to derogate from privileges, immunities, and other benefits granted to personnel described in paragraphs (A) to (D) under other agreements.

ARTICLE XIII

Any state desiring to become Party to this Agreement shall notify the Governing Board through the Executive Director. The Governing Board shall provide such a state with certified copies of this Agreement through the Executive Director. Upon approval by the Governing Board, that state shall be permitted to accede to this Agreement. This Agreement shall enter into force for that state on the thirtieth (30th) day after the date on which its instrument of accession is deposited. In the event that a state or states of the CIS and Georgia accede to this Agreement, that state or those states shall comply with the obligations undertaken by the Government of the Russian Federation in Articles VIII, IX(C), and X–XII.

ARTICLE XIV

Although nothing in this Agreement limits the rights of the Parties to pursue projects without resort to the Center, the Parties shall make their best efforts to use the Center when pursuing projects of character and objectives appropriate to the Center.

ARTICLE XV

(A) This Agreement shall be subject to review by the Parties two years after entry into force. This review shall take into account the financial commitments and payments of the Parties.

(B) This Agreement may be amended by written agreement of all the Parties.

(C) Any Party may withdraw from this Agreement six months after written notification to the other Parties.

ARTICLE XVI

Any question or dispute relating to the application or interpretation of this Agreement shall be the subject of consultation between the Parties.

ARTICLE XVII

With a view to financing projects as soon as possible, the four Signatories shall establish necessary interim procedures until the adoption of the Statute by the Governing Board. These shall include, in particular, the appointment of an Executive Director and necessary staff and the establishment of procedures for the submission, review, and approval of projects.

ARTICLE XVIII

(A) This Agreement shall be open for signature by the European Atomic Energy Community and European Economic Community, acting as one party, the United States of America, Japan and the Russian Federation.

(B) Each Signatory shall notify the others through diplomatic channels that it has completed all internal procedures necessary to be bound by this Agreement.

(c) This Agreement shall enter into force upon the thirtieth (30th) day after the date of the last notification described in paragraph (B).

IN WITNESS WHEREOF, the undersigned, being duly authorized thereto, have signed this Agreement.

Done at Moscow on 27 November 1992, in the Danish, Dutch, English, French, German, Greek, Italian, Japanese, Portuguese, Russian, and Spanish languages each text being equally authentic.

(Followed by five signatures)

For the European Atomic Energy Community
For the European Economic Community
For the United States of America
For Japan
For the Russian Federation

Appendix C

STATUTE

Adopted by ISTC Governing Board
March 17, 1994

This Statute is adopted pursuant to Article IV of the Agreement Establishing An International Science and Technology Center (hereinafter referred to as "the ISTC Agreement"). In the event of a discrepancy between it and the ISTC Agreement, the latter shall prevail.

ARTICLE I
[NAME, LOCATION]

A. The International Science and Technology Center (hereinafter referred to as "the Center") is established pursuant to Article I of the ISTC Agreement. Pending its entry into force, the Agreement shall be provisionally applied pursuant to Article I of the Protocol signed in Moscow on December 27, 1993.

B. The Headquarters of the Center is located at Moscow, in the Russian Federation.

ARTICLE II
[POWERS]

A. Article II of the ISTC Agreement provides as follows:

"The Center" shall develop, approve, finance, and monitor science and technology projects for peaceful purposes, which are to be carried out primarily at institutions and facilities located in the Russian Federation and, if interested, in other states of the CIS and Georgia.

The objectives of the Center shall be:

[i] To give weapons scientists and engineers, particularly those who possess knowledge and skills related to weapons of mass destruction or missile delivery systems, in the Russian Federation and, if interested, in other

states of the CIS and Georgia, opportunities to redirect their talents to peaceful activities; and

[ii] To contribute thereby through its projects and activities: to the solution of national or international technical problems; and to the wider goals of reinforcing the transition to market-based economies responsive to civil needs, of supporting basic and applied research and technology development, inter alia, in the fields of environmental protection, energy production, and nuclear safety, and of promoting the further integration of scientists of the states of the CIS and Georgia into the international scientific community.

B. The Center is authorized to carry out the activities enumerated in Article III of the ISTC Agreement and shall use its resources solely for the accomplishment of its objectives.

C. Without prejudice to the privileges and immunities provided by the ISTC Agreement, the Center and individuals related to its activities and the implementation of projects on the territory of the Russian Federation shall respect the national legislation of the Russian Federation.

ARTICLE III
[PARTIES, NEW PARTIES]

A. The United States of America, Japan, the Russian Federation, and, acting as one Party, the European Community and European Atomic Energy Community (hereinafter referred to as "the Parties") are the initial Parties to the ISTC Agreement.

B. Accession to the ISTC Agreement:

[i] A state desiring to accede to the ISTC Agreement shall so inform the Governing Board (hereinafter referred to as the "Board") through the Executive Director and shall provide information required by the Board. The Board shall, inter alia, require information concerning the requesting state's anticipated contributions to the Center and its expected proposals and activities.

[ii] The Executive Director shall transmit requests for accession to the Board without delay and shall place the request for accession on the agenda of the first Board meeting after the receipt of the information requested in accordance with subparagraph [i] of this Article.

[iii] The Executive Director shall communicate the Board's decision to the State requesting accession.

[iv] Upon approval by the Board, the acceding state shall be permitted to deposit its instrument of accession with the Board through the Executive Director.

ARTICLE IV
[BOARD PURPOSE, MEMBERSHIP, PROCEDURES]

A. The Board has the responsibilities set forth in Article IV of the ISTC Agreement.

B. Each initial Party has one vote on the Board. The United States of America, Japan, the Russian Federation, and, acting as one party, the European Community and the European Atomic Energy Community, have each appointed their representatives.

C. It is intended that the Board's membership be expanded from the size provided for in paragraph B. of this Article.

[i] A Party acceding to the ISTC Agreement may request Board membership through the Executive Director.

[ii] A Party is eligible for membership on the Board when the Board approves and upon such terms and conditions, in particular as to voting rights, as the Board may determine. Such terms and conditions must not be inconsistent with the ISTC Agreement.

[iii] One acceding Party that is a state of the CIS will have membership on the Board, in accordance with subparagraph [ii] of this Article. The term of that Party's representative shall be one year or a period until another such state has acceded, whichever is longer. A representative from another acceding state that is a state of the CIS shall be appointed subsequently to a one-year term.

[iv] A Party joining the Board under subparagraph [iii] of this Article shall not be eligible to vote on applications for accession or Board membership by other states of the CIS.

D. The Board shall select its Chair, who shall serve for one year.

E. The Board shall meet as needed, but not less than four times annually, upon thirty (30) days prior notice from the Chair, except whenever a shorter period of notice is agreed to by all Parties. At the request of the representatives of two Parties on the Board to the Chair, an extraordinary meeting of the Board shall be held upon fifteen (15) days prior notice except whenever a shorter period of notice is agreed to by all the Parties.

F. The Board shall decide its own rules of procedure, which shall address, inter alia, the method by which representatives to the Board shall cast their votes and the participation of non-Board members, including Parties, governments, inter-governmental organizations, non-governmental organizations, in Board meetings, and the establishment of any committees and task forces.

ARTICLE V
[SECRETARIAT]

A. The Secretariat of the Center consists of the Executive Director, Deputy Executive Directors, and other staff.

B. The Executive Director supervises the daily administration of the Center and is responsible for implementing the policies and decisions of the Board. The Deputy Executive Directors report directly to the Executive Director. In addition, the Executive Director directly oversees the chief officers for administration, procurement, and finance. The Executive Director is appointed for a two-year term by, and may be dismissed upon the decision of, the Board.

C. There are initially three Deputy Executive Directors, who are appointed by the Board for two-year terms and who may be dismissed upon the decision of the Board. Without prejudice to paragraph B., the Board shall designate one Deputy Executive Director as a Principal Deputy Executive Director, who shall fulfill the duties of Executive Director in the absence of the Executive Director for a period up to three months. After three months' absence, or upon the earlier permanent incapacity of the Executive Director or Deputy Executive Director, the Party which nominated the Executive Director or Deputy Executive Director will have the option to nominate a new Executive Director or Deputy Executive Director, who will be approved by the Board, for the remainder of the term.

D. After consultation with the Deputy Executive Directors, the Executive Director shall recommend to the Board the division of responsibilities among them.

E. Staff other than the Executive Director and the Deputy Executive Directors shall be nominated by the Parties and approved by the Executive Director, consistent with decisions of the Board. In approving staff nominations, the Executive Director shall consider the paramount importance of employing staff of the highest standards of efficiency, technical competence, and integrity.

F. Under the guidance of the Executive Director, the Secretariat shall be responsible for, inter alia:

[i] Disseminating information about the Center, including its objectives and functions;
[ii] Receiving project proposals and information required in accordance with this Statute and preparing proposals for transmission to the Board;
[iii] Responding to statements of interest from institutions in the CIS;

[iv] Assisting the Parties and participants in the development of project proposals;

[v] Collating the advice on the scientific and technical merit of project proposals given pursuant to Article VIII of this Statute;

[vi] Communicating with those who submit project proposals;

[vii] Bringing together specialists in the CIS with other specialists with similar interests;

[viii] Proposing the Center's activity plan and a budget for each year;

[ix] Preparing Annual Reports of the Center's activities, with the first Report to be submitted to the Board at the end of 1994;

[x] Making the necessary arrangements for handling business confidential information, as defined in Article XIII.A., in the Center Secretariat. The Center personnel shall conclude confidentiality agreements with the Secretariat for the period of their work at the ISTC and two years thereafter. Upon a complaint or on his or her own initiative, the Executive Director shall take appropriate administrative actions, up to and including dismissal, against an ISTC employee who has disclosed business confidential information; and

[xi] Other functions assigned to it by the ISTC Agreement, this Statute, or the Board.

G. In respect of the ISTC Agreement, the Executive Director shall, in fulfilling the following functions of a depository, notify the Parties of:

[i] Deposits of instruments of accession;

[ii] Amendments and their dates of entry into force; and

[iii] Notifications of a Party's withdrawal.

ARTICLE VI
[SCIENTIFIC ADVISORY COMMITTEE]

A. Within seven (7) days of the ISTC Agreement's entry into force, each initial Party may appoint not more than two (2) persons to the Scientific Advisory Committee (SAC), which is established pursuant to Article IV.D. of the ISTC Agreement. The Board may allow any state admitted to membership under Article III to appoint, alone or in conjunction with others, another such person. The persons appointed shall be prominent members of scientific disciplines relevant to the Center's objectives. The Parties are encouraged to appoint members with expertise in a broad range of scientific disciplines.

B. The SAC members shall serve in their personal capacities and shall not serve as representatives of the Parties appointing them.

C. The SAC shall meet at least once a year to advise the Board on fields of research and application to be encouraged. Its first meeting shall occur within thirty (30) days of the ISTC Agreement's entry into force.

D. In addition to meetings described in paragraph C. of this Article, the SAC shall meet upon request of the Board, to provide advice on questions referred to it by the Board. To this end, a SAC member may ask his or her Party or the Chair of the Board to recommend that the Board call a meeting of the SAC.

ARTICLE VII
[PROPOSAL SUBMISSIONS]

A. Any person, institution, government, or inter-governmental or non-governmental organization may submit a proposal.

B. Proposals shall be made through the Executive Director.

C. Each acceptable proposal shall comply with the instructions of the Center, which shall set forth requirements concerning information to be contained in proposals and the format for proposals. These instructions are prepared by the Executive Director and approved by the Board. At a minimum, the instructions shall require for each proposal:

[i] A summary of the project, including the name of the project manager; a short narrative description of the project's purpose, activities, anticipated results, location, and participants; and the project's estimated duration and costs, identified by element of expense to include at least: salaries, equipment, materials, travel, and standard overhead of up to 10% of direct costs, excluding equipment and travel;

[ii] A description of all program and financial aspects of the project, including anticipated commercial results and intellectual property rights;

[iii] A statement of whether concurrence has been obtained from participating individuals, institutions, and state(s) in which work is to be carried out and an acknowledgement that such concurrence is required prior to Board consideration: and

[iv] Monitoring and auditing assurances sufficient for implementing obligations of Article VIII of the ISTC Agreement.

These instructions should help ensure that each proposal contains information sufficient for the Executive Director, Scientific Advisory Committee, and Board to fulfill their responsibilities under this Statute and the ISTC Agreement.

D. Each Party is encouraged to disseminate the Center's instructions within its territory.

E. The Center will give due regard to preventing, in soliciting proposals, disseminating proposals and related reports for review, and making available project results:

[i] the seeking or disseminating of any information of a national security nature;

[ii] the transfer of sensitive information that is prohibited under relevant international rules and practices for the nonproliferation of weapons and other sensitive technologies, in particular information related to special nuclear materials; and

[iii] unauthorized disclosures of proprietary and business confidential information.

Proposers are responsible for ensuring that their proposals comply with applicable laws and regulations regarding sensitive information.

F. Proposals are regarded as submitted when the Executive Director determines that the information required in paragraph C. of this Article is substantially complete.

G. The Executive Director shall transmit proposals to the State(s) in which work is to be carried out within five (5) days of their submission, in order to obtain the prior concurrence required in Article VI of the ISTC Agreement, unless such concurrence has been obtained. When no response is received within 30 days of the request's transmission to the state(s), the Executive Director shall so notify the Board. In accordance with Article VI of the ISTC Agreement, the Executive Director must obtain the concurrence of the state(s) in which work is to be carried out before transmitting the proposal to the Board for approval.

ARTICLE VIII
[SCIENTIFIC AND OTHER PROFESSIONAL ADVICE]

A. The Executive Director shall send each submitted proposal to at least one SAC member of each Party no more than five (5) days after its submission. The Executive Director shall include at least the information required in Article VII.C. and other information he or she deems relevant, and a form on which the review shall be completed. The Executive Director shall prepare that form after consultation with the SAC.

B. Each SAC member may obtain, without expense to the Center, up to three (3) expert scientific, economic, or other professional reviews for each project.

C. Not more than thirty (30) days after receiving the proposal from the Executive Director, each SAC member shall return a single completed form synthesizing the reviews obtained in accordance with paragraph B. of this Article, together with copies of those reviews and his or her own recommendation as appropriate; or confirmation that no review has been undertaken.

D. A completed review shall contain:

[i] The reviewers' names and qualifications, including any qualifications related to the specific proposal;
[ii] An analysis of the scientific and technical merit and importance of the proposals;
[iii] An opinion as to whether the project's objective can be accomplished within the framework proposed and time allowed;
[iv] An analysis, to the extent possible, of the qualifications of the proposed participants and of the skills necessary to meet the project's objectives; and
[v] Recommendations for the proposal's improvement.

E. When the Executive Director receives all reviews of a proposal, but no later than forty-five (45) days after its submission, he or she shall either:

[i] Transmit the proposal to the Board, accompanied by all reviews and other relevant information; or
[ii] Consult with the proposer to consider revision in accordance with the reviews. The Executive Director shall decide whether a revised proposal requires further review by the SAC before it is transmitted to the Board. If a proposal is being revised, the Executive Director may extend the forty-five (45) day period as necessary. The Board will be informed of the status of such proposals which are under revision within the forty-five (45) day time period.

ARTICLE IX
[PROJECT APPROVAL]

A. The Executive Director shall transmit proposals to at least one member of the Board of each Party, along with the information required by this Statute. The Executive Director shall also attach:

[i] An initial assessment by the Executive Director as to whether the project is in accordance with the objectives of the Center, as described in Article II of the ISTC Agreement;
[ii] The results of scientific and professional reviews of the project proposals conducted in accordance with Article VIII of this Statute, if available; and
[iii] Recommendations by the Executive Director, when he or she deems it appropriate.

B. Approval of projects by the Board:

[i] Unless the Board decides otherwise with regard to a specific proposal, it shall have at least forty-five (45) days to consider a proposal after the proposal has been transmitted to it by the Executive Director. It shall consider the proposal no later than its first meeting after the forty-five (45) day period ends.

[ii] The Executive Director shall communicate the Board's decision to the person, institution, or government proposing the project.

C. In deciding whether to approve a project, the Board will be guided by criteria and priorities established according to Article IV.B.[v] of the ISTC Agreement. The Board shall adopt these criteria at its first meeting.

D. Each project approved by the Board shall be subject to a project agreement that is binding upon the participants in the project before the project is carried out.

E. In approving each project, the Board shall consider financing for the project.

ARTICLE X
[PROJECT AGREEMENTS]

A. For each approved project financed through the Center, the Center, acting through the Executive Director or his or her designee, shall enter into a written project agreement for the project with the recipient entity or entities. The project agreement shall expressly provide that it is subject to the provisions of the ISTC Agreement and the Statute, which shall govern in the case of conflict with the project agreement. The Secretariat shall ensure that this is the case.

B. At a minimum, the Project Agreements referred to in paragraph A. of this Article shall contain provisions which:

[i] specify conditions under which costs shall be eligible for reimbursement and ensure that they are allowable under the terms of the Project, reasonable as to amount, and properly allocated to the Project;

[ii] Designate responsibility for performance of technical and financial tasks under the project and delineate procedures to be followed in the resolution of disputes;

[iii] Establish a schedule for performance and conditions to be met in order to obtain payment;

[iv] Provide for each Party which wholly or partly finances a project and for the Center the right of full ISTC Agreement access, after notice of not

less than twenty (20) days or as specified in the project agreement, to carry out on-site monitoring and audit of all activities of the project; specify the portions of the facilities, equipment, documentation, information, data systems, materials, supplies, personnel, and services which will concern the project and so will be accessible for the monitoring and audit; such specification shall permit the recipient entity the right to protect those portions of facilities which are not related to the project.

[v] Require the recipient entity to account for resources used, to identify the types of records required to support expenditures for the project, and to return unspent funds within a stated time;

[vi] Require regular technical and financial reports detailing the expenditures made against the projects by the same elements of expense identified in the approved proposal, including accounting for any interest earned by the recipient on funds accepted from the Center;

[vii] Require that allowable costs not include, inter alia, any element of profit;

[viii] Set a standard contribution for overhead costs up to 10% of direct costs, excluding equipment and travel;

[ix] Require that allowable costs not include amounts imposed for taxes of any kind, including profit tax, value added tax, personal income tax, local taxes as well as any other tariffs, dues, custom duties, import taxes, fees, or any other similar taxes or charges;

[x] Prohibit the transfer of sensitive information that is prohibited under relevant international rules and practices for the nonproliferation of weapons and other sensitive technologies, in particular information related to special nuclear materials, and unauthorized disclosures of proprietary and business confidential information.

[xi] Provide for the termination of the project as follows:

(a) When the agreement is terminated other than pursuant to paragraph (b) below, costs shall be limited to the allowable costs incurred by the recipient entity prior to the termination and such other costs as the Center considers to be fair and reasonable, having regard to commitments reasonably entered into and which cannot be canceled or avoided. The recipient entity shall comply with any directions of the Center in the termination notice to reduce or mitigate these costs.

(b) When the Center or the financing Party(s) determines that the recipient entity has not complied with the terms and conditions of the project agreement, the recipient entity shall, upon demand, promptly return all payments and equipment contributions previously made.

(c) Any disputes on the above matter shall be settled by a procedure involving, in case of appeal, a final decision of the Board.

C. When an approved project is financed other than through the Center, the persons or institutions providing financing shall conclude a project agreement with the recipient entity and with the Center, represented by the Executive Director. The project agreements shall take fully into consideration the provisions specified in paragraph B. of this Article and be fully consistent with the provisions of the ISTC Agreement.

ARTICLE XI
[CONTRIBUTIONS TO THE CENTER]

A. Without prejudice to Articles XII and XIV, each Party may deposit any or all of its monetary contribution to the Center for operating costs, projects, and all other expenses in accordance with its laws and regulations into an account in the name of the Center or directly into the Center project and administrative accounts. At the discretion of the financing Party, this contribution may be made subject to a written agreement with the Center and may be maintained in any currency.

B. Funds that are deposited in the Center's bank accounts pursuant to paragraph A. of this Article shall be disbursed from the bank account by the Executive Director or his designee in accordance with procedures approved by the Board and/or any agreement between the Center and the relevant financing Party.

C. The Russian Federation shall provide at its own expense an appropriately furnished facility suitable for use by the Center along with maintenance, utilities, and security for the facility and vehicles. The Russian Federation shall also provide full financial resources to cover its personnel in the Center Secretariat.

D. Contributions made to the Center by persons, states that are not Parties to the ISTC Agreement, inter-governmental organizations, or non-governmental organizations may be maintained in a Center account established by the Executive Director, with the approval of the Board. Disbursement procedures for these funds shall be established by the Board.

E. In financial transactions, the Center shall not pay in the Russian Federation taxes of any kind, including profit tax, value added tax, personal income tax, local taxes as well as any other tariffs, dues, custom duties, import taxes, fees, or any other similar imposed taxes or charges.

F. Disbursements of funds for projects may be made to the appropriate organizations and individuals in hard currency or local currency.

ARTICLE XII
[FINANCING PROJECTS THROUGH THE CENTER]

A. The Center shall establish appropriate project and administrative hard currency bank accounts outside the CIS and also appropriate accounts as approved by the Board, in each of the States of the CIS that are Parties to the ISTC Agreement, in order to consolidate financing for projects and administration.

B. Each Party which has undertaken responsibility to finance a project through the Center shall do so in a written commitment to the Center and will ensure that funds are available for use by the Center in those amounts required to execute the project agreement.

ARTICLE XIII
[INTELLECTUAL PROPERTY RIGHTS]

A. For the purposes of the Agreement and this Statute:

"Intellectual property" shall have the meaning defined in Article 2 of the Convention Establishing the World Intellectual Property Organization, done at Stockholm on July 14, 1967.

"Business confidential information" means information containing know-how, trade secrets, or technical, commercial or financial information, which either:

[i] Has been held in confidence by its owner;
[ii] Is not generally known or available from other sources;
[iii] Has not been made available by its owner to other parties without an obligation concerning its confidentiality; or
[iv] Is not available to the receiving party without obligations concerning confidentiality.

B. Each project agreement shall provide for the adequate protection of intellectual property and business confidential information exchanged or provided in the course of a project.

C. Each Party shall use its best endeavors to ensure that rights acquired are exercised in such a way as to encourage, consistent with the Statute:

[i] The dissemination and use of non-confidential information created, provided, or exchanged in the course of a project;
[ii] The adoption and implementation of international technical standards; and

[iii] Fair competition in areas affected by the Agreement.

D. Entities having rights should make adequate efforts to exploit their intellectual property rights consistent with the objectives of the Agreement. To that end, except as provided in paragraph E. of this Article, each project agreement shall provide that:

[i] All rights worldwide to intellectual property arising from the project, including patent protection for industrial property, shall be held by the recipient entity (or its designee), which shall provide adequate protection of such intellectual property (except as provided below). If the recipient entity (or its designee) decides not to protect the intellectual property in the territory of a Party other than the recipient entity's Party, each such Party and the financing Party have the option to protect the intellectual property in that territory.

[ii] Each Party and the Center shall be entitled to a non-exclusive, irrevocable, royalty-free license with the right to sub-license in all countries to translate, reproduce, and publicly distribute scientific and technical journal articles, reports, and books directly arising from the project. When the objective of a project is only to produce an article, report, or book that is expected to be valuable in itself, the provisions of paragraph E. of this Article shall be applied.

[iii] (a) The recipient entity (or its designee) shall grant the financing Party (or its designee) an exclusive, irrevocable, royalty-free license (with the right to sub-license) for commercial purposes in that Party's territory. In such cases, the financing Party and recipient entity shall agree on appropriate compensation for persons named as inventors. Costs of protection in that territory shall be borne by the licensee. When the benefits from the exploitation of intellectual property arising from the project are expected to exceed significantly the financing Party's expected contribution, the provisions of paragraph E. of this Article shall be applied.

(b) When two or more Parties finance a project, it is expected that the provisions of paragraph E. of this Article shall be applied. When the Parties and the recipient entity agree not to do so, in such cases the co-financing parties (or their designees) shall agree on the allocation among themselves of the rights received pursuant to this paragraph.

(c) Upon the request of the financing Party (or its designee), the recipient entity (or its designee) shall enter negotiations for licenses in additional territories on fair and reasonable terms.

(d) Upon the request of a non-financing Party (or its designee), a non-exclusive license for commercial purposes, with the right to sub-license, shall be granted in that non-financing Party's territory, on fair and reasonable terms to be mutually agreed, taking into account that non-financing Party's contribution to the establishment and operation of the ISTC; the financing Party (or its designee) shall be entitled to a license on the same terms in that non-financing Party's territory.

(e) The financing Party will, if requested, provide assistance to the recipient entity in managing the intellectual property;

[iv] A non-exclusive, irrevocable license on transfer conditions for non-commercial purposes, with the right to sub-license, shall be granted to the Center and to each Party (or its designee) for the territory of each Party in which the intellectual property is protected. Upon request the Parties will exchange information on licenses and sub-licenses granted under this paragraph;

[v] Persons named as inventors shall receive not less than 15% of any royalties earned by the executing entity;

[vi] All publicly distributed copies of a copyrighted work arising from cooperation under the project shall indicate the names of the authors of the work unless an author explicitly declines to be named;

[vii] The recipient entity shall grant on reasonable conditions access rights for intellectual property and information owned by the recipient entity necessary for the exploitation of intellectual property arising from the project, provided that the recipient entity is free to disclose such intellectual property or information, that no major business interests of the recipient entity oppose the granting of access rights, and that in making this opposition such interests are not abusively restricting the exploitation of such rights.

E. The financing Party (or its designee) and the recipient entity (or its designee) may agree to protect, allocate, and manage intellectual property arising under the project agreement differently than paragraph D. of this Article provides, consistent with the principles of the Agreement and their laws and regulations. In order to avoid increasing the work of the Center's staff, any provisions agreed under this paragraph will be provided by those entities to the Center for inclusion in the project agreement.

ARTICLE XIV
[FINANCING OF ADMINISTRATIVE EXPENSES]

A. The fiscal year of the Center shall be the calendar year.

B. By November 15 of each year, the Executive Director shall submit to the Board the annual budget estimates for the expenses of the Center. The Center's budget shall exclude costs of facilities, materials, services, and vehicles provided by the Russian Federation free of charge pursuant to the Memorandum of Understanding between the Center and the Government of the Russian Federation. The Board shall approve the annual budget with any amendments and return the budget for execution to the Executive Director by December 31 of that same year. The initial budget shall be for the remainder of the fiscal year in which it is submitted.

C. Upon the approval of the annual budget by the Board, the Board will establish and inform each Party of the amount of its share, if any, of the Center's annual operating budget. In accordance with this budget, each Party shall ensure that funds are credited for their share for use by the Center.

D. Any funds remaining uncommitted at the end of each fiscal year shall be applied to the budget for the following year.

E. Withdrawal by a Party from the ISTC Agreement shall not affect its budgetary contributions committed under paragraph C. of this Article to the Center's administrative account.

F. In addition to financial contributions, the Parties will be encouraged to second staff and provide other support to the Center at no cost to the Center's budget. The Center may, as necessary, enter into agreements concerning these secondments and support.

ARTICLE XV
[FINANCIAL PROCEDURES]

A. Periodic financial reports shall be provided to the Parties and the Board on the Center's administrative costs, project awards, and expenditures in the format and detail required by the Parties and the Board.

B. An annual audit by an auditor approved by the Board shall be conducted of the Canter's expenditures and related financial activities. Results of the audit shall be reported to the Board within thirty (30) days after completion.

ARTICLE XVI
[AUDITING AND MONITORING)

A. All funds contributed for a project through the Center shall be subject to audit by the Center or by a Party represented on the Board with regard to projects it finances or their representatives in accordance with the following principles:

[i] Audit of costs shall assure that costs reimbursed are allowable under the terms of the project agreement;

[ii] The Center, a Party represented on the Board with regard to projects it finances, or audit organizations as specified by the Board may perform such audits, or engage others to do so.

[iii] Accounting systems used by project recipients must be acceptable to the Center or the Party represented on the Board in regard to projects it finances and shall be subject to review and audit.

[iv] Audit reports pertaining to a project shall be available to the entities audited, to the Center, and to all Parties represented on the Board.

[v] Allowable costs based on the result of an audit shall be determined by the entity performing the audit or engaging others to do so. Any disputes shall be settled in accordance with resolution of dispute procedures contained in the project agreement.

[vi] Provisions for each Party which wholly or partly finances a project and for the Center to have the right of full ISTC Agreement access, after notice of not less than twenty (20) days or as specified in the project agreement, to carry out on-site monitoring and audit of all activities of the project; specifications of the portions of the facilities, equipment, documentation, information, data systems, materials, supplies, personnel, and services which will concern the project and so will be accessible for the monitoring and audit; such specification shall permit the recipient entity the right to protect those portions of facilities that are not related to the project. After completion or termination of a Center project the recipient entity may utilize the facility or portion of the facility previously used for the Center project for other work; however, all documentation and records including those associated with equipment, data systems, materials, supplies, and services utilized on the Center project must be maintained for up to two years following such completion or termination and such documents and records and personnel must be available to the auditor for up to two years following such completion or termination.

B. Approved projects funded other than through the Center shall be subject to audit by the financing Party and/or their representatives, taking into account the principles set forth in paragraph A of this Article.

ARTICLE XVII
[SUPPLEMENTARY AGREEMENTS]

Each Party may conclude supplementary written agreements with the Center as approved by the Board consistent with the ISTC Agreement in order to comply with its national laws, rules, and regulations applicable to the Center.

ARTICLE XVIII
[AMENDMENT OF STATUTE]

This Statute may be amended by unanimous consent of the Board.

Statements on the Statute by the Parties

Statements of the United States, European Community, and Japan:

"Any element of profit" in Article X.B.[vii] is recognized to include contributions to pension funds, social insurance, and other social funds.

"The Russian Federation, as part of its in-kind contribution, has agreed to indicate on each project proposal transmitted to the Board its contribution of the costs listed above."

Statement of the Russian Federation:

"The Russian Federation interprets 'fair and reasonable terms' referred to in Article XIII.D.[iii]. as terms established at the moment on the international license market."

Appendix D

Protocol on the Provisional Application of the Agreement Establishing an International Science and Technology Center

The United States of America, Japan, the Russian Federation, and the European Atomic Energy Community and the European Community, acting as one party, hereinafter referred to as the "Signatory Parties," recognizing the importance of the Agreement Establishing an International Science and Technology Center, signed in Moscow on November 27, 1992, hereinafter referred to as the "Agreement,"

HAVE AGREED AS FOLLOWS:

Article I

(1) The Agreement shall be provisionally applied in accordance with its terms by the Signatory Parties from the date of the last notification of the Signatory Parties of the completion of internal procedures necessary for entry into force of this Protocol.

(2) The Agreement shall be applied provisionally until its entry into force in accordance with Article XVIII thereof.

Article II

The Agreement shall be subject to review by the parties two years after the beginning of provisional application of the Agreement notwithstanding the provisions of Article XV(A) of the Agreement.

Article III

Any of the parties may withdraw from this Protocol six months from the date on which written notification is provided to the other parties.

Article IV

(1) Any state desiring to become a party to the Agreement in accordance with Article XIII thereof, after fulfilling the conditions set forth in that Article, and after completing its internal procedures that will be necessary for accession to the Agreement, shall notify the Signatory Parties of its intention to provisionally apply the Agreement in accordance with this Protocol.

(2) The provisional application by that state shall begin from the date of notification referred to in Paragraph (1) of this Article.

Done in Moscow on December 27, 1993, in the English and Russian languages, each text being equally authentic.

For:
The United States of America, Japan, The Russian Federation, and The European Atomic Energy Community and the European Community
(with four appropriate signatures)

Appendix E

DECREE

Of the President of the Russian Federation

On the Establishment in Russia of an International
Center for Supporting Scientists and Specialists

1. To agree with the proposal of the Ministry of Foreign Affairs of Russia on establishing an international center for supporting scientists and specialists.

2. To give the Ministry of Atomic Energy of Russia responsibility to propose a place for locating the Center.

3. To instruct the Ministry of Atomic Energy of Russia, the Ministry of Industry of Russia, and the Russian Academy of Sciences with the agreement of the Ministry of Science of Russia and the Ministry of Foreign Affairs of Russia to ensure that the Russian component of the Center will have qualified specialists, including the participation of our representatives in its governing bodies.

President of the Russian Federation
B. Yeltsin

Moscow, Kremlin
18 March 1992

No. 258

Translated by Glenn Schweitzer

ORDER

Of the President of the Russian Federation

On the Signing of the Agreement on the Establishment
of the International Science and Technology Center

1. To approve the draft agreement between the Russian Federation, the United States of America, Japan, and the European Community on the Establishment of the International Science and Technology Center.

2. To authorize the Ministry of Foreign Affairs of the Russian Federation to sign the said agreement for the Russian side. To authorize the Ministry of Foreign Affairs of the Russian Federation, with the agreement of the other interested ministries and agencies, to make necessary changes in the text of the draft Agreement which are not of a significant character.

3. To assign to the Ministry of Atomic Energy of the Russian Federation the responsibility for the organizational-technical support of the activities of the International Science and Technology Center.

4. To instruct the Ministry of Atomic Energy of the Russian Federation to sign a Memorandum with the International Science and Technology Center about Russian support for the activities of the Center on Russian territory in accordance with its responsibilities.

5. To direct the Ministry of Labor of the Russian Federation in agreement with the Ministry of Finance of the Russian Federation and in accordance with proposals of the Ministry of Atomic Energy of the Russian Federation to establish the salaries and other aspects of pay for the Russian staff members of the Secretariat and for service personnel of the International Science and Technology Center.

6. To direct the Ministry of the Economy of the Russian Federation and the Ministry of Finance of the Russian Federation to resolve the question of financing all capital investment amounting to 92 million rubles during the

fourth quarter of 1992 (in prices of the third quarter of 1992) for technically equipping and for partial reconstruction of the working space of the Scientific Research Institute of Pulse Technology of the Ministry of Atomic Energy of the Russian Federation designated for staff offices of the Center and for acquiring its automobiles.

To direct the Ministry of Finance of the Russian Federation to consider each year the continuing allocation to the Ministry of Atomic Energy of the Russian Federation with an inflation index for support of the staff members of the Center, and also for supporting the use of the facilities of the Center and for its security, beginning from the fourth quarter of 1992. (On the basis of estimates of the Ministry of Atomic Energy of the Russian Federation.)

7. To direct the Ministry of Communications of the Russian Federation to work on an agreed basis with interested organizations for ensuring the communications and information transmittal between the International Science and Technology Center and Russian scientific-research centers and organizations participating in the programs financed by the International Science and Technology Center.

8. To instruct the Ministry of Atomic Energy of the Russian Federation, together with the Ministry of the Economy of the Russian Federation, the State Committee of Industrial Policy of the Russian Federation, the Ministry of Science, Higher Education, and Technology Policy of the Russian Federation, the Ministry of Defense of the Russian Federation, the Ministry of Security of the Russian Federation, and the State Technical Commission of the Presidency of the Russian Federation, to form an Interagency Council for coordinating the activities of Russian agencies and organizations, connected with the program of the International Science and Technology Center and also to develop and present during the fourth quarter of 1992 for approval by the Government of the Russian Federation proposals about the activities of the Council and a proposal about the order of selection of projects proposed for realization through the International Science and Technology Center.

9. To instruct the ministries and agencies of the Russian Federation, at installations where the projects of the International Science and Technology Center are located, to undertake the necessary organizational measures for protecting state secrets.

10. To name as the Russian representative on the Governing Board of the

International Science and Technology Center Sergei Ivanovich Kisliak (Ministry of Foreign Affairs of the Russian Federation).

President of the Russian Federation
B. Yeltsin

8 November 1992
No. 662-rp

Translated by Glenn Schweitzer

Appendix G

ORDER

Of the President of the Russian Federation

On the Provisional Application of the Agreement for
Establishing the International Science and Technology Center

To accept the proposal of the Ministry of Foreign Affairs of the Russian Federation on the provisional application of the Agreement for Establishing the International Science and Technology Center, signed in Moscow on 27 November 1992.

To instruct the Ministry of Foreign Affairs to negotiate this issue with the parties which signed the said Agreement and to reach agreement on the preparation of the necessary documents.

President
Of the Russian Federation
B. Yeltsin

17 December 1993
No. 767-rp

Translated by Glenn Schweitzer

Appendix H

Issues About the ISTC Raised by the Supreme Soviet

List Prepared by the Supreme Soviet in April 1993

1. May the Center finance projects which are not of interest to Russia?

2. May the Center monitor work of a military character?

3. Will the staff of the Center have the opportunity to enter closed enterprises; and, in that case, how will state secrets be protected?

4. Won't the Western scientists use the knowledge they receive from Russian projects for their own military development?

5. Won't there be discrimination of the Russian staff members of the Secretariat in comparison with Western staff members, in pay and in travel abroad?

6. Won't the reorientation of weapons scientists to peaceful topics weaken the military readiness of the country?

7. Won't the Russian scientists, the enterprises, and the nation as a whole lose because of the loss of legal entitlement to the intellectual property created by Russian scientists?

8. How will the activity of the Center facilitate the transition to market relationships?

9. How can the scientists of Russia and the CIS countries be stimulated to participate in activities of the Center?

10. What will be the relationship between the Governing Board and the Executive Director of the Center in the main decisions concerning the financing and carrying out of the projects of the Center and in the use of the results of the activities of Russian specialists in projects?

11. Isn't the procedure for initiating the projects too long?

12. Isn't it simpler to create direct bilateral connections (minus the Center) between Russia and foreign organizations where the customers are located?

13. Why is the Russian parliament considering an agreement on establishing a Center not only with Russia but also with other CIS countries?

14. What is the procedure for other CIS countries to adhere to the Agreement?

15. Which country will designate the arbitrator to decide questions concerning violations of the Agreement and project agreements?

16. What is meant by the phrase "and also services" in Article 9 about the responsibilities of the Russian Government in providing material support for the Center?

17. Who will pay for expanding the premises of the Center when other countries accede to the Agreement?

18. Why are the foreign staff members of the Center exempted from paying Russian income tax?

19. Why is the financial support received by specialists participating in Center projects not subject to income tax?

20. Won't the sale of foreign currency on the internal exchange market of Russia be harmful to Russia?

21. Won't Russia be harmed from the exemption of the staffs of non-Russian organizations from paying customs on their personal property which they or their families can repeatedly bring into Russia?

22. Aren't there too many diplomatic immunities for the foreign staff of the Center?

23. Won't there be the possibility for legal action against the foreign staff of the Center in the event of a crime?

24. Won't the Center attract the best scientists of the country to the projects for further work abroad?

25. Won't the use of the "cheap working labor" of Russian scientists and participants in Center projects enrich the Western countries which participate in the Agreement?

26. May countries with clear dictatorial regimes join the Agreement?

27. In what currency will the calculations be made for countries of the CIS which have their own foreign currency?

28. Will financing of the Center reduce humanitarian aid for Russia and other CIS countries?

29. What are the perspectives of the activities of the Center in the near future if the Supreme Soviet ratifies the Agreement?

30. Will the activities of the Center be increased in the future from the point of view of additional financial assistance from abroad?

31. Are the Center and Russia interested in attracting internal Russian capital investment for supporting projects of the Center without the participation of Japan and France?

List Prepared by Supreme Soviet in May 1993

1. Doesn't the organizing of the ISTC on the material base of the most advanced Russian scientific centers create a one-way street of disseminating leading technology abroad with nothing in return?

2. Will there be analogous research carried out at leading institutes in the United States, Japan, and the European Community in the fields of microelec-

tronics, computer technologies, and biotechnologies with the participation of Russian scientists? Since the Agreement doesn't envisage such cooperation, how will there be partnerships and equality?

3. The ratification of the Agreement will not only be an organizational step but will also authorize the broad proliferation of intellectual achievements of Russia.

4. The Agreement should provide for compensation for the COCOM ban on the import of leading technologies into Russia.

5. If there is no change in the COCOM ban on imports of technologies into Russia, there should be bans on exports of technologies from Russia.

6. It should be noted that in Russia there is no internal legal basis for organizing a legal structure similar to the ISTC.

7. There is no legal basis for transferring advanced technologies of dual-use significance from state scientific organizations to the commercial structure and to foreign parties.

8. There is no legal basis for protecting and transferring intellectual property.

9. There is no government system for registering advanced and dual-use technologies such as a state register and procedures for their transfer through sales or exchanges.

10. It is essential that ratification be supported by the Ministry of Defense, the Ministry of Security, the Intelligence Service, the Committee for the Defense Industry, and others.

11. It is not clear whether the Center can engage in commercial activities.

12. It is not clear if the Secretariat will be able to monitor projects which are financed through channels other than the ISTC.

13. It is not clear how the customs exemption will be carried out (licenses, quotas) in connection with items that are regulated in response to specific decisions of the President and the Government.

Translated by Glenn Schweitzer

Appendix I

Projects Approved by the ISTC Governing Board

March 18, 1994

002   Monitoring Krypton–85

003   Theoretical and Numerical Models of Severe Reactivity-Initiated Accidents of Nuclear Reactors and Calculation of Radioactive Pollution Source Parameters

007   Information Network of Scientific Centers for Scientific-Technical Projects and Conversion Programs

008   Conversion of Expertise in Missile Navigation to Mathematical Geophysics and Particularly to the Problems of Ecology and Natural Disasters

009   Z-pinch X-ray Source for Medicine and Microelectronics

012   Laser Separation of Middle Mass Isotopes

015   Electronics of Organic Materials

029   Hydrodynamical Aspects and Turbulent Mixing for Optimization of Laser Target Compression

030   Physics of Controlling Pulse Technology for Diamond Synthesis and Compaction

034   Development and Improvement of ISTC Projects (administered by ISTC Secretariat)

040   System Design for Safeguarding Nuclear Materials Utilized at Complex Nuclear Facilities

041   Development of Pulsed Plasma Source for Technological Processes

047   Mathematical Simulation of Atmospheric Pollutants—Mesoscale Transport and Transformation

048   Models for Transport and Transformation of Atmospheric Trace Contaminants

049   Development of Industrial Accelerometer for Vibration Diagnostics of Nuclear Power Plant Equipment

051   Development and Testing of Models to Calculate Migration of Radioactivity in Groundwater

056   Installation to Detect Explosives in Luggage and Postal Packages Based on Pulsed Neutrons and X-rays

059   Disposal and Long-Term Storage in Geological Formations of Solidified Radioactive Wastes from Plutonium Production for Military Purposes and from Radiochemical Reprocessing of Spent Fuel of Atomic Power Plants

064   Design of a Nuclear Reactor Core-Melt Catcher on the Basis of Zirconium Concrete

065   Techniques of Forecasting Loads on Nuclear Reactor Containment during Severe Accident Conditions

066   Accelerated Flame Propagation and Deflagration-Detonation Transition in Large Volumes of Hydrogen-Steam-Air Mixtures and Reduction of Loads on Nuclear Reactor Containment under Severe Accident Conditions

068   New Generation of Integrated Program Tools for Portable Parallel Program Development at Nuclear Power Plants

075   Development of Acoustic Sensor Equipment for Tightness Checks at Nuclear Power Plants

June 18, 1994

001   Theoretical Research on Propagation of Seismic Waves from Underground Explosions and Earthquakes

017   Feasibility Study of Technologies for Accelerator-Based Conversion of Military Plutonium and Long-Lived Radioactive Waste

019   Interactions between Tritium and Candidate Materials for Use in Fusion Reactors

023   Data Base on Benchmark Calculations of Solar and Long Wave Atmospheric Radiation Transfer Parameters for Climate Studies

031   Development of a High-Capacity Content-Addressed Neuron Network

033   Nuclear Waste Management and Disposal at Mayak Site

037   Femtosecond Photoelectronic Diffraction Measurement Techniques

050   Experimental and Theoretical Simulations of Plasma-Type Neutron Source

052   Hardware and Software for Medical Area Network

067   Program Codes for Simulation of Dynamic Processes in Nuclear Power Reactor Facilities

073   Monograph on Self-Quenching Pulse Reactors

074   Shock Waves and Extreme States of Matter

076   Atomic and Radiation Processes in Plasmas, Gases, and Solids

079   New Forms of Condensed Carbon: Quasi-Two-Dimensional Graphites and Fullerenes

091   Design of Recombinant Protein-Peptide Immunomodulators

092   Testing of Feed System for Nuclear Propulsion for Exploration of Mars

106   Environmentally Safe Means for Utilization of Chemical Weapons Technology in Hydrometallurgy and in Cleaning Waste Waters and Gases

107   Generation of Ultrashort, High Power Laser Pulses for Investigation of Interactions of Superintense Light Fields with Matter

110   Development of Technology for Catalytic Fluidized Bed Destruction of Organic Wastes Containing Radionuclides

119   Development of Recombinant Immunobiological Preparations for Cleaning Up Oil Pollution

123   Research on Cardiac and Anti-Tumor Drugs

124   Investigations of Initiation and Development of Chemical Explosions in Industrial Reactors and Facilities

125   Medical Preparations for Treatment of Hyper-Beta-Lipoproteinemia, Atherosclerosis, and Heart Disease

127   New Pharmaceutical Compounds Based on Phosphilipids and Nucleosides with Anti-HIV and Immunoadjuvant Activity

132   Preparation for Production of Inactivated Vaccine against Hepatitis A

133   Technical Specifications for Production of Live Measles Vaccine for Oral Administration

136   Synthesis and Evaluation of Alpha Fluorine-Substituted Derivatives of Phosphonic Acids as Analogs for Natural Phosphates and Phosphonates

143   Development of Process Induction Slag Melting of Radioactive Metal Wastes

144   Development of Three-Dimensional Dosimetry Planning System for Radiation Therapy

161   Gamma Ray Spectroscopy of Tokamak Plasmas

CIS–10 Building Blocks for Semiconductors Based on Gallium Arsenide and Related Compounds (in Georgia)

September 23, 1994

016   Development of Electrokinetic and Chemical Methods for Rehabilitation of Soil and Groundwater Contaminated with Nuclides and Heavy Metals

034   Development and Improvement of ISTC Projects (supplemental funding)

040   System Design for Safeguarding Nuclear Materials Utilized at Complex Nuclear Facilities (supplemental funding)

058   Technology Based on Metal Hydrides (conditionally approved)

060   Potential Health Risks Resulting from Worker and Public Exposure to Toxic and Radioactive Substances in Chelyabinsk Region

085   Environmental Radiation Ambient Monitoring System

086   Modelling System for Investigations of Ecological Problems and for Design of Ecological Monitoring Systems

103   Microencapsulated and Gel-like Chemical and Pharmaceutical Products for Health Care, Agriculture, and Polymer Materials

111   Demonstration of Producing Quasi-Stationary Electromagnetic Field Sources for Fundamental Investigations of Matter

126   Gasification for Extraction of Coal Wastes for Utilization of Substandard Coals (conditionally approved)

138   Low-cost Hemispherical Resonator for Small Commercial Navigation Systems

139   Whispering Gallery Effect for Steering Synchrotron Radiation Beams and Testing Supersmooth Concave Surfaces

145   Library of Evaluated Nuclear Data on Charged Particles for International Thermonuclear Reactor Program and Other Fusion Applications

149   Conversion of Military Infrared Laser Technology for Dentistry

150   Contamination of Agricultural Products and Countermeasures for Management of Contaminated Lands

159   New Type of Tokamak Fusion Reactor "Globus M"

173   New Fuel Elements for Water Cooled Power Reactors

176   Measurements of Activation Reaction Cross Sections Important for Fusion Applications

183   Measurement of Neutron Energy Spectra of Spontaneous Fission of Curium Isotopes

192   Reaction Engine with Microwave Power Supply (conditionally approved)

CIS–3   Evaluation of Actinide Nuclear Data (conditionally approved in Belarus)

December 9, 1994

March 31, 1995

June 30, 1995

222   Blast Wave Perturbations

228   Biological Methods for Treatment of Polyphenyl Soils

251   New Active Medium on the Basis of Rare-earth Scandium Borates and Development of Laser Sources

269   Conceptual Design of Modular Helium Reactor with Gas Turbine

273   Radiation in Nuclear Fuel Cycle Based on Reprocessed Uranium and Mixed Uranium-Plutonium Fuel

276   Book on Past Research on Pulsed Reactors at Chelyabinsk–70

277   Elaboration of High Precision Measurement System on Basis of CCD Sensors

289   Electron Phase Transition in Condensed Matter

302   Autonomous Hydroelectric System without Dams (feasibility study)

307   Quantitative Criteria for Geological Suitability for Long-Term Waste Storage as Shown at Krasnoyarsk Mining Complex (feasibility study)

309   Expert System for Signs of Hazardous Chemical Production

312   Modelling of Neurochemical Mechanism of Neurodegenerative Disorders and Development of Efficient Neuroprotectors

332   Safe Storage of Large Amounts of Plutonium after Dismantlement of Weapons (feasibility study)

333   Spectral Method for Analysis of Inverse Algorithms for Ill-Conditioned Matrices

339   Monograph on High Energy Phenomena in Electric Discharges in Dense Gases

348   Physical Methods and Pilot Equipment for Detecting and Identifying Radioactive Materials

350   Model of Closed Tritium Loop for Simulation of Plasma Effects on Reactor Systems in Support of ITER

352   Research on High Temperature Component Technologies

363   New Generation of Biopesticides

369   Feasibility and Economics of Using Weapons Plutonium and Civilian Plutonium as Fuel for Fast and Thermal Reactors

CIS–12   Safety Aspects of VVER-K Reactor under Increased Seismic Activity (in Kazakhstan)

September 26, 1995

106   Environmentally Safe Means for Utilization of Chemical Weapons Technology in Hydrometallurgy and in Cleaning Waste Water and Gases (Supplemental Funding)

Index

Access to sensitive facilities, 28–29,
47, 90–92
AID, 182, 203–204
American–Israeli binational
foundation, 189
Applied industrial research, 164–165
Armenia
interest in ISTC by, 77–80
Arzamas–16
access to, 90–91
Chetek activities at, 122–123
conversion interest of, 140
strikes threatened at, 226
support for ratification efforts by,
57–58

Baker, James, 19
Belarus
interest and membership in ISTC by,
77–80
Benevenides, Pablo, 20
Biological warfare
BIOPREPARAT, responsibility for, 69
Yeltsin's adviser on, 68
Boeing Company, 156, 186
Bosnia
relevance of ISTC model to, 207–210
Brain drain, 161–162, 168
Budgets for research
allocation by projects of, 164–165
decline of, 167–168

Canada
interest in ISTC by, 77–80
interest in Ukrainian science center
by, 205
Central Aerohydrodynamics Institute,
156
CERN, 177

Chelyabinsk–70
access to, 90–91
conversion at Institute of Technical
Physics in, 151–152
Chemical Physics Institute
(Chernogolovka), 51
Chemical warfare
Yeltsin's adviser on, 68
Chernogolovka, 50–52
brain drain from, 51–52
Chemical Physics Institute in, 51
Landau Physics Institute in, 51
mascot of ISTC from, 52
research on rocket fuels at, 51
research on industrial explosions at,
51
Chernomyrdin, Viktor, 178
Chetek
nuclear explosion technology of,
122–123
China
relevance of ISTC model to, 211
Clinton, William, 74, 178
Commercialization of technology, 149
CONVERSBANK, 38
Conversion
concept of, 142–144
Russian industrial problems in, 139
Russian priorities in, 148
skepticism regarding, 141
U.S. experience in, 144–145
western partners for projects in, 147
Crime in Russia, 6
Croatia
relevance of ISTC model to, 207–210

Department of Commerce, 184, 187
Department of Energy, 179–181, 203

About the Author

Glenn E. Schweitzer, Director of the Office for Central Europe and Eurasia at the National Academy of Sciences/National Research Council, was the first Executive Director of the International Science and Technology Center in Moscow. He is the author of *Techno-Diplomacy: U.S.-Soviet Confrontations in Science and Technology* (Plenum, 1989) and *Borrowed Earth, Borrowed Time: Healing America's Chemical Wounds* (Plenum, 1991).